THE NEW WORLD DISORDER

Peter R. Neumann is Professor of Security Studies at King's College London, where he directed the International Centre for the Study of Radicalisation (ICSR) for many years. As an internationally sought-after expert, Neumann served as advisor to the USA at the United Nations in 2014. In 2017 he was special representative to the Organisation for Security and Co-operation in Europe (OSCE). He also writes for *The New York Times* and *Der Spiegel*, among others. His book *The New Jihadists* was a bestseller. He lives in Oxford.

David Shaw works as a journalist for Germany's international broadcaster, Deutsche Welle, as well as translating from several languages, including German, Dutch, Russian, and French. He lives in Berlin.

THE NEW WORLD DISORDER

How the West is Destroying Itself

PETER R. NEUMANN

SCRIBE

Melbourne • London

Scribe Publications
18–20 Edward St, Brunswick, Victoria 3056, Australia
2 John St, Clerkenwell, London, WC1N 2ES, United Kingdom
3754 Pleasant Ave, Suite 100, Minneapolis, Minnesota 55409, USA

First published in German as *Die neue Weltunordnung*
by Rowohlt Berlin Verlag GmbH in 2022
Published in English by Scribe 2023

Typeset in Fairfield LT Std by J&M Typesetting

Printed and bound in the UK by CPI Group (UK) Ltd, Croydon CR0 4YY

Scribe is committed to the sustainable use of natural resources and the
use of paper products made responsibly from those resources.

978 1 915590 14 5 (UK hardback)
978 1 761380 24 2 (Australian edition)
978 1 957363 63 9 (US edition)
978 1 761385 40 7 (ebook)

Catalogue records for this book are available from the National Library
of Australia and the British Library.

scribepublications.com.au
scribepublications.co.uk
scribepublications.com

CONTENTS

Introduction

THIS IS A BOOK ABOUT IDEAS AND THEIR (OFTEN UNINTENDED) consequences. It describes how the West — still considered 'invincible' only thirty years ago — is now in the process of bringing about its own downfall. This book documents the developments that have played a part in that process. And it demonstrates that the West's downfall is ironically due to the same ideas that once made it so strong. The conclusion is not that the West needs different ideas, or that it needs no ideas at all. Rather, the conclusion is that the West must do better at learning from its mistakes, and that its core ideas must be reconsidered and reformulated in order for liberal modernity to survive.

But what is 'the West', anyway? As used in this book, the West is neither a point on the compass nor a political alliance; it is, first and foremost, a state of mind. Its origins lie in the ideas of the Enlightenment, which began to spread in the 17th century, first across Western Europe and then North America. The pioneers of the Enlightenment include scholars and philosophers like

Francis Bacon in England and René Descartes in France, who were interested in questions of metaphysics and epistemology. The answers they came up with were revolutionary by the standards of the time, and provoked much fierce debate among intellectuals in the coffeehouses and Masonic lodges of the day. They included the ideas that human beings did not have to submit to their fate; that progress is possible; and that everything can be understood through a process based on reason, logic, and measurement.[1]

Those ideas were a declaration of war on the status quo. The notion that all human beings have a capacity for reason and can be masters of their own fate was incompatible with the absolute authority claimed by the Church and feudal rulers. Consequently, over the course of time, this intellectual revolution developed into a political one. One hundred and thirty-five years after Descartes formulated his famous statement 'I think, therefore I am', the people of the Thirteen British Colonies in North America proclaimed their right to 'life, liberty, and the pursuit of happiness'. And a further decade later, French revolutionaries stormed the Bastille in the name of 'liberty, equality, fraternity'. Those were the most important and, even to this day, most influential events that gave the liberal modern age, and with it, the West, its substance. They created the conditions for what the British historian Niall Ferguson called the 'killer apps' of Western modernity: broadly speaking, a combination of science and technology, economic competition, the rule of law, and democracy.[2]

One pivotal reason for the successful spread of these ideas around the world was that, right from the outset, they were deemed to be universal — meaning they applied to every human being as a matter of principle: all people, not just the French or the Americans, were politically equal and had the right to fundamental freedoms and dignity. And, although slavery and colonialism showed that there was often a wide gap between aspiration and reality, these ideas had enormous appeal, even far beyond the reaches of Western Christian culture. The dissemination of Western ideas became a historical 'mission': few people doubted that a world in which everyone enjoys the benefits of modern, liberal — that is, Western — values would be a more just, free, prosperous, and peaceful world.

Today, the ideas of the liberal modern age appear so self-evident to us that barely anyone can imagine how it could be any other way. In countries where society is aligned with Western ideas, people are living longer. Diseases that once killed millions have been eradicated. The market economy has brought unprecedented prosperity. Almost all states shaped by Western ideas are democracies with free elections, independent judiciaries, and individual civil liberties that protect their citizens from state persecution. The maxim coined by the English philosopher Thomas Hobbes in the 17th century, that human existence is always 'solitary, poor, nasty, brutish, and short', is now true only for a minority of people in Europe and North America.

In reality, however, liberal Western modernity is a paradox. Many of the causes of the 'disorder' described in this book are rooted in the very values and ideas that have made Western societies so successful. Modern technology, science, and competition form the basis of prosperity in the West, but at the same time, they are also partly responsible for the divisions within it. Democracy, liberty, and universal human rights are the West's greatest achievements, but when they are 'exported', they are often met with resistance.

The dark side of the West has become particularly apparent over the past decades. One reason for that is globalisation, which gave extra centrifugal force to liberal modernity. The global market has replaced individual national economies, with production and supply chains now spanning the globe. The internet has made universal connectivity possible. Open borders and low transportation costs mean we can now reach places previous generations could only dream of. Most people now have a greater awareness of events in other parts of the world, rather than just their neighbourhood or country.[3] These developments are positive for many people, but not everyone has benefitted equally from them by any means. Globalisation has not only 'shrunk' the world, but it has also made it more demanding — more efficient and prosperous, but also faster, more complex, and more aggressive. According to the Polish-British sociologist Zygmunt Bauman, globalisation has led to the radicalisation of the modern age.[4]

Such criticism of the West is nothing new. A century ago, the conservative French philosopher René Guénon had already identified a 'crisis of the modern world' and predicted its imminent demise. The developments he blamed for this crisis were the very same ones that gave supporters of liberal modernity reason for optimism. Rather than seeing modern science and technological development as progress, Guénon saw them as the cause of psychological uprootedness and a loss of spirituality. In his opinion, ideas such as democracy and equality were not just wrong, they were responsible for destroying the natural order of things and propelling societies into chaos and misery. For Guénon, the entire history of the Enlightenment was a spiritual catastrophe that could only be averted by returning to 'traditional' — that is, pre-modern — values.[5] There is an Italian saying that sums this up perfectly: 'Si stava meglio quando si stava peggio' — 'Things were better back when they were worse.'

But that's certainly not the line taken in this book. The achievements of the West are undisputed. The clock cannot be turned back. No one wants to 'switch off' the internet or abandon modern medicine; political concepts such as equality and universal human rights are deeply rooted in our mindset — and cannot easily be removed from it, thank goodness. This book is not a manifesto for abandoning liberal modernity as Guénon wanted. It is a call for a renewal. It presents guiding principles for a version of the West that should be more honest with itself and with others, and which, most importantly, needs to be more pragmatic and inclusive in the way it functions.

Ideas or interests?

Of course, this is not the first book to deal with the problems and contradictions of the West. The questions of what the West is, what it stands for, and whether it has a future have occupied researchers and commentators for decades.[6] Broadly speaking, there are three main schools of thought. The first is the left-wing, or 'anti-imperialist' tradition, represented in my native Germany by writers such as the commentator Michael Lüders, and in the United States by the linguist Noam Chomsky.[7] They see the supposedly altruistic ideas of the West as a mere pretext for enforcing its brutal economic and power-political interests. In their eyes, the real rogue states are not China, Russia, or Iran, but the US and its European junior partners.

In opposition to that is the liberal school of thought, which is exemplified by the historian Heinrich August Winkler in Germany and by his fellow historian Niall Ferguson in the English-speaking world.[8] Unlike the anti-imperialists, liberals believe the West is sincere about its ideas, that it is defined and held together by them, and that spreading those ideas is the West's historic mission. That does not mean that the West never makes mistakes, or that it never pursues its own vested interests. But what distinguishes the West from other political philosophies, power alliances, or empires, according to Winkler, is that it is self-correcting. Precisely because the West is liberal and democratic, he argues, its mistakes have never been able to be swept under the carpet for long and — sooner or later — their consequences eventually had to be faced. Thus, Winkler rejects the claim of the anti-imperialists that Western values are nothing but a pretext, arguing that they are the basis for long-lasting resilience and adaptability. His optimistic conclusion is that 'the corrective power of this project has [...] proved that it is far from exhausted'.[9]

The third position is that of the 'realists', who include the security policy researcher Carlo Masala in Germany and the political scientist John Mearsheimer in the US.[10] Like the idealists, the realists believe that Western politics is determined by modern, liberal ideas. But unlike the idealists, they believe this is a mistake. In their opinion, it is the modern, liberal mission that has plunged the West into so many unnecessary and costly adventures that its dominant position is now in question. In contrast to the anti-imperialists, they do not see this as a reason for the West to stop pursuing its interests. On the contrary, they believe the West should finally get serious about doing so. Masala believes that 'realistic foreign and security policy [...] begins with accepting the situation as it is and no longer chasing after the dream of a liberal world order'.[11]

While this book builds upon these three schools of thought, it advocates for a position which differs from them. The anti-imperialists are right when they say that the West pursues not only its values, but also its own interests. But it is not the case that Western values are just a pretext. As many of the chapters in this book will show, the desire to spread modern liberal ideas has often been a sincere — and enthusiastically pursued — concern of the West. When ideas and interests have come into conflict with each other, there has often been an attempt to reconcile the two. And in many cases, the supposed interests were defined by values ('a united Europe', 'a democratic world', 'free trade') to such an extent that the two could no longer be separated.

So the idealists are correct when they claim that Western values are the deciding factors more often than we think. But their notion that the West has had an exclusively positive effect on the world, or that its mistakes have always been corrected rapidly, is naïve. While it is true that democratic institutions have enabled Western countries to react more quickly to societal changes — for instance, by affording equal rights to women and minorities — mistakes made outside of the Western countries themselves have often taken decades, if not centuries, to be replaced by right and morally correct views. Colonialism, for example, from which Western countries profited for centuries, did not end because resistance to it developed within Western societies, or due to some self-corrective will, but because the colonies themselves fought against it.

All this means that the 'realistic' position comes closest to actuality in its description of the problem. With its naïve, values-driven politics, the West has often shot itself in the foot and, rather than correcting itself as the idealists hoped, it has often made its own mistakes worse. However, the conclusion the realists draw from this is not only wrong but also self-contradictory: if the West is a community of ideas, then declaring its own conceptual framework to be defunct would be tantamount to self-destruction. If Western nations were to pursue only their own interests, they would no longer have any common ground and in Europe especially, it would be 'every country for itself'. Thus, the answer to the crisis of the West cannot lie in the West's abandoning its own values, but rather — if anything — in reinventing them.

The demand expressed in this book, therefore, is something new: neither cynical anti-imperialism nor naïve idealism, but a realistic analysis of the current crisis without throwing the successful and identity-forming ideas of the West overboard. Most recently, the war in Ukraine has shown that many people want values-based politics, and that such a basis is what makes the implementation of joint policies possible at all. The 'trick' is to identify key problems and then solve them through the smart application of modern liberal means.

About this book

This book is the result of many years studying questions of foreign and security policy, although many of its chapters are concerned with political developments in the domestic, economic, or technological realm. The common thread is the modern liberal ideas that dominate thinking among the political elite in Western nations and the West's attitude to new political challenges — whether they concern domestic, foreign, or economic policy. If the resulting analysis says anything about those ideas themselves, it is how all-encompassing their influence is, and how closely they are intertwined.

The book does not present grand ideas for a 'new world order' in the way that scholars of international relations usually do. Instead, it should be read as a short history of Western unipolarity, which demonstrates how liberal ideas have influenced Western thinking and, on many occasions, hindered the West's own success. Its purpose is to re-examine that history, identify key mistakes, and — in doing so — make sure that they are not repeated.

In this context, the term 'elite' is a necessary, albeit ill-defined construct. The elites — or, depending on the context, 'political elites', 'business elites', or 'security elites' — are people who shape ideas on politically relevant issues, and thereby gain influence over the way decision-makers think, or over the decision-making process itself. In very rare cases, that happens in secret, but more often it takes the form of commentaries, media publications, interviews, speeches, or other interventions which are public, but often little-noticed by the general population.

As this book shows, there are different elites, who are not in agreement with one another at all times — or on all issues. In order to gain an idea of which views were influential at certain points in time, I carried out 75 semi-structured interviews with experts and decision-makers who witnessed or helped shape many of these debates.[12] The picture these give of the ideas and sentiments involved may not be exhaustive, but it is more nuanced and more empirically well-founded than that seen in most books of this kind.

Then there is the view of Europe. Many books about the West concentrate almost exclusively on the role played by the United States, treating Europe as an appendage that can be dominated, dragged along, or 'seduced' as America chooses. However, although the US is undoubtedly the most important Western state when it comes to politics, economics, and military matters, European states, as well as Australia and New Zealand, have also played an important — and independent — role in many events. They are similarly based on modern liberal ideas to America and also try to stand up for those ideas with great self-confidence, albeit in a rather different way. It is for this reason that this book reflects the debates not only in the US, but also, where necessary, in other Western countries.[13]

The main section of this book consists of 18 chapters, each dealing with a particular key event or development. Most follow a similar pattern: the first stage is to understand the debate on a given issue; then comes an understanding of the political decisions that followed from that debate; and — finally — the consequences of those decisions. As mentioned at the outset, this book is about ideas and their consequences.

The thematic chapters are grouped into four sections,

structured chronologically. The first part — 'Optimism' — covers the 1990s and shows the initial optimism of elites about the future of the West. Rather than considering the new risks, they hoped for a world in which the West's victory in the Cold War was a permanent one, where there were no more ideological opponents and where democracy and the market economy would prevail throughout. Their rude awakening came with the terror attacks of 11 September 2001.

The second part — 'Hubris' — is mainly about the defiant reaction to that shock, which was shaped by the West's exaggerated self-confidence and led to the disastrous wars in Afghanistan and Iraq. One chapter deals with the global financial crisis, which spelled the end of the illusion that the West's economic and financial system was superior.

The third part describes the resulting disillusionment in the first half of the 2010s. The clearest manifestation of this was the grossly inadequate response of the West to the Arab Spring, which drastically worsened the situation in Libya and Syria and further aggravated global challenges like terrorism and migration. Perhaps most important from the current perspective: during that period, Vladimir Putin's revanchist, anti-liberal Russia was developing into an authoritarian counter-project to the liberal West, although its aggressive anti-Western campaign went totally unnoticed, especially by elites in Germany.

The final part — 'Backlash' — deals with the present situation: with the European project in crisis and the West tearing itself apart in a conflict between liberal and authoritarian forces; on the other hand, a rising China, whose technocratic version of the 'authoritarian modern age' appears to many to be stronger, more successful and more forward-looking than the West; and the existential challenges posed by climate change, to which neither the liberal nor the authoritarian version of modernity has so far managed to find a convincing response.

Can the West be saved? This book concludes that it can, but only by reinventing itself and ushering in a new and more sustainable modernity.

PART I
Optimism:
1990-2000

CHAPTER 1
The New World Order

THE IDEA OF A NEW WORLD ORDER AS PURSUED BY WESTERN politicians after the end of the Cold War was an optimistic liberal fantasy. The first person to attempt to claim it for himself was the US president, George H.W. Bush. In September 1990, less than a year after the fall of the Berlin Wall and America's victory in the Gulf War, he spoke of the dawn of a new era in which 'the nations of the world [...] can prosper and live in harmony'. After the end of the East–West conflict, Bush continued, there was an opportunity to create a world where 'the rule of law supplants the rule of the jungle. A world in which nations recognize the shared responsibility for freedom and justice. A world where the strong respect the rights of the weak.'[1]

Bush used the term 'new world order' almost 50 times in the months following that address, but its precise meaning was never clear. Bush's comments were vague, and no policy or strategy document ever appeared defining the term in more detail. The 'new world order' suddenly stopped appearing in Bush's statements in May 1991.[2] Indeed, the phrase is practically absent from his foreign policy autobiography.[3] Bush's security advisor and co-author, Brent Scowcroft, later said the expression was 'a mere slogan'.[4]

Apparently, the only people who knew what the term really meant were the conspiracy theorists. They interpreted the new world order to be some kind of globalist dictatorship allegedly sought by the Freemasons, Illuminati, Satanists, Jews, and other 'dark powers'. During the nineties, they believed Bush's aim was to abolish America and replace it with a world government. Flyers claimed millions of 'American traitors' had already been trained to be 'slave-masters under the New World Order'. Every helicopter sighted anywhere in America was taken as the harbinger of an imminent invasion.[5] Speeches in which Bush promised partnership with Russia and a greater role for the United Nations were cited as proof.

However, the true meaning of Bush's new world order lay not in its substance, but in its symbolism. From America's point of view, the West had not just ended the Cold War, but won it. The people who took to the streets in Eastern Europe were not demonstrating for better, more efficient communism, but for freedom and democracy. To Bush and his allies, it seemed obvious that a 'more Western' world order would be a fairer and more just one. They saw no contradiction between American leadership and a stronger role for the United Nations. Although Bush and the US government did not yet have a clear idea of what it would look like, the new world order was an expression of liberal optimism, which shaped America's geopolitical stance throughout the nineties.

And it wasn't only the Americans. The optimistic idea that the newly developing world order would be both more peaceful and more democratic was also, and perhaps particularly, prevalent in Europe. Klaus Naumann, who was Chief of Staff in the armed forces of a newly reunified Germany, recalls:

> The Cold War was an enormous strain. When it ended, the first feeling was one of huge relief: We did it! That was followed by a feeling of optimism, which culminated in the Paris Charter of November 1990. It framed the idea of a single 'security zone from Vancouver to Vladivostok' in which there would be a rejection of violent force, respect for national borders, freedom. That was when we in Europe hoped we really would be able to create a zone of understanding, of peace, in the wake of the tension of the Cold War. We all shared that hope.[6]

The later chapters in this part of the book deal with the various policy areas where that optimism had a particularly powerful impact on political thinking: security policy, hopes for a process of transition towards democracy in Russia and China, technological progress, and belief in an end to terrorism. This chapter is about the vision itself — and the limits it came up against very early on, even on apparently friendly territory.

Free people

The liberal optimism of the 1990s was based on two widely held beliefs among the Western political elite. The first was confidence in liberal democracy's inexorable march of triumph. One of the most prominent supporters of this idea was the political scientist Francis Fukuyama, who published the provocatively titled article 'The End of History?' just a few months before the fall of the Berlin Wall.[7] In his essay, Fukuyama explains that the collapse of communism was not just an accident or a concatenation of fortunate conditions, but the result of a historical dialectic. Over the course of two centuries, Fukuyama argues, liberal democracy had prevailed over monarchy, fascism, and communism as the best — and ultimate — form of government. According to Fukuyama, no system was better suited to satisfying all fundamental human needs. No other system could provide more efficient means of solving conflicts. And no other system had better expressed the pursuit of individual dignity and the quest for 'mutual recognition', already described in the philosophical dialectics of the 19th-century thinker Georg Wilhelm Friedrich Hegel.

Fukuyama did not proclaim an end to violent conflict in the future. What he meant by 'the end of history' was that the competition between opposing ideologies was at an end. The collapse of communism meant liberal democracy had triumphed over its last great rival. Of course, there may be wars in the future, says Fukuyama, but the great conflicts between rival systems seen in the 20th century were now, literally, 'history'. As long as there is no significant state that can offer an attractive ideological alternative, nothing could now stand in the way of the spread of liberal democracy.[8]

Fukuyama's article captured the spirit of the times. The edition of *National Interest* in which it appeared sold out after just a few weeks. The world's leading newspapers dedicated entire pages to discussing it. *The New York Times* called 'The End of History?' one of the hottest topics of the summer.[9] And, although there was opposition, scepticism, and differing interpretations of it, Fukuyama's thesis was very quickly accepted. The position taken by Henry Nau, a leading Republican Party foreign policy expert and senior official during Ronald Reagan's presidency, was typical. Like many of his colleagues, Nau rejected the bold and, in his opinion, misleading phrase 'the end of history', and stressed the fact that the triumph of liberal democracy was by no means guaranteed. But his conclusions were identical to those of Fukuyama. The 'emancipation of individual human beings which grew out of the Reformation and Enlightenment', writes Nau, 'gives liberal societies a material edge in the acquisition and use of wealth and power [...] If nations or regional actors aspire to succeed in the struggle for power in the future, they will have to succeed to some extent in the struggle for individual liberty as well.'[10]

The political consequence of Fukuyama's analysis was obvious. Apart from a couple of isolationists who called for a geopolitical 'retreat',[11] and some realists who (unsuccessfully) attempted to elevate Germany and Japan to the position of America's new 'challengers',[12] almost all foreign policy thinkers agreed that the West should support the advance of liberal democracy.

If there were differing positions at all, they concerned only the means of achieving that aim. For liberal institutionalists like the Harvard Professor Joseph Nye, the world had become not only more free, but also more complex. Instead of two superpowers, each keeping 'order' in their sphere of influence, there were now new states with weak institutions, internal conflicts, and ill-defined borders. It was the job of the West to promote democracy and human rights without causing chaos. If America did not want to act as the 'world's policeman', says Nye, it must act to strengthen multinational organisations like the United Nations and the Organisation for Security and Cooperation in Europe (OSCE).[13]

The so-called neoconservatives took a different approach. In their view, America was now the only unchallenged superpower that could assert its own interests alone or together with willing partners. Multilateral organisations were, at best, obstacles, and, at worst, opponents. However, unlike 'regular' nationalists, who defined power-political and economic interests in purely self-centred terms,[14] neoconservatives stressed the fact that America's most important interest lay in spreading universal values — i.e., democracy and individual freedom. In summer 1996, two leading neoconservative thinkers, the journalist William Kristol and the historian Robert Kagan, argued that America had become a 'benevolent hegemony' after the end of the Cold War, and claimed that 'its moral goals and its fundamental national interests are almost always in harmony'.[15] For that reason, America should not hesitate to pursue an active — and if necessary, military — policy of seeking 'regime change' in authoritarian countries like China and Iran. The aim must be, the authors argued, to drive dictators, ayatollahs, communist apparatchiks, and the like from office and replace them with democratically elected governments.

Free markets

The second belief that underpinned the liberal optimism of the nineties was not political in nature, but economic. As early as the late 1950s, the American sociologist Seymour Martin Lipset had presented evidence of a positive correlation between virtually all economic development indicators — industrialisation, overall prosperity, and education, for example — and democracy, which means that economic development would always be followed (sooner or later) by political freedom.[16] The prime example of this was 19th-century Europe, where industrialisation led to the rise of a tax-paying bourgeois middle class that was no longer willing to accept a system in which only the aristocracy had a say in matters of public interest. The further economic modernisation progressed, the greater the section of society that could participate in the political process — the late 19th century saw the inclusion of working-class men, with women joining them in the early 20th century.

Lipset's theory has come in for a lot of criticism over the years — for instance, for its failure to consider social and cultural factors adequately;[17] or because observations showed that overly rapid modernisation leads to instability.[18] But the idea that 'free people' and 'free markets' are two sides of the same coin, and that economic liberalisation must eventually lead to political liberalisation, was already an integral part of the Western elite's thinking even before the fall of the Berlin Wall.

Added to this, the 1990s witnessed the phenomenon of globalisation and, along with it, the belief that closer economic integration would become the motor that would drive a worldwide process of democratisation. The most popular proponent of this idea was the *New York Times* journalist Thomas Friedman, who wrote a series of books extolling the benefits of globalisation, and whose talks at the annual World Economic Forum in Davos always drew capacity audiences. According to Friedman, globalisation had a 'revolutionary character', and its consequences were at least as significant as those of the end of the Cold War. He believed globalisation involved a process of 'creative destruction', in the course of which nation states would lose their power, and international borders would become meaningless.[19]

Alongside free trade and permanently low energy prices, Friedman argued, the principal driving force was technological progress, especially the 'digital revolution'. The global networking of people and markets would result in Western companies moving their production abroad, where well-paid jobs would be created. In addition, this would provide people everywhere with more access to independent information:

> Thanks to the information revolution [...] no wall in the world is secure anymore. And when we all increasingly know how each other lives, it creates a whole new dynamic to world politics. [...] And when it comes to some opportunities being enjoyed in some bright corner of the world, leaders no longer have the option to deny them to their people, only not to deliver them. [...] And when they can't deliver, they have a problem.[20]

Friedman knew that the economic benefits of globalisation come at a price. States seeking increased economic growth and prosperity would have to put on the 'Golden Straitjacket', which in practice means accepting a long list of neoliberal reforms. They include keeping inflation low, shrinking state bureaucracies, maintaining balanced state budgets, eliminating tariffs on imported goods and government subsidies, removing restrictions on foreign investment, deregulating the capital markets, and of course, privatising all important industries. By the early nineties, this set of policies had already become the standard for 'reform programmes' prescribed by international financial institutions, under the name 'Washington Consensus'.

Such measures, Friedman was convinced, would benefit the vast majority of people, not only in the form of higher incomes, but also because they would kickstart a process towards political openness. Western companies investing in foreign markets would demand transparency and clear standards from foreign governments. Corruption, nepotism, and cronyism would no longer be tolerated. And the demand for reliable information about the state of the economy would — eventually — result in the development of a free press. Friedman named the process by which foreign influence would lead to democratic reforms 'revolution from the beyond', or, in a word, 'globalution'.[21]

A community of democracies

With hindsight, the optimism of thinkers like Fukuyama and Friedman appears naïve. However, neither intellectuals nor politicians at the time were able to come up with any popular alternatives. Other than that of the supposed advance of liberal democracy and the market economy, there was no 'great idea' for a new world order that might have gained currency with the Western political elites. One reason for this was that the liberal optimism was well-founded: dozens of countries did indeed become democracies within a few years, and in countries like India and China, millions of people were lifted out of poverty. Equally important, however, was the fact that this liberal optimism confirmed the West's view of itself, as embodying the universal, enlightened values that made the West what it is and gave America and its European partners the feeling that their policies did not serve their own interests, but the (global) common good.

The commitment to spreading liberal democracy was particularly strong in the United States. Unlike most European countries, America saw itself from the outset as a country with a mission. Abraham Lincoln described the US Declaration of Independence as the document that 'gave liberty, not alone to the people of this country, but hope to the world for all future time'.[22] In that tradition, victory over the Soviet Union was for many Americans not just a success for their country, but the triumph of American ideas, and spreading those ideas throughout the world was not just a strategy but a historical calling. This made it easy for the political elites to persuade their compatriots of a new, liberal world order, as long as the United States was its global champion.

The change of government in January 1993 brought no change in that regard. The Democrat Bill Clinton was even more convinced than Bush that America should advocate for a world of free people and free markets. He mentioned 'promoting democracy' in every important foreign policy speech he made. The introduction to his

National Security Strategy, published in summer 1994, reads, 'The more that democracy and political and economic liberalisation take hold in the world [...] the safer our nation is likely to be and the more our people are likely to prosper.'[23]

However, before Clinton's presidency was out, the limits of this doctrine had already become apparent. A good example of this is the 'Community of Democracies', one of the most important foreign policy initiatives from Clinton's second term as president. The idea was to create a kind of United Nations of Democracies as a forum for liberal democratic countries to meet amongst themselves and develop strategies to promote freedom and human rights. The initiative was suggested by US Secretary of State Madeleine Albright, who was born in Czechoslovakia and fled to the United States with her parents at the age of eleven. Fighting communism and other forms of authoritarian rule was close to her heart, and the creation of an association in which democratic states would support each other became a personal priority for her. As Albright says in her memoirs, 'Democracy was my theme.'[24]

After several years of preparatory work, the 'Community of Democracies' was constituted at a conference in Warsaw in June 2000, at the end of which representatives from one hundred and six participating countries signed a statement of democratic principles. But the initiative quickly lost momentum. Even during the preparations, there was disagreement over which countries should be invited to join. The United States' six co-conveners all had very different ideas of what a democracy is. They eventually agreed to admit as many countries as possible. That's why the founding members included not only the 'old' and 'new' democracies of Western and Eastern Europe, but also countries like Morocco and Jordan, which were important partners for America, but not democracies.

A further problem was that most of the countries did not share America's missionary zeal. Although many had fought hard to establish democracy, very few wanted to adopt promoting it as the guiding principle of their foreign policy. Ted Piccone, then a young State Department official who worked on the Warsaw conference's closing statement, recalls how smaller states and developing countries in particular were anxious about the issue of sovereignty. Their fear was that public declarations targeting violations of human rights and liberties by other states would be seen as 'interfering', and would — sooner or later — lead to interference in their own affairs. In short, it became clear that the participating states had less in common than they originally thought. Despite their democratic identity, Piccone says, they 'lacked the will to reach a consensus. There was no cohesion.'[25]

However, the biggest problem was America itself. Despite Madeleine Albright's efforts to include other countries in the organisation, the 'community' was seen primarily as an American project. And although most participating states had friendly relations with the US, none wanted to be seen as taking orders from America. Piccone also eventually reached the conclusion that America's dominance was a hindrance:

> [The 1990s] were the peak of American power, and we
> wanted to capitalise on that. We said, 'This is the world
> in which democracy is becoming the dominant form of

government. That's good for us and it's good for you.' […]
But paradoxically, America was possibly *too* big and *too*
powerful at the time to be able to give other states the
feeling that they could be equal partners.[26]

The 'Community of Democracies' organised several follow-up
conferences and opened a secretariat office in Warsaw, but it barely
engaged in any concrete activity. After the United States' invasion
of Iraq in 2003 (see chapter 8), the initiative was effectively dead.

'European standards'

At first glance, Europe was more cautious about promoting
democratisation. France rejected the idea of a 'Community of
Democracies' and refused to sign the Warsaw Declaration. The
French foreign minister at the time, Hubert Védrine, made it clear
that he opposed 'the Anglo-Saxon approach' to promoting democracy.
Speaking to journalists, he said, 'Democracy is not like a religion
that lends itself to converts but rather a process of evolution that
involves long [and psychological] maturing processes.'[27] He later
told Albright that he found the initiative too American and that his
country had no desire to play second fiddle on the international
stage.[28]

Germany also had reason to be reticent. The consequences of
German reunification consumed a lot of energy and attention.[29]
Furthermore, German politicians were conscious of the fact that
many of the country's partners still had reservations about a new,
bigger Germany, so its foreign policy priority was to avoid making a

bad impression. Wolfgang Ischinger, who was political director of
the German Foreign Ministry in the nineties, described Germany's
foreign policy at that time as 'inhibited':

> We didn't dare give our opinion [...] The motto in Berlin
> was, to put it in casual terms, to act like a hare in an open
> field: to keep our ears down and make ourselves as small
> as possible so no one sees us.[30]

As a consequence, Germany, France, and the other Western
European states avoided the word 'democratisation' and pursued a
different approach which was more focused on institution building.
However, they were involved in another ambitious democratisation
project — namely the enlargement of the European Union to
include ten Central and Eastern European states.[31] The German
chancellor, Helmut Kohl, never missed an opportunity to stress that
European unification must be 'irreversible'.[32] The vision that he and
many other Western European politicians articulated was one of a
Europe that was 'united, free, and at peace'.

   The process that was meant to lead to the realisation of that
vision included not only negotiations about the single market or
agricultural policy, for example, but also — and primarily — the
expectation that accession states should conform their 'internal
constitution' to 'European standards' when it came to issues such
as democracy, the rule of law, and the protection of minorities.
In practice, those 'negotiations' were not talks between equal
partners struggling to reach a compromise; they were a process of
assimilation, in which the Eastern accession states accepted the

norms, laws, and procedures of the West.[33] In many cases, it was the EU Commission that decided what 'freedom' meant in detail.

Of course, the Eastern European candidate countries were willing partners in that process, and there is no doubt that pressure from Brussels helped to secure protection for minorities, prevent conflict, and strengthen democratic structures. But the accession states often had other priorities. Their focus was not on a vision of a united and democratic Europe, but the protection of their newly gained sovereignty. Their approach was not idealistic, but instrumentalist in nature.[34] Access to Western markets and their own security were more important to them than 'European values'.

In this vein, many accession states saw Russia as a threat long before Vladimir Putin became president. That was particularly true of Poland, as well as the Baltic states, which had been part of the Soviet Union until 1991. Bernd Mützelburg, Germany's ambassador to Estonia at the time, who later became a foreign policy advisor to Chancellor Gerhard Schröder, recalls:

> They wanted protection from the Great Bear that was still feared by many for historical reasons. That's why the Balts, the Poles, and the Czechs were primarily interested in joining NATO and the security guarantees that came with that membership. Only after that did they ask themselves what joining the community of values [the EU] meant for their own internal constitution.[35]

The clearer it became that the 'European project' did not correspond precisely to their own immediate interests, the more sceptical they became. The market-economy 'straitjacket' placed on Eastern Europeans by the EU led to social hardship. Special regulations, for example in the case of the free movement of people, increased their feeling that they were second-class Europeans, and the constant reprimands from Brussels for not implementing every EU Directive in exactly the way it was intended by the European Commission gave people in the accession states the impression that they were not masters in their own house, despite their regained freedom.

While approval of EU membership was running at almost 100 per cent in all accession states at the beginning of the decade, opposition had become significant ten years later: 25 per cent in Estonia, 26 per cent in Poland, and 31 per cent in Latvia.[36] Mützelburg monitored that change in public mood closely:

> At first, there was massive relief that they had got rid of their Soviet overlords [...] [But later] the mood changed. People were saying, 'Hang on a minute, we used to be told what to do by the Soviets, and now the people in Brussels are trying to boss us around. That's not what we wanted. We wanted freedom and self-determination, and we believed we would get that in the European Union.[37]

The feeling of being bossed about by foreigners was never strong enough to threaten the success of the EU's enlargement to the East. But the tensions between the liberal, universalistic approach of the political elites in the West and the desire for sovereignty and the self-interest among Eastern Europeans became a permanent line of conflict and caused a whole series of political rifts in the ensuing decades — not least during what came to be known as the refugee crisis in 2015 (see chapter 14). Just like America, Europe was forced to recognise that its own, supposedly universal values were not as automatically accepted in its own European 'back yard' as it had believed, and their spread was not as inevitable as the theory of the triumph of liberal democracy would have it.

CHAPTER 2
Perpetual Peace

The liberal optimism of the 1990s also heavily influenced security policy. Within three weeks of being elected British prime minister in May 1997, Tony Blair ordered a wide-ranging review of the country's defence policy. Blair was convinced that the British military was stuck in the logic of the East–West conflict and was determined to change that as quickly as possible. The resulting document — the *Strategic Defence Review* — was an exemplary reflection of the 'new thinking' that had taken hold everywhere in the West during the decade.[1]

Rather than averting dangers for the country, its population, or its allies, the task of defence policy in the future was to be to solve all the world's problems.[2] It was no longer the job of the military to fight, but rather to stabilise democratic governments, promote economic development, and deal with humanitarian crises. The greatest challenge was no longer considered to be waging war, but combatting the risks from 'globalisation and interdependence' —

including drug trafficking, terrorism, and ethnic conflicts, but also 'inequality and human suffering'.[3] There was no longer any reason for 'real' — that is, existentially threatening — wars, but insecurity, instability, and risks were lurking round every corner.

The worldview reflected by this 'new thinking' was that of Fukuyama and Friedman. As already mentioned, even Fukuyama never claimed there would be no more violent conflict; his assertion was merely that those conflicts would no longer pose an existential threat, and that the triumph of democracy would result in an ever-expanding zone of peace. Precisely that was the hope of the security policy elites, who considered a 200-year-old theory that democracies don't wage war on each other to be an 'empirical law'.[4] This theory — or a highly simplified form of it — became the basis of the West's security policies. But rather than leading to 'perpetual peace', implementing it resulted in a lost decade in which 'humanitarian intervention' was overemphasised, new threats were underestimated, and security capabilities were systematically scaled back.

Democratic peace

The idea that democracies interact with each other more peacefully than authoritarian forms of rule already existed before modern democracies themselves did. It was first fully articulated in an essay by Immanuel Kant entitled *Perpetual Peace*. In that work, Kant opposed the view that the absence of war was exclusively the result of alliances and balances of power. He stressed that it was dependent on a state's 'internal constitution' and claimed that, ultimately, only republican states are capable of perpetual peace. His reasoning was that the human and financial costs of conflict were borne by the citizens, who were therefore usually more pacifist than their rulers, which meant that when citizens were involved in decisions on war and peace, war would occur less often.

Kant also outlined an organisation of states in which allied republics would offer each other mutual protection. Almost 200 years before Fukuyama, he formulated the idea of a kind of democratic peace zone, which would expand and eventually lead to 'perpetual peace'. In his words:

> If Fortune ordains that a powerful and enlightened people should form a republic, [...] this would serve as a centre of federal union for other states wishing to join, and thus secure conditions of freedom. [...] Gradually, through different unions of this kind, the federation would extend further and further.[5]

The French philosopher Charles Montesquieu offered a further argument. His book *The Spirit of Law* — one of the most important texts of the Enlightenment — was an attempt to explain why the republican form of government was superior to other systems of rule, such as monarchy or 'despotism'. As Montesquieu saw it, one of the main reasons was the fact that republican states are more commercially successful, and trade among them results in connections, common interests, and mutual dependencies which make war more difficult — if not all together impossible. 'Two nations who traffic with each other become reciprocally dependent,' writes Montesquieu, 'for if one has an interest in buying, the other has an interest in selling; and thus their union is founded on their mutual necessities.'[6]

Historians and political scientists have also repeatedly examined the idea of a 'democratic peace'[7] — particularly following the end of the Cold War.[8] The arguments made in such articles were in principle the same as those made by Kant and Montesquieu. The difference was only that the contemporary writings were now underpinned by empirical evidence. The political scientists Zeev Maoz and Bruce Russett, for example, came to the conclusion that there had been no war between two democratic states in the period from 1946 to 1986.[9] Their fellow academic Michael Doyle considers that period to have begun as far back as 1815.[10]

However, the academic debate that triggered such articles revealed some important nuances. For example, the degree to which democratic peace was 'perfect' depended on the definition of 'war' and 'democracy'. Points that required clarification included, for instance, the question of whether states in the 19th century, in which the right to vote was reserved for white, wealthy men could be considered democratic from today's perspective. It also became clear that the arguments put forward by Kant and Montesquieu were in many ways questionable. The historian Christopher Layne cites several crises which *almost* led to war as examples of times when normative considerations played virtually no part in the decisions of politicians, although strategic considerations and power politics certainly did.[11]

Perhaps the most important objection was that young democracies still in the process of consolidating their democratic status were often not more peaceable, but more aggressive in their relations with other states. The political scientists Edward Mansfield and Jack Snyder concluded that democracies were twice as likely to go to war in the first decade after their transition to democracy as authoritarian states were. Mansfield and Snyder argue that this is due to weak state institutions and the fact that democratic transition is often accompanied by a resurgence of nationalist sentiment.[12] The widespread assumption that authoritarian states become more peaceable after they transition to democracy was thus both false and misleading. Therefore, as political scientist John Owen also found, the crucial factor was not whether states had a democratic constitution, but whether they had internalised liberal norms.[13]

Little of such objections and nuances featured in the public debate or in the minds of politicians. In his books, Thomas Friedman popularised the concept of democratic peace in the form of his 'Golden Arches Theory', based on the claim that no two countries that both have McDonald's (supposedly an indicator of economic liberalisation) have ever fought a war against each other.[14] That theory was already incorrect by the time it was published, (for example, Serbia and all the countries it went to war with had McDonald's restaurants), but nonetheless it — and with it the notion of democratic peace — came to be seen as an ironclad rule among politicians and in foreign ministries in the West and was used to justify government action and even war.

The fact that the theory of democratic peace was only valid for dealings *between existing* democracies, the existence of significant exceptions, and — as highlighted by Mansfield and Snyder — the fact that young democracies are often more war-prone than autocracies, were neither acknowledged nor understood by Western political elites. Clinton's 1994 State of the Union address simply states: 'The best strategy to ensure our security and to build a durable peace is to support the advance of democracy elsewhere.'[15]

Alternatives?

Other theories did not fit so well with the optimistic liberal zeitgeist. The most prominent was undoubtedly Samuel Huntington's theory of the 'Clash of Civilisations', which was first published in an article in the journal *Foreign Affairs* in summer 1993 as a response to his former student at Harvard, Fukuyama. Huntington argued that future wars would not be waged over ideologies or economics, but over culture. He considered Fukuyama's prediction that universal values would triumph to be a dangerous illusion, because Western ideas of democracy and human rights are not universal but *Western*, and their spread is not seen as a liberation but as 'cultural imperialism'.[16] Huntington describes eight so-called civilisations and predicts conflicts will break out at their borders. In his opinion, Islamic culture was particularly problematical, as it was in conflict with all its 'neighbours'. 'Islam has bloody borders,' he concludes.[17]

The article generated a huge response and soon became the most-read and most-cited piece in the history of the journal *Foreign Affairs* because it appeared to offer a credible explanation for the resurgence of nationalist and religious conflicts such as that in the former Yugoslavia. Left-wing conspiracy theorists saw it as part of a 'campaign' aimed at inciting anti-Muslim sentiment among the American public (see chapter 5).[18] But in reality, Huntington's theory had barely any impact on Western political elites. This was partly due to the fact that many points made by Huntington were misleading or implausible — not least of all the (more or less) arbitrary division of the world into eight civilisations and the idea that future conflicts would principally play out *between* them, when it was already foreseeable that conflicts *within* civilisations (for example between Sunni and Shi'a Islam), would be at least as significant.

This was compounded by the fact that Huntington's theory was deemed racist. Although he denied this, his statements on 'Islam' were so sweeping and negative that he became a figure of hate for the left-wing and a pariah for the mainstream. Intellectuals usually only mentioned Huntington in order to distance themselves from him, and no major Western politicians subscribed to his theories. The attitude of the former German foreign minister, Joschka Fischer, was typical: 'No sensible Western political system can take this theory seriously,' he wrote, 'as it would be a simply nightmarish view of the 21st century.'[19]

Another alternative to 'democratic peace' was the theory of the American author Robert Kaplan, whose essay 'The Coming Anarchy' appeared in *The Atlantic* in early 1994.[20] In deliberate contrast to Fukuyama, he concentrated on parts of the world that were excluded from the supposed triumph of democracy. He pointed out that the collapse of nation states, high population growth, and infectious diseases had brought parts of Africa and Asia to a state of chaos and left them in the control of criminal gangs. This was compounded by environmental crises such as climate change and water shortages, whose impacts could heighten existing tensions and trigger violent conflict. Kaplan was anything but optimistic. What he saw was not democratic peace, but a world in crisis.

Like Huntington's, Kaplan's essay was popular but had little political impact. Academics ignored him because he was 'just a journalist', and foreign policy elites considered his view overly pessimistic. Kaplan himself quickly realised that his message did not fit with the spirit of the time:

> Despite the war in Yugoslavia, the global elites were very optimistic. The assumption was that the triumph of democratic movements in Central and Eastern Europe would continue into Africa and Asia and that the events in Central and Eastern Europe would be a kind of model for the rest of the world. Those — like me — who spoke of conflict, development, the environment or culture in that situation were quickly labelled reactionary.[21]

And indeed, it was not until the terror attacks of 11 September 2001 (see chapter 6) that there was a willingness in Western capitals to re-examine their own optimistic assumptions about the state of the world. Until then, their belief in a 'democratic peace' — or, more accurately, an abbreviated interpretation of the idea — was almost unshakable.

Humanitarian interventions

The enthusiasm among Western political elites for the idea of 'democratic peace' had real-world consequences. The first was an increasing number of so-called wars of choice, where there was no direct or existential threat to Western interests. Most of these military missions, for example in Haiti, Bosnia, or Sierra Leone, were described as 'humanitarian interventions' and were an expression of the conviction that the 'international community' had an opportunity (and a moral obligation) to 'interfere' in the internal affairs of states which seemed unwilling or unable to ensure the security of their population — for example in the case of national disasters, civil war, or 'crimes against humanity'. The term 'responsibility to protect' was coined for this phenomenon in the nineties, a phrase that was popularised internationally by Canada in particular, but also by other Western states, and that was enshrined as a non-binding norm in the statutes of the United Nations in the middle of the following decade.[22] This was new in international law[23] and left-wingers and left-leaning liberals hoped it would put an end to the focus on states and national sovereignty and contribute to a new human security policy that was more oriented towards human rights.[24]

The problem was that publics' tolerance of failure in such 'non-existential' wars was generally very low. People in the West commonly had no problem with their military being deployed for 'cosmopolitan' reasons, but only as long as they were not costly. When missions lasted too long, became too expensive or too complex, or if Western troops were killed, the mood often swung rapidly — especially if the mission had not yet been brought to a successful end.

One of the first examples of this was Operation Restore Hope in Somalia. In 1992, following reports of a humanitarian disaster, the Bush administration decided to send 25,000 troops to join the UN-led mission. The aim was to protect the population and ensure the supply of essential goods — especially food and medicine. The conflict turned out to be more complex than expected, however, and an attempt to arrest members of an enemy militia in October 1993 ended with the death of 19 American soldiers. Although President Clinton, who had succeeded Bush in the meantime, did not want to give the impression that there was a direct connection, he ordered the withdrawal of American troops just a few weeks later. That did not escape the attention of America's enemies: the leader of Al Qaida, Osama bin Laden, would later say that this incident convinced him that the supposedly toughest military power in the world was in fact a 'paper tiger' with no will to fight.[25]

The most tragic consequence of the Somalia mission occurred the following year. Shortly after the last American troops had left Somalia, unrest broke out in Rwanda in Central Africa, which escalated in the spring of 1994 and eventually led to a genocide in which at least half a million people died. Although all states had vowed 'never again' to allow a genocide to happen after the Holocaust, no nation was prepared to intervene militarily in Rwanda. Madeleine Albright, who was America's ambassador to the UN at the time, later admitted that one of the main reasons for that reluctance was the fiasco in Somalia. Although the two situations were unrelated, her boss, President Clinton, was wary of launching another potentially hazardous mission in Africa that would not have had public backing so soon after the failure in Somalia.[26] 'The only solution,' wrote Albright, 'would have been a large and heavily armed coalition led by a major power, but because of Somalia, the US military wasn't going to undertake that.'[27]

The collective failure of the international community in Rwanda exposed the arbitrary nature of humanitarian intervention.

In most cases, whether and when Western states intervened in humanitarian crises was not dependent on the scale of the crisis itself, but on media coverage, alliance obligations, and the vicissitudes of domestic politics. There was no way to justify the fact that there was an intervention in Somalia but not in Rwanda on the basis of humanitarian arguments. The British prime minister, Tony Blair, recognised the problem and, in the spring of 1999, he presented a series of criteria aimed at making military interventions more predictable.[28] Those stipulations were useful but they did not amount to a clear, universally binding doctrine.[29] Even the left-leaning liberal philosopher Jürgen Habermas — a vociferous supporter of the principle of 'the responsibility to protect' — was later to criticise what he called the 'unclear [political] conflict situation', which had not ended antagonism between states but intensified it.[30]

Nationalist revival

Another consequence of the 'new thinking' was the underestimation of nationalist and religious-fundamentalist forces (see also chapter 5). Although Fukuyama and Friedman had mentioned 'ethnic and religious violence' in their articles, it was mostly only in passing. They saw such violence as a 'remnant' of a bygone era that would diminish in significance, albeit gradually, along with the increasing spread of Western values.[31] One of the few who appeared to understand the 'modernity' of such violence was the American sociologist Benjamin Barber, who released a book called *Jihad vs. McWorld* in 1995. Barber's theory was that, rather than being an

anachronistic fringe phenomenon, the revival of nationalism and
religion was the dark side of globalisation:

> What I have called the forces of Jihad [...] may appear
> to be directly adversarial to the forces of McWorld.
> Yet Jihad stands not so much in stark opposition as in
> subtle counterpoint to McWorld and is itself a dialectical
> response to modernity whose features both reflect and
> reinforce the modern world's virtues and vices — Jihad
> *via* McWorld rather than Jihad *versus* McWorld.[32]

Barber's arguments were nuanced and intelligent, but — just like
those of Kaplan — they received little attention from politicians.

The most drastic example of nationalist and ethnic violence
during this period is the conflict in Yugoslavia. For European
politicians, the breakup of the multi-ethnic state beginning in 1990
and continuing over the following ten years was not the sign of a
nationalist renaissance, but — more than anything — a surprise.
Boris Ruge, a young diplomat who had just joined the Yugoslavia
section of the German Foreign Ministry at the time, puts it very
plainly: 'The idea that there might be an actual war was new and
unfamiliar. It was a shock.'[33]

Although the Luxembourg foreign minister, Jacques Poos,
declared ending the conflict to be 'Europe's big moment', it took
years for the European elite to understand the dynamics of the war.
At the beginning of the decade in particular, there was a belief in
the capitals of Europe that the conflict was an 'archaic' problem
which would be able to be solved if only all sides would realise

that they were now part of a 'new Europe'. The British conflict researcher James Gow was an advisor to European governments at the time, and he sees the attitude of European elites during that period as both arrogant and naïve:

> EU leaders had hardly any serious ideas, but we had optimism, overweening ambition, and people who completely overestimated their own abilities and resources. There was a naïve, almost messianic belief that Europe could settle the issue simply by being interested in Yugoslavia.[34]

The situation changed little until the launch of American air strikes in 1995. But even Washington baulked at the idea that the conflict was a sign of a 'new nationalism'. Rather than seeing it as a clash between rival nationalisms, American politicians interpreted it as a conflict between nationalism and democracy.[35] That was true, insofar as the Serbian president Slobodan Milošević and his allies pursued a particularly aggressive form of nationalism and committed far worse atrocities than the leaders of other former Yugoslavian states. However, Milošević's attitude to democracy was less different from that of the other leaders than the Americans thought. For example, just like the Croatian president Franjo Tuđman, Milošević stood in (relatively) free elections, and for a long time enjoyed the support of 'his people'. Nationalism was neither a help nor a hindrance, nor, as Madeleine Albright believed, a relapse to the Stone Age.[36] On the contrary, nationalism was a relatively typical trait of the 'young', often 'war-prone' democracies described by Edward Mansfield and Jack Snyder in their research.

Peace dividend

Another direct consequence of the idea of a supposed 'perpetual peace' was drastic reductions in national security budgets and the scaling back of the corresponding state institutions. President Bush had expressed the idea of a 'peace dividend' as early as 1990, by which he meant that a portion of the funds previously spent on arms and defence should flow into education, healthcare, or infrastructure projects. However, the advent of the Gulf War, in which America and its partners defeated the Iraqi dictator Saddam Hussein within a few weeks in early 1991, prevented the most radical of those proposals from being realised. Nonetheless, Western political elites agreed with Bush in principle that the end of the East–West conflict offered opportunities to scale back spending on security and defence and use the money for supposedly better, more socially 'useful' purposes. One paper published by the International Monetary Fund in autumn 1991, for example, suggested slashing global defence budgets by almost \$200 billion annually. According to *The Washington Post*, this was based on the premise that 'nobody has enemies now'.[37]

Although hopes of more social spending were quickly dashed, almost all Western nations did cut their security budgets in the nineties — in some cases drastically. Figures published by the Stockholm-based research institute SIPRI show global expenditure on defence fell by an (inflation-adjusted) figure of more than \$200 billion between 1990 and 1998. The proportion of global economic output dedicated to defence also fell — from 2.6 to 1.7 per cent. In the United States, the proportion of economic output that went on defence spending fell from 5.3 (1990) to 2.9 (2000) per cent;

in Germany it fell from 2.7 to 1.5 per cent. Of course, there were exceptions,[38] but the trend was clear: rather than *restructuring*, Western governments in the nineties pursued a policy of *reducing* their armed forces and security apparatus.

That trend affected not just the military, but also intelligence services. The intelligence services of the West had concentrated heavily on observing the Eastern Bloc until the end of the Cold War, so there was no question that they needed to change. But when politicians spoke of 'reorientation' what they usually meant was less funding. Hansjörg Geiger, president of Germany's Federal Intelligence Services (BND) in the mid-nineties, suggested his agency should concentrate on 'new issues' such as terrorism, migration, or the effects of environmental crises. However, his suggestion didn't go down particularly well with his bosses. 'It was my job [...] to reduce the organisation's workforce from 7,500 to 6,500 people as part of the "peace dividend". It was difficult [to initiate new thematic priorities, because] the staff who would have been needed for those thematic priotities were often quite different people.'[39]

The only advocates of more spending on defence and security in the nineties were the American neoconservatives. They complained that many conservatives had bowed to public sentiment and were talking of balanced budgets and a peace dividend rather than thinking about how America would be able to win future wars. In a 1996 article, William Kristol and Robert Kagan called for an increase, rather than a cut, in the defence budget of one third so that America would be able to maintain its role as a 'benevolent hegemon' and deter potential challengers. They argued that the country must be prepared for all eventualities, because 'who knows what will happen'.[40]

Unlike most of the Western political elites, the neoconservatives did not see liberal optimism (which they shared in principle) as a reason to lean back and dream of a future 'with no enemies', but as a chance to expand America's supremacy and reckon with its remaining enemies — the so-called rogue states. If not during the nineties, then after the attacks of 11 September 2001 at the latest, they were in a better position with their view than the liberal 'dreamers' who were keen to believe there would be no more serious conflicts.

CHAPTER 3
Who's Afraid of Russia and China?

THE CONTRADICTORY CONSEQUENCES OF LIBERAL OPTIMISM WERE also evident in the way other world powers were seen. Throughout the 1990s, one of the top priorities of the West's foreign policy was the democratisation of Russia. Just like all his fellow Western heads of government, Clinton was a passionate supporter of the Russian president Boris Yeltsin, who was seen as a bulwark against any resurgence of communism or ultranationalism. Clinton advocated in the US Congress for economic aid, supported Yeltsin's re-election campaign, lauded his diplomatic successes, and avoided criticising him publicly over the war in Chechnya, in which his government attempted to put down a separatist uprising. During his last visit to Moscow as US president, Clinton showered Yeltsin with praise ('Russia was lucky to have you'), spoke of how much the two had achieved together ('We did some good things. They'll last.'), and assured him, 'You've got the fire in your belly of a real democrat.'[1]

However, the West's policies towards Russia resulted in less democracy rather than more. It had already become clear towards the end of Yeltsin's presidency that little remained of the Russian democracy which emerged out of the collapse of the Soviet Union. Contrary to the claims of the later US secretary of state, Condoleezza Rice, the problem was not that the Clinton administration became 'bogged down' in strategically unimportant conflicts like those in Haiti and Somalia, causing it to neglect major powers like Russia and China;[2] the problem was that the foreign policy pursued by Western governments was naïve and, ultimately, counterproductive.

In both China and Russia, the West pursued a policy of market-based modernisation, which it hoped would rapidly lead to more growth, prosperity, and freedom. But in doing so, the West unwittingly contributed to two important causes of a (later) backlash. In Russia, the policy helped hasten the collapse of the state and contributed to a resurgence of nationalism, while in China, it helped the Communist Party consolidate its authoritarian rule.

Shock therapy

The close connection between economic and political demise was evident in the collapse of the Soviet Union. During the severe economic crisis in the summer of 1991, communist hardliners attempted to grab power in a coup. On 19 August, they confined the then General Secretary of the Communist Party, the reformer Mikhail Gorbachev, to his dacha on the Black Sea, sealed off the capital, Moscow, and declared a state of emergency on public radio. The coup failed within forty-eight hours, however, and the then president of the Russian Soviet Republic, Boris Yeltsin, seized the opportunity. Before the year was out, he declared Russian independence and the Soviet Union — until then one of the world's two superpowers — was wiped from the map virtually overnight.

However, Russia's declaration of independence solved none of the country's economic problems. On the contrary, the sudden breakup of the Soviet Union's internal market into fifteen independent states led to the collapse of supply chains and made the shortages of vital goods even more severe than they already were. The young, free-market reformers led by Yegor Gaidar, whom Yeltsin had appointed to his cabinet, were convinced that a long-lasting improvement in the economic situation could not be brought about by gradual reform, and a radical break with the Soviet system was necessary. 'I was absolutely sure that there was no other way,' Gaidar would later say, 'and I was absolutely sure that [a] delay [would be] suicide for the country.'[3] The programme of reforms introduced in rapid succession from the beginning of 1992 included the unfixing of prices and the rapid privatisation of practically all state-owned enterprises. The term used to describe this policy was 'shock therapy'.

The reformers were not alone when administering this 'shock therapy'. In addition to Western-dominated financial institutions — the International Monetary Fund, the World Bank, and the European Bank for Reconstruction and Development — Western governments also sent dozens of economic experts to Moscow, who worked closely with the reformers and enthusiastically pushed their programme. Most of those consultants had precise ideas about how Russia should go about fixing its economic crisis. Andrei Shleifer and Daniel Treisman, two American professors who supported the Russian government with its reform programme in the early nineties, later published a book in which they made no secret of their ideological convictions:

> Markets should be free. Property should be private and secure. Inflation should be low. Trade between countries should not be obstructed. To achieve these goals, a country's government must leave prices alone, avoid owning or subsidising firms, enforce contracts, regulate responsibly, balance its budget, and remove trade barriers. Any government that does all this can expect national income to grow.[4]

This was the same formula that Friedman described in his books as the 'Golden Straitjacket' (see chapter 1), which the Western consultants hoped Russia would implement as quickly and as fully as possible. Two of its most important proponents, star economists David Lipton and Jeffrey Sachs, wrote as early as the spring of 1992 that the gains resulting from those reforms were potentially huge — 'much greater than is commonly supposed'.[5] The question was no longer which economic path Russia should follow, but how consistent it would be in following it. Possible objections — for example, concerning the pace of change, the social hardship it caused, or the weakness of Russia's state institutions — were considered to be secondary.[6] Instead of quibbling, Lipton and Sachs argued, Western governments should do everything in their power to support the market reformers.

The shortcomings of the reform package soon became apparent. When Gaidar and his associates lifted almost all price controls on 1 January 1992 with the aim of getting goods back onto empty shop shelves, they triggered massive inflation that wiped out many Russian people's savings in one fell swoop. In January alone, prices rose by over 200 per cent, and by the end of the year the inflation rate had reached 2,500 per cent.[7]

This was precisely the point at which the reformers chose to implement their next reform phase: the privatisation programme. All Russian citizens were issued with coupons that they could exchange for shares when state enterprises were auctioned off. In Yeltsin's view, this was an unprecedented democratisation programme,[8] but in practice, only a small number of Russians profited from it. The historian and Russia expert Mark Galeotti was living in Russia at the time and soon recognised the absurdity of the procedure:

> There were people who had lost everything [due to the unfixing of prices]: pensioners standing outside metro stations selling toothpaste. And those people were told, 'Here's your coupon, invest it, and in ten or twenty years you might make a profit.' It was no wonder that those people — indeed, most Russians — sold their coupons for a fraction of their value to middlemen or criminals.[9]

Tens of thousands of businesses, including the major oil and gas companies, thus fell into the hands of a tiny group of businessmen who later became known as 'oligarchs'.[10] What is more, starting in 1995, the state sold off the rest of its assets in a series of special auctions (the 'loans for shares' scheme) to the very billionaires who subsequently financed Yeltsin's re-election campaign.[11] By the end of the decade, it was not only Russian industry that belonged to the oligarchs, but the entire state.

Humiliation

The reforms had catastrophic consequences for Russian society. In the first half of the 1990s, Russia's economic output shrank by more than 50 per cent, taking it below the level of many developing countries. More than two thirds of the population — around a hundred million people — fell into poverty. Many scraped a living by selling old clothes, pots and pans, books, or their war medals at street markets, or bartered them for food. Others moved to the countryside, retreating to their dachas and growing their own vegetables. In six years, the average life expectancy for males fell from 64 to 58. This was due to a collapse of the healthcare system and the return of long-forgotten diseases, but also — and above all — to a rapid increase in murders, suicides, and alcohol and drug-related deaths. According to the journalist Paul Klebnikov, no country had ever declined so far so quickly during peacetime.[12]

There was a similar effect on state institutions, which had been an object of pride for many Russians. Three years after the collapse of the Soviet Union, little remained of the Soviet Army — the force that had defeated the Nazis in World War II and stood up to the Americans to the last. Yeltsin slashed the defence budget by 75 per cent, discharged more than a million soldiers, and ordered the remaining troops to become 'self-maintaining'. 'Parts of the army,' writes the conflict researcher Michael Mandelbaum, 'were reduced to scavenging for food and shelter like bands of primitive hunters, often relying on local authorities rather than on the national government in Moscow.'[13] Every year, several thousand soldiers died of suicide, while others sold their weapons and military equipment to the highest bidder.[14] The CIA imposed a halt on recruitment because so many members of the Russian military wanted to work for the Americans.[15] Many joined criminal gangs instead, or became mercenaries in the private armies of the oligarchs.[16]

The collapse of the state was also manifest on the international stage. Many Russians were humiliated by the fact that Russia was made a fool of by a 'gang of Caucasian rebels' in the war in Chechnya, or that NATO was expanding to include states that had previously been within the Soviet 'sphere of influence'. Another factor was the president himself. At the beginning of the decade, Yeltsin had portrayed himself as a dynamic fighter in the cause of democracy, but by the middle of the nineties, he had become a seriously ill, constantly drunk man who suffered from bouts of depression and would — without explanation — disappear from public view, often for weeks at a time. He was also clearly being controlled by a tiny circle of people made up of oligarchs and corrupt advisors. There was no greater symbol of Russia's decline than its own highest representative.

To what extent was the West responsible for all this? The current debate over this period often focuses on NATO's eastward expansion (see chapter 13). However, during the 1990s, the crucial factor was Russia's catastrophic economic situation — and the feelings of humiliation it engendered.[17] If the West bore any responsibility, it was largely for the fact that Western advisors did little to dissuade Gaidar and his circle from implementing dubious ideas like the coupon-based privatisation, or the selling off of Russia's natural resources. Indeed, many of those ideas were lifted from neoliberal textbooks; they were part of the modern liberal orthodoxy and relentlessly pushed by Western advisors. Mark Galeotti describes the dynamics as follows:

> Firstly, there were ambitious American economists with large egos, who saw Russia as the largest laboratory they had ever had; secondly, there was Gaidar, who wanted quick, simple solutions and so readily accepted the Americans' proposals; and, thirdly, there was the fear [on the part of both] of a return of the communists which caused them to want to make the process of privatisation irreversible as rapidly as possible.[18]

The consequence of Western involvement, if only from the outside, was that Russians increasingly lost faith in Western democracy and blamed the collapse of their country's economy on America, 'the West', or 'Western influence'. As early as the mid-nineties, communists and ultranationalists had become the two strongest political forces. The only party *not* to take an explicitly anti-Western position was Grigory Yavlinsky's liberal Yabloko party, which garnered barely 7 per cent of the vote in the 1995 legislative election and just 4.3 per cent in the early 2000s. From a Western perspective, this meant that there was no longer any political alternative to Yeltsin from 1993 onwards, and the entire Russia policy was therefore geared towards keeping him in office as president for as long as possible. To that end, Western governments were willing to turn a blind eye to many of the most problematic developments that were detrimental to democracy. That included human rights abuses in the war in Chechnya, for instance, as well as the increasingly open corruption among Yeltsin's advisors and — not least of all — the health of the president himself.[19]

Despite regular attempts by Western politicians to paint a rosy picture of the situation — after a state visit to Russia, for example, Clinton spoke of meeting young Russians who were 'intelligent, idealistic, and fiercely committed to democracy'[20] — the aim of turning Russia into a 'stable European democracy' had clearly failed.[21] Instead, the West's policies nurtured instability and facilitated the return of an aggressive, anti-liberal — and ultimately anti-Western — nationalism under Yeltsin's successor Vladimir Putin, who was to declare war on the West a little more than a decade later.

Trojan horses

In contrast to Russia, it was always clear that China would not undergo political change in the 1990s. The lesson that the Chinese leaders learned from the student protests and the Tiananmen Square massacre in the spring of 1989 was not that they must create space for debate and peaceful protest in future, but that such activities must be nipped in the bud. Politburo members who had advocated for concessions during the protests were placed under house arrest and removed from their leadership positions in the Chinese

Communist Party. 'From that point on,' says the China expert Moritz Rudolf, 'the chapter on liberalisation was closed.'[22] The political reforms introduced shortly afterwards in Eastern Europe were seen as a cautionary tale, motivating the state leadership to isolate itself even more from democratic influences. State premier Li Peng told the US secretary of state, 'What we did in Tiananmen Square was correct, just look at what is happening now in Central and Eastern Europe!'[23]

But despite that clear rejection of political reform, the political elites in the West remained convinced that China could be 'democratised'. Their intellectual champion was the American professor John Ikenberry, who penned many articles on the subject. Ikenberry shared the optimistic liberal worldview of many of his fellow intellectuals. He believed that democracy would spread, that it was the West's mission to promote that process, and that the key to achieving it lay in increasing mutual dependencies — in other words, in trade, international exchange, and economic ties.[24]

In the case of China, this entailed supporting the modernisation of the country's economy by any means necessary. In Ikenberry's analysis, it followed that the West had three aims: firstly, China must open up, by which he meant opening up to Western investment, trade, technology, and cultural exchange; next, the country must be integrated into the liberal institutional order, i.e., into regional and international agreements; and thirdly, China must be bound to its partners in Asia and the West through security agreements.[25] The aim of those three elements — which Ikenberry calls 'opening up', 'tying down', and 'binding together' — was to turn China into a responsible actor in the (Western-created) international system, despite its huge size.

Ikenberry and other Western intellectuals hoped the first stage in particular — 'opening up' — would boost the process of democratisation and eventually lead to the end of one-party rule. The richer China became, the bigger its middle class would grow and the greater the influence of the West would be, leading to a corresponding rise in the demand for freedom and democracy.[26] The Western elites saw investment, technology, and prosperity as the 'Trojan horses' that would help introduce democracy into China. That the Chinese leadership would succeed in separating economic from political freedom was not considered likely or even possible by anyone.

The supposed blueprint that gave the liberal optimists such confidence was provided by the 'Asian Tigers' — Taiwan, South Korea, Singapore, and Hong Kong — which had gone from being developing countries to industrialised nations in just a few decades, and whose economic growth had led (in varying degrees) to political liberalisation. Jeffrey Bader, a diplomat who was responsible for Asian affairs at the State Department during Clinton's presidency, hoped that China's development would follow a similar course:

> We called it a model for Asian development. Just like China, all those countries had started out poor. All made similar modernisation efforts, all were one-party states. All fought corruption and backed export-oriented economic growth [...] In time, they all became richer. The richer they got, the more likely it was that a political

opposition would emerge. And that [...] led to press freedom and greater political openness. [...] We never spoke of 'democratisation', but for many of us that was a desirable and plausible path for China that we were working towards.[27]

Despite the — sometimes very great — differences between those countries and China,[28] the West's entire policy was based on that model. China's entry into the World Trade Organisation (WTO), which came in 2001 after more than ten years of preparations, was seen as that policy's crowning achievement. The move integrated China fully into the world economy, giving it access to the largest global markets. George H.W. Bush had earlier pointed out that 'No nation on Earth has discovered a way to import the world's goods and services while stopping foreign ideas at the border.'[29] Clinton, who had concluded the negotiations, hoped for 'prosperity in America, reform in China and peace in the world'.[30] Even Condoleezza Rice, who had called for a 'more robust' approach to China, concluded that greater integration into the global economy would result in political change there. More trade and economic exchange are good, she wrote in *Foreign Affairs*, since 'trade in general can open up the Chinese economy and, ultimately, its politics too'.[31]

Wishful thinking

In reality, however, those hopes were little more than wishful thinking. One reason for this was that Western governments had no idea what was actually happening in China. Although it was the most populous country in the world, Western intelligence services and media had paid little attention to it during the Cold War. And even in the nineties, China was slow to come to the fore. As Nigel Inkster, director of operations for the British intelligence service MI6 at the time, confirmed: 'As far as the West's attention is concerned, China was tangential for a long time. Anyone could project their hopes and ideas of what China was and what it would become into the evolving situation.'[32] It was believed that improvements in the economic situation would result in an increase in the West's influence and louder calls for freedom of the press. However, if the economic situation worsened — as it did during the so-called Asian financial crisis in 1997 — it was predicted that social, economic, and ethnic tensions would result.[33] So, whatever happened, the collapse of the one-party system always appeared to be just around the corner.[34]

Another reason was that the Chinese government understood the West's intentions perfectly well and did everything it could to prevent the liberalisation that the West hoped for. The best example of this was the rise of the internet, which Western elites believed was 'uncensorable' and would spell the end of the state's monopoly on information.[35] However, Beijing was aware of that danger from the outset.[36] During the first decade of this century, the Chinese government set up its 'own' internet that was isolated from the rest of the world and which filtered foreign content for its potential to inflict political damage. It was an enormous undertaking,[37] but, contrary to Western expectations, as in other areas, the state was successful in stripping technology of its potentially subversive influence. The creation of a 'sovereign', 100-per-cent state-controlled infrastructure also facilitated the development of local internet giants and a digital surveillance system that later became the hallmark of a Chinese-style 'authoritarian modernity' (see chapter 17).

Britain's experience in Hong Kong was similar to that of America. In 1993, four years before the return of the British Crown colony to Chinese control, the government in London appointed the Conservative politician Chris Patten as governor. After taking office, Patten introduced a series of democratic reforms aimed at ensuring that the residents of the city could retain their (relatively) liberal constitution after the 'reunification' with China. Patten also secretly hoped that the city's economic success would prove to be 'contagious' and pave the way for the spread of democracy throughout the whole of China.[38] 'In Patten's view,' says former British diplomat Kerry Brown, 'Hong Kong was supposed to show the rest of China that democracy and the rule of law could function in the Chinese context.'[39]

However, Patten overestimated the significance of both his own role and of Hong Kong. Although Hong Kong had been China's richest city in the 1990s, its contribution to China's economic output sank over the subsequent decades from more than 20 per cent to just 2 per cent. In other words, China's economic development was so rapid that the (relative) significance — and potential influence — of Hong Kong quickly declined.[40] Added to this was the fact that the Chinese leadership was aware of Patten's hopes from the start. Jeffrey Bader, a personal friend of Patten's, recalls China's reaction to his proposals: 'He went to Beijing to explain his plans for the period after 1997. But they didn't want to hear any talk of democracy. Their response was, "You must be joking! This is our last meeting." And it was.'[41] According to Bader, Patten's experience was no exception. 'The Chinese were polite, but they were not interested in any ideas that did not correspond to their ideology. Especially when they came from the West.'[42]

That attitude was neither new nor surprising. It reflected China's approach to political reform since the leadership of Deng Xiaoping, the 'father' of economic liberalisation. According to Moritz Rudolf, China 'only ever wanted to learn from the West what could be integrated in the Chinese context. And they always said that'.[43] As a consequence, there was little change to the authoritarian status quo in the nineties and the supremacy of the communist party was never at risk. In the end, it was not China that became politically dependent on the West as economic interdependence increased, but the other way around. Just as with the fall of Russia, albeit under different auspices, the policy of promoting democratisation based on (neo-)liberal economic assumptions showed itself to be not only ineffective, but actually counterproductive.

CHAPTER 4
Techno-optimism

PROBABLY THE MOST IMPORTANT CHANGE TO TAKE PLACE DURING THE
1990s was not political, but technological in nature. At the start of
the decade, many Americans had never even heard of the internet.
Less than 5 per cent of the US population had an email address.
And even in 1995, it was necessary to explain to readers what email
even is. A report by the RAND think tank included the following
information about the service:

- Both parties to the transaction need not be on-line at
  the same time — e-mail is stored in an electronic 'inbox'
  until accessed.

- The information arrives in a 'machine-readable' form
  such that it can be stored, retrieved, forwarded, cut-
  and-pasted into new messages, replied to, and reused
  in flexible ways.

- It is fast, with most messages arriving (worldwide) within minutes of being sent.

- Messages may contain combinations of text, pictures, diagrams, voice annotations, even video clips.[1]

This passage shows how drastically life in Western societies has changed in little more than a quarter of a decade. While most people these days spend virtually their whole time online, and life without the stimulation of the internet, smartphones, and social media is unimaginable for many, only a generation ago the idea of communicating with others via a computer was completely alien to the vast majority of people.

Just like the Industrial Revolution in the 18th and 19th centuries and the technological quantum leaps that accompanied it, the 'digital revolution' was an achievement of the Enlightenment. The Enlightenment was based on a belief in progress, the 'scientification' of the world, and a political and economic system that not only guaranteed individual personal development, but actively promoted it. So it was no accident that the internet was a product of the West.

Just as typical, however, was the excessive optimism that accompanied the rise of new technology. As the British philosopher John Gray has shown, a faith in human progress through science — known as positivism — was one of the 'fundamental beliefs' of the modern age from the late 18th century onwards,[2] and there is a long tradition of modern and liberal thinkers, such as Henri de Saint-Simon, Auguste Comte, Bertrand Russell, and Karl Popper, who saw technological and political progress as inextricably linked.[3]

The emergence and spread of the internet was accompanied — once again — by great, often utopian hopes that it would liberate people and solve our social problems. The basic idea, writes Gray, remained unchanged:

> For Saint-Simon and Comte, technology meant railways and canals. [...] For neoliberals, it means the internet. The message is the same. Technology — the practical appliance of scientific knowledge — produces a convergence in values. This is the central modern myth, which the Positivists propagated and everyone today accepts as fact.[4]

As with pervious technological revolutions, the 'techno-optimists'[5] of the 1990s believed the latest revolution was unique, that its consequences would be so dramatic as to dwarf all previous technological progress, and that it would help make the world 'healthier, happier, more efficient, and more democratic than ever before'.[6]

The American historian Howard Segal suspects that the 'ahistorical contemporary visionaries' making such predictions had read too much of Fukuyama's ideas about 'the end of history'.[7] And indeed, in a similar way to Fukuyama's geopolitical ideas, the techno-optimism of the nineties led to an overestimation of the positive potential of change and an underestimation of the risks it entailed.

The electronic agora

It is often said that the internet was created in the 1960s, but that is not exactly true. The main precursor to the internet was a computer network set up by the American Department of Defence in the late sixties to enable decentralised communication in the case of a nuclear attack. That resulted in a technical protocol which was used to facilitate academic networks in the 1970s, and from the eighties onwards it was used in what was called Usenet, which could be dialled into with an analogue telephone via a modem. In 1990, America's National Science Foundation decided to open up its network for use by the general public, allowing internet providers to start selling connections on the free market. Another boost came from the invention of the World Wide Web, which made electronic content more readily available and more easily displayed by browsers. It was not until the mid-nineties that the internet became generally known beyond the realms of the military, academia, and small communities of tech enthusiasts.[8] From that point, the new technology began to spread increasingly rapidly. By the end of the nineties, a third of the population in developed countries had access to the internet; by the end of the 2000s, that had risen to nearly 70 per cent.

As the internet expanded from the mid-nineties onwards, there were many so-called techno-utopians who saw the digital revolution as a chance to build a new world. One of the most important left-wingers was the author Dale Carrico, who saw technological progress as the last remaining social force 'that could plausibly be described as potentially revolutionary'. Rather than resisting them, he thought the political left should become champions of 'disruptive' technologies like the internet, genetic engineering, and nanotechnology, which all challenge existing power and market monopolies, albeit in different ways.[9] On the right were the so-called techno-libertarians like the investor George Gilder, who advocated in his books for aggressive individualism and rejected any idea of state or social order.[10] Gilder believed the best mechanism for any form of social and economic selection lay in a market perfected by technology.[11] This worldview was so prevalent among young programmers, entrepreneurs, and technophiles in Silicon Valley that it became known as 'The California Ideology'.[12]

Politicians were principally inspired by the (less radical) techno-optimists, who prioritised more conventional (and typically liberal) aims such as democracy, education, and prosperity. Their political model was the 'agora' — a marketplace near the Acropolis where the freemen of Athens would gather in the 6th century BCE to discuss political issues and make suggestions to their representatives. In the view of the techno-optimists, the free exchange of ideas would lead to the best solution to any problem, and the more of it that took place, the freer the 'marketplace' where ideas are 'traded', and the better the final result would be. Even false, crazy, or extreme ideas would not constitute a problem in this environment since, they believed, 'good' ideas will always prevail over 'bad' ones in a society led by reason. So, the response to 'bad' ideas should be *more* exchange, rather than less. This was also the view of an American federal court that threw out a law aimed at regulating the internet in 1996. 'As the most participatory form of mass speech yet developed, the internet deserves the highest protection from government intrusion,' concluded one of the presiding judges, 'just as the strength of the internet is chaos, so the strength of our liberty depends upon the chaos and cacophony of the unfettered speech.'[13]

The techno-optimists believed such a 'marketplace' could be created with the aid of the internet. Then — as today — there was much criticism of the way the political discourse was conducted. As the techno-optimists saw it, the ideas and concepts that play a part in that process were not, in practice, chosen by a democratic collective of free citizens as they (supposedly) were at the original agora, but by a small group of editors, publishers, and media moguls whose political interests were often completely at odds with those of their 'consumers'. Only the internet had the potential to break that oligopoly of opinion-making. They believed the internet to be democratic and egalitarian, in contrast to traditional media such as newspapers, radio, or television: everyone has access, and no one can be excluded. Communication no longer took place in one direction, but in many — ideally *from* everyone *to* everyone. Instead of being information consumers, people were active information producers on the internet.[14] In other words, the techno-optimists saw the internet as a modern version of the agora, which would help solve social problems and improve democratic processes.[15]

Virtual visions

There were three main areas where the techno-optimists hoped to see progress. The first was the issue of social cohesion. One of the most influential contributions in this regard was the 1993 book *The Virtual Community* by the journalist Howard Rheingold. In that work, Rheingold relates his experiences as a member of one of the first online communities. He found everything there that he would expect to find in a community in 'real life', and more. Just like in the 'real world', on the internet there was love and hate, solidarity and envy, good will and ill will. But Rheingold found the virtual community superior in many ways to the one outside his front door. Those who joined the online community had sought out and found like-minded people rather than being thrown together with them by accidents of geography. They treated each other with more respect: since at the time chatting was purely text-based, race, gender, and disability were irrelevant, as, unless a user specifically wanted to talk about their membership of a particular group, there was no way others could know. This was one reason why Rheingold saw the internet as one of the key answers to the breakdown of traditional communities: 'Perhaps,' he concluded, 'cyberspace is one of the informal public places where people can rebuild the aspects of community that were lost when the malt shop parlour became a mall.'[16]

A common criticism of Rheingold's book was that the online community mainly consisted of affluent, educated people who were also well-integrated into 'real life' and therefore were not an accurate representation of American society as a whole — or of its problems. However, many of Rheingold's insights were presumably also true of more socially deprived communities. One study carried out by the RAND Corporation in 1995 investigated the effects of email use in various places and concluded that people from ethnic minorities, older people, and socio-economically disadvantaged groups benefited particularly from the new medium. An email account gave users access to other online services — such as newsgroups and chatrooms — and allowed them to take a more active part in discussions about problems in their local community. The researchers also found that the internet enabled users to find relevant information more easily, to organise themselves, and to speak with a united voice. In the southern Californian city of Santa Monica, for example, homeless people used an online petition to convince the municipal administration to open its shower facilities earlier in the day and provide lockers free of charge. Rheingold's observations about the supposedly egalitarian nature of online communication also seemed to be confirmed. Troublemakers and extremists were soon called to order by a majority of other members. 'The only basis for discrimination,' said one user from Seattle, 'is your typing speed.'[17]

The second area where techno-optimists hoped to see progress was public participation in politics. It seemed obvious that the internet offered opportunities to improve the democratic process, because it provided a way for more people to participate more easily in political debates. Many experts envisioned a kind of 'deliberative democracy', in which citizens would regularly participate in the formation of political opinion, express their views, and reach decisions in dialogue with politicians. The sociologist Benjamin Barber believed citizens would be able to use the internet to gather information, question politicians and experts, hold discussions in digital town hall meetings, and vote electronically on important issues.[18]

Social movements and non-governmental organisations campaigning for such causes as minority rights, environmental protection, or action against poverty received particular attention. The Canadian political scientist Jeffrey Ayres saw an opportunity for such movements to organise themselves more quickly and cheaply, as well as — most importantly — more internationally with the aid of the internet, enabling them to put pressure on not only their own governments but also multinational companies and transnational organisations.[19] The protests of December 1999 that took place at the World Trade Organisation (WTO) Ministerial Conference in Seattle and which objected to environmental destruction and the exploitation of developing countries were seen as the first success of such internet-based global activism.[20]

The third area in which positive change was anticipated was international politics. Although only around 2 per cent of people outside of the developed world had access to the internet at the end of the nineties, techno-optimists were confident that the entire world would be networked within the space of a few years. Futurologists John Arquilla and David Ronfeldt believed that a completely new kind of international politics would emerge from the spread of technology and the increased influence of non-governmental organisations. Alongside traditional *Realpolitik* — meaning the competition among states for more influence — the researchers believed the spread of ideas, values, and norms would become increasingly important in the future. A state's power would no longer depend on the strength of its military or its economy, but on its ability to influence the global exchange of ideas.[21]

A similar concept that emerged at the same time was Joseph Nye's idea of 'soft power'. His argument was that the attractiveness of societies, their ability to convince others of their ideas, to set agendas, and build coalitions, are just as important a way of exercising power as threats, sanctions, and violence — which Nye calls 'hard power'. Nye was concerned with far more than just the internet, but he argued that new communications technologies play an important part in the rise of soft power: 'The information revolution makes states more porous. Governments now have to share the stage with actors who can use information to enhance their soft power and press governments directly, or indirectly by mobilising their publics.'[22] More even than Arquilla and Ronfeldt, Nye saw the spread of the internet as a means of propagating democracy and, like Friedman and Clinton (see chapter 3), he believed that increased access to independent information would contribute to a process of liberalisation in authoritarian states such as China.[23]

Of course, most techno-optimists realised that the internet could also have a 'dark side'. Rheingold pointed out that users' data could be misused for surveillance purposes. Barber feared that media giants would commercialise the internet, destroying its democratic potential in the process. Ayres warned of 'global electronic riots', and Arquilla and Ronfeldt spoke of possible 'information wars'. But enthusiasm for the 'emancipatory character' of the new medium often drowned out such objections. Lawrence Grossman's 1996 bestseller *The Electronic Republic* is a good example of this. In his book, the former television producer described the risks and dangers that could emerge from the internet, and warned of the spread of populist or extremist ideas. In his conclusion, however, he brushed aside all doubts and reservations and, with great pathos, declared that America — and with it, the entire world — was on the brink of a new era of democracy. Through electronic media, Grossman argued, 'Many more citizens are gaining a greater voice in the making of public policy than at any time since the direct democracy of the ancient Greek city-states some 2500 years ago.'[24]

Internet policy

The most notable political pioneer of these ideas was Al Gore, who became Bill Clinton's vice president in 1993. Unlike most politicians, who only began to show interest in the internet when it started to catch the media's attention, Gore had been involved in the emergence of computer networks as early as the 1980s. He advocated for the expansion of 'supercomputers' while he was a senator in the mid-1980s — when only 5,000 computers around the world were connected in a network. He also called for an infrastructure to be created so that such computers could communicate with each other.

A 1991 law initiated by Gore provided the financing for a 'national information superhighway' to enable different networks to be combined to form a so-called internet. The term 'information superhighway' was more than just an analogy for Gore; it was an expression of his deep commitment. Just as the creation of a national network of highways in the mid-20th century had led to more trading between US states and a more active exchange of people and ideas, Gore believed it was the duty of politicians at the end of the 20th century to create a 'data highway' that would have an even greater and more positive effect on both business and society.[25] Two of the 'fathers' of the internet, computer engineers Robert Kahn and Vinton Cerf, later acknowledged Gore's vision, saying that even though he was not the 'inventor' of the internet,

'Al Gore was the first political leader to recognise the importance of the internet and to promote and support its development.'[26]

Like all techno-optimists, Gore believed that social progress was the consequence of technological advances and that this was especially true for democratic participation. In a speech to delegates of the International Telecommunications Union (ITU) in the spring of 1994, he explained that connecting computers in networks enabled them to pool their capacities and so find solutions to more complex problems more quickly, saying that the greater the exchange between computers, and the faster and simpler that exchange is, the more likely it is that fitting solutions could be found quickly. Gore hoped for a similar result from the internet and the information superhighways he was proposing in his speech — not just more trade or solutions to complex scientific problems, but a larger 'market of ideas':

> The Global Information Infrastructure will not only be a metaphor for a functioning democracy, it will in fact promote the functioning of democracy by greatly enhancing the participation of citizens in decision-making. And it will greatly promote the ability of nations to cooperate with each other. I see a new Athenian Age of democracy forged in the fora the GII will create.[27]

The idea of an 'electronic agora' that so fired the imagination of the techno-optimists had thus become official American policy.

In Europe, there was no equivalent to Al Gore, enthusiastically advocating for the development of this technology from the outset, who also had the necessary sway to promote it politically. But starting in the mid-nineties, Europe began to see a similar debate. As well as democracy, education was one of the central issues in that discourse. The British Prime Minister Tony Blair, for example, considered nationwide access to the internet to be one of his main election promises and he was keen to make good on it during his premiership. Even before that, when he was leader of the opposition, he proposed offering telecommunications companies privileged access to the market in return for ensuring that every state school and library was connected to the internet. Blair spoke of a 'supreme national effort', something he considered necessary to create 'an advanced system of further education for the electronic age', which would allow single parents, the unemployed, and the self-employed to study or train from home.[28] Once prime minister, Blair was one of the first to address the social gap between those with access to information technology and those without: 'This technology is revolutionising the way we work, the way we do business — the way we live our lives,' he said at an education conference in the spring of 2000, 'Our job is to make sure it is not the preserve of an elite — but an internet for the people.'[29]

In Germany, the focus of interest lay on the internet's economic potential. At a time when mass unemployment was the main political issue, politicians from all parties hoped the internet would provide an 'innovation boost', resulting in higher incomes and high-quality jobs. Although Germany had a relatively good telephone and data network compared to other countries, there was a fear that the country would fail to keep pace with the digital revolution, costing the economy hundreds of billions in lost output. One of the most dogged advocates of the 'transformation to an information society' was the Social Democrat politician Wolfgang Thierse, who regularly accused the government at the time of 'missing opportunities'. 'We are in the midst of a fast-moving process that will provide new opportunities and livelihoods in the very immediate future,' he told parliament in 1997. 'That process can only be compared with the Industrial Revolution, which changed social life totally within the space of two hundred years.'[30] Like many other parliamentarians, he warned that 'an industrialised society that hampers or sleeps through the modernisation of information technology will not be able to profit from it,' which in turn meant, 'It will not be able to maintain the existing level of employment, but will have to accept an enormous loss of jobs.'[31]

Thierse, Blair, and Gore had no interest in addressing the risks and dangers associated with the digital revolution. Thierse did call for the 'social and ecological' consequences of the internet revolution to be considered, but his primary objective in doing so was to raise the level of public trust in the new technologies. The political scientist Abel Reiberg examined the emergence of Germany's internet policy extensively and found that issues like child safety and data protection were only discussed if there was a suspicion that such questions might negatively affect people's acceptance and 'general positive use of the internet'.[32]

Reiberg also points out that there was a particular lack of serious debate about the impact the digital revolution would have on political discourse. Instead of provoking critical reflection, the rise and spread of the internet followed a positivist tradition that associated new technologies with social progress. Almost no one imagined that the internet could become a tool for autocrats and even terrorists. And it seemed just as inconceivable that the new medium would contribute to the polarisation of political discourse rather than its improvement. At that time, technology was considered intrinsically 'good' — and the vision of the techno-optimists was not just accepted; it became a political imperative.

CHAPTER 5
The New Terrorism

JUST AS THEY UNDERESTIMATED THE POLITICAL CONSEQUENCES OF the 'digital revolution', the liberal optimists also failed to recognise the danger of jihadist terrorism. That was evident as early as February 1993, when the World Trade Center in New York was targeted by terrorists for the first time. Six people were killed after a truck bomb denotated in the parking garage under the North Tower. The FBI arrested the first suspects within days, all of whom were part of a network run by a blind Egyptian cleric, Omar Abdel-Rahman.

The American public had heard little of Islamist extremism before the attacks of 11 September 2001, and so the group was no more than a curiosity for them. Newspapers portrayed it as some kind of cult of loons and fanatics gathered around a charismatic leader. Thomas Friedman — who, it should be noted, had experience as a Middle East correspondent — denied the group had any importance at all. Friedman described the bomb maker, a Pakistani man by the name of Ramzi Yousef, as 'the quintessential Super-

Empowered Angry Man'.[1] The FBI also had a hard time interpreting the significance of the case. Three dozen members of the group were convicted over the next few years, but the word 'terrorism' never appeared in any of their indictments. Their international connections were never investigated. And following the end of the final trial in 1997, the FBI discontinued all further investigations.[2] It's difficult to imagine from today's perspective, but the incident was practically forgotten until the attacks of September 2001; it was considered an isolated incident.

The National Commission on Terrorist Attacks Upon the United States, also known as the 9/11 Commission, later criticised the handling of the February 1993 attacks as grossly negligent. The 'Blind Sheikh' turned out not to be some crazed cult leader, but the spiritual head of a jihadist group that later joined forces with Al Qaeda. Yousef was not a 'crazy lone wolf'; he had met with Osama bin Laden several times and received money from his uncle, the terrorist planner Khalid Sheikh Mohammed, to fund the attack. Many of those convicted had fought in Afghanistan and had trained in bin Laden's training camps. Furthermore, bin Laden's name appeared on a list of 'unindicted co-conspirators' that the FBI prepared for trial, but never followed up on.[3] Long before anyone realised it, America had already been a victim of the Al Qaeda terrorist network.

The FBI's reaction to the February 1993 attack, as well as that of the American public, was symptomatic of the hesitant approach of Western political elites to the threat of jihadist terrorism in the 1990s. The danger was ignored for years, and even when it was recognised, it was not understood. The root of the problem was what the 9/11 Commission described in its conclusions as a 'failure of imagination'. After the end of the Cold War, there was not only a lack of the resources required to recognise the danger, but for a long time there was also a lack of will or ability among Western elites to even imagine such a direct challenge to the Western state system and its values.

Nihilist terrorism

Although terrorists are (usually) not state actors, there was a tacit acknowledgement during the Cold War that the main terrorist groups were 'sponsored' by states. Libya and Syria, for example, were involved in many conflicts in this way without getting their own hands dirty. Even the Soviet Union and the countries of the Eastern Bloc supported terrorist organisations, typically with the aim of destabilising Western states or US-backed governments.[4] In the early 1980s, the American author Claire Sterling published a book entitled *The Terror Network*, in which she attempted to prove that virtually all terrorist groups existing at the time were controlled by the Kremlin. According to her theory, international terrorism was Moscow's 'secret war on the West'.[5] Many saw that as hyperbole, but the idea that terrorist groups relied on the support of states was considered plausible by the intelligence services of most Western countries.[6]

Many experts hoped the end of the Cold War would lead to a decrease in terrorism, since many of the states that had supported terrorist groups would no longer have an interest in proxy wars, or had to exercise more restraint. And indeed, although it didn't happen overnight, half a dozen Marxist groups — such as the Baader-Meinhof Group in Germany — did vanish over the course of the following decade. The Middle East saw the development of the Oslo peace process, which led to the recognition of the Palestinian Liberation Organisation — formerly labelled a terrorist group — as the official representative organisation of the Palestinian people. And even in places that were not directly affected by the Cold War, such as Northern Ireland, there was a hope of peace, resulting ultimately in the 1998 Good Friday Agreement. In short, the end of the East–West confrontation brought movement into many deadlocked conflict situations, and it appeared as if, in particular, the left-wing and 'anti-imperialist' terrorism that had been sponsored during the Cold War by Eastern or Soviet-aligned states, would soon be a thing of the past.

However, while the 'old' terrorists were gradually retiring from armed conflict, experts like the Israeli-American historian Walter Laqueur recognised the rise of a more brutal terrorism that was seemingly of a totally different kind. The attack on the World Trade Center in February 1993, which the perpetrators hoped would kill up to a quarter of a million people, was just a first indication of that. In March 1995, members of the Japanese Aum Shinrikyo cult sprayed toxic sarin gas in a crowded Tokyo metro train during the morning rush hour. Their aim was to trigger a global Armageddon.[7] Less than a month later, a right-wing extremist veteran blew up a government building in the US state of Oklahoma, killing 169 people. And in the summer of 1998, Osama bin Laden came to the world's attention once more, when suicide bombers belonging to his network attacked the US embassies in two East-African countries, killing 224 people, most of them Africans. This was very different to the kidnappings and attacks of the seventies and eighties, which were often carried out for the benefit of television cameras and resulted in relatively few deaths.[8] The old maxim that 'terrorists want lots of people to watch, not lots of people to die' was no longer true.[9]

This 'new terrorism' turned out to be not only more brutal, but also more complex. No amount of probing could identify one single all-powerful state-sponsored 'octopus' controlling all the attacks and networks. In addition, the attackers were usually completely unknown, and their groups had a loose, rather than hierarchical structure. Security services began to speak of 'networks' rather than organisations, and those networks were constantly changing, with the ability to re-form as needed. In many cases, their motivation did not go back to any kind of clearly defined ideology as was the case in the Cold War, but was based on a diffuse mixture of personal frustration, hatred of the world, conspiracy theories, and — above all — apocalyptic interpretations of religion. Perhaps the most worrying aspect was the interest shown, and sometimes actively pursued, by many groups in chemical, biological, radiological, and nuclear weapons. This 'new terrorism' was extremely dangerous, and could not be reduced to one common denominator.[10]

The crux of the matter from the point of view of Western political elites was that this 'new terrorism' did not have a single, shared goal or a common enemy, and — most importantly — there was no central coordination or support from an enemy state trying to harness different groups for its aims. In the West's view, the many deaths in attacks by the 'new terrorists' were tragic, and states should do everything in their power to prevent existing stockpiles of chemical, biological, and radiological material from getting into the hands of terrorists. However, combatting this kind of 'nihilist' terrorism was not a political task; rather it was the job of psychologists and the police.[11] This was precisely the same view as that held by Fukuyama, who had warned of an increase in terrorism in his article on the end of history back in 1989, which he did not, however, believe would halt the spread of Western values.[12]

For a long time, with the exception of a handful of academics and journalists,[13] no one recognised that an ideologically coherent and globally operating network had formed out of that seemingly amorphous mass of 'angry young men', which could rely on astonishing resources as it energetically plotted to take on the West, its politics, and its value system. In the 1990s, two of France's leading Middle East experts published very influential books in which they both came to the conclusion that Islamism had already passed its peak.[14] Until the attacks of 11 September 2001, paying attention to supposed fringe figures like Osama bin Laden was 'frowned upon' in Germany, too.[15] Only the Muslim Brotherhood in Egypt and Palestinian Hamas occasionally received some attention, although they were seen as 'local issues'.

The only group that was already considering the rise of the jihadists in their political calculations were the US conservatives. Since long before the 9/11 attacks, they had argued that the greatest strategic danger to America's security was the proliferation of weapons of mass destruction and — more particularly — the 'nexus' between 'rogue states' and apocalyptic terrorists.[16] This was later to become one of the main justifications for the Iraq War (see chapter 8).

A regional problem?

A narrative that became popular among conspiracy theorists was that America had deliberately 'built up' Islam as the new enemy after the end of the Cold War. Once the Soviet Union was defeated, they argued, the West was in urgent need of a new opponent as a way of keeping its own population in check, distracting from its own failures in economic and social policy and, not least of all, in order to justify the financing of the 'military-industrial complex'. The description by the 'establishment academic' Huntington of a 'clash of cultures' and 'Islam's bloody borders' fitted well with that narrative. Thus, even before the 9/11 attacks, a number of commentators believed Islam was supposed to replace communism as the 'new bogeyman'.[17]

There was no evidence at all to support this narrative. For a large proportion of the 1990s, Western political elites all but ignored the threat from jihadist terrorism, and when they finally woke up to it, there was a lack of will to confront it politically or militarily. At the same time as Huntington was writing his article on the 'clash of cultures', the US Department of Defense was carrying out a confidential study to determine which of various possible conflict scenarios the American military should prepare for. None of those scenarios identified 'radical' or 'fundamentalist' Islam as a potential adversary. The only terrorists mentioned in the study were Latin American 'narcos'; drug dealers who it was feared could seize control of the Panama Canal.[18]

Even more importantly, America withdrew almost completely from Afghanistan in 1992, after supporting the 'Afghan resistance' — the 'mujahidin' — in its fight against the Soviet occupation in the previous decade. While the country had been an important battlefield in the fight against communism, it lost all significance after the end of the rivalry between East and West. Following the Soviet withdrawal, and even more so after the collapse of the Soviet Union in 1991, America no longer had any reason for engagement in the impoverished country.[19] Contrary to commonly made claims, there was no evidence that bin Laden was recruited by the CIA, or that he ever had contact with that agency or any other section of the US government.[20] The focus of America's relations then shifted almost completely to Pakistan, which wanted to end the civil war in its neighbour and establish a conservative religious government there that would be hostile to its arch-enemy India.[21] When America suddenly became interested in Afghanistan again towards the end of the decade, it was already too late, in the opinion of Michael Hurley, a senior CIA official: 'We had concentrated on other parts of the world and completely lost sight of the situation in Afghanistan.'[22]

The tardiness of Western intelligence services in recognising the danger posed by bin Laden's network is now historically well-documented. Until the late nineties, for example, few people were aware of the fact that former fighters from the war in Afghanistan had been involved in the firefight in October 1993 in which 19 US soldiers were killed and that led to the withdrawal of American troops from Somalia. As previously discussed, the part played by international jihadist networks in the bombing of the World Trade Center in February 1993 went unstudied until the end of the decade. It was not until 1996, when bin Laden issued a fifteen-page statement declaring war on America, that the CIA set up a special unit to monitor his activities.

The British were also largely In the dark. The UK's intelligence services were drastically cut after the end of the Cold War, and most of the staff that remained continued to concentrate on the Eastern Bloc and Northern Ireland. David Omand, who was appointed director of the intelligence monitoring service, GCHQ, in 1996, reported that the British intelligence agencies 'at the time [had] about three people who knew about international terrorism. It was not until the 9/11 attacks that we understood that it was a threat to us.'[23]

Part of the problem was that Western intelligence services had long considered the jihadist movement to be a 'regional issue'. And there were good reasons for that assumption — initially, at least. When many of those who had fought in the Soviet–Afghan War returned to their home countries, they were not initially concerned with waging war on the West but with overthrowing the leaders in their home countries. This explains the many terror campaigns throughout the Middle East and North Africa in the early nineties involving so-called Afghan veterans. Even those who had managed to make it to Europe as asylum seekers and were now living in places like London or Hamburg, were primarily concerned at the time with supporting their 'brothers' in their home countries. Gerhard Conrad, one of the foremost Middle East experts with Germany's Federal Intelligence Service (BND), recalls:

In the 1990s, we saw [jihadist] terrorism primarily as a regional problem, not as a global problem or one directed specifically at the West. It was clear that it was a bit anti-American, as the US was more exposed [with its troops] in the region [...] So we tried to keep an eye on those people, as there was always someone who went astray. But by and large, the European view was that terrorism was regional and we believed it did not concern us![24]

The situation remained unchanged into the mid-nineties, although it was becoming ever clearer that the jihadists were changing their strategy and beginning to shift their focus towards the 'far enemy', i.e., the West. The attacks that took place in France in 1994 and 1995 were seen as a 'special case' because of the civil war in Algeria and France's role as the former colonial power there.[25] Even bin Laden's 1996 'declaration of war' failed to prompt any change in this attitude, as the wording of his statement seemed to indicate that the Al Qaeda leader was primarily concerned with the presence of US troops in Saudi Arabia and the misdeeds of the Saudi monarchy.

It was not until bin Laden's second 'declaration of war' and the attacks on American embassies in East Africa in 1998 that it became impossible to deny that what had been assumed to be a regional problem had now gone global. In the opinion of Gerhard Conrad, it was only then that Western intelligence services recognised the full extent of bin Laden's intentions and his 'operational capacity': 'Before, no one really saw it, because no one really looked.'[26]

Manhunt

It took even longer for the danger to be recognised on the political level. Even after the attacks in East Africa, the Americans at first refused to believe that bin Laden was responsible. Ali Soufan, an FBI agent of Lebanese extraction who had already turned his attention towards bin Laden, found his suspicions fell on deaf ears at his agency. 'I argued with my headquarters [the day after the attacks] because I was sure it was bin Laden. But my bosses just said, "bin Laden would never attack us directly".'[27]

When investigations revealed that Soufan was right, the US security services pounced on this new threat. In the late 1990s, there were numerous investigations, international sanctions, and a military 'punishment strike' targeting bin Laden's camps in Afghanistan and an alleged poison gas factory in Sudan. But these measures were not systematic. They chiefly targeted bin Laden personally, rather than the global infrastructure he had built up over the course of the nineties. Writing in his autobiography, Bill Clinton described the efforts of his administration to combat Al Qaeda as a kind of manhunt, aimed first and foremost at ascertaining bin Laden's whereabouts in order to kill him with a cruise missile.[28] Estimates say the retaliatory strikes he ordered after the 1998 attacks hit a maximum of thirty Al Qaeda members. Bin Laden himself was never in danger.[29] The fact that the problem was not one single man, but a worldwide movement aimed at destroying America and the West, seems simply not to have fit with Clinton's optimistic view of the world.

The consequence of this was that important action that could have prevented the attacks of 11 September 2001 was not taken. Ali Soufan believes that no systematic pressure was put on Pakistan during Clinton's presidency, that communication between different intelligence services was abysmal, and that no one was concerned with raising awareness of the existence of a strategic threat.

After another attack on an American target — this time, on the destroyer USS *Cole* while in harbour in Yemen — the White House still resisted the obvious conclusion that the jihadist movement had declared war on America. According to Soufan, 'nobody in Washington wanted to hear that bin Laden was behind this attack. Because that would have meant something needed to be done.'[30] Thus, the attack, which after all claimed the lives of seventeen American sailors, remained without consequences for Al Qaeda. In contrast to the 1998 attacks, this one did not even provoke a retaliation strike.

Little changed in this respect under Clinton's successors. It almost seemed as if jihadist terrorism suited their ideas even less than those of Clinton's administration. Bush's principal foreign policy goal was to cement America's dominant position and the focus in doing so was on states that might represent competition or a threat to the US. Two months after he took office, Bush's top cabinet members outlined their priorities in a State Department journal: for Secretary of State Colin Powell, it was China, Russia, North Korea, Iraq, and NATO; Secretary of Defense Donald Rumsfeld mentioned missile defence and peacekeeping missions; and National Security Advisor Condoleezza Rice was interested in 'major powers and rogue states'.[31] None of them mentioned jihadist terrorism.

Rice in particular seemed to consider the issue to be of secondary importance. In the eight months before 9/11, she downgraded the position of National Coordinator for Counterterrorism and removed the holder of that office's access to the Principals Committee, where major security policy decisions were made. Richard Clarke held that position at the time. He found it difficult even to get a meeting with Rice. 'Like so many of the Clinton administration's actions,' writes Clarke in his memoirs, Rice found Clinton's fixation with bin Laden, 'rather odd'.[32]

The theory that the West systematically built Islam up as the 'new enemy' during the nineties is thus inconsistent with the facts. The real 'crime' was not that the West was intent on starting a conflict with Islam, but that the growing threat from the jihadist movement went completely unrecognised for so long. Though the reasons for it were varied, the idea that an aggressive global movement might exist which not only rejected Western values but actively fought against them, was inconceivable to Western political elites in the decade after the end of the Cold War. In fact, as late as July 2001, the former CIA analyst Larry Johnson was moved to write an article in which he criticised what he saw as the completely exaggerated view of the threat posed by terrorism. He claimed that Islamist terrorists were not gaining in strength, and nor was America in increasing danger of becoming a target. He concludes the article with the words, 'I hope for a world where facts, not fiction, determine our policy [...] Terrorism is not the biggest security challenge confronting the United States, and it should not be portrayed that way.'[33]

Only two months later, the threat posed by terrorism would prove to be far from fictitious. The real fiction turned out to be the ideas of 'perpetual peace' and the inexorable spread of democracy that blinded Western political elites to the new dangers during the 1990s.

PART II
Hubris
2001-2010

CHAPTER 6
Wake-Up Call 9/11

THE LIBERAL OPTIMISM OF THE 1990S CAME TO AN END EARLY IN THE morning of 11 September 2001, when terrorists crashed two passenger planes into the Twin Towers of the World Trade Center in New York, causing the skyscrapers to collapse and killing thousands of people. The immediate reactions were similar everywhere. The first was one of shock. People across the entire world were stunned as they watched the planes fly into the towers. It was unimaginable that one of the tallest and most recognised landmarks in the world could be reduced to rubble in the space of just a few seconds; it was inconceivable how much suffering the attackers were willing to cause. This was followed by the realisation that 11 September 2001 was a watershed moment. Just hours after the attacks, people were aware that everything would be different from then on — even if no one yet knew exactly how America would respond. The only thing that seemed certain was the thought expressed a few days later by the American writer Paul Auster: 'And so the twenty-first century finally begins.'[1]

That insecurity was due not only to the scale of the attacks but also to the fact that the terrorists gave no clue as to what their aims were.[2] Although there was little doubt within a few days that bin Laden's Al Qaeda network was behind the attacks, there was no video or text claiming responsibility. Conservative commentators therefore pounced on the attackers' religion and identified Islam as the reason for their fanaticism. Like the British historian Bernard Lewis, for example, they argued that religion was the main reason for the intolerance and propensity for violence in traditionally Muslim societies.[3] The left focused on America's foreign policy. Less than a week after the 9/11 attacks, the American writer Susan Sontag described them as 'a consequence of specific American alliances and actions' and criticised the sanctions against Iraq that were in place at the time,[4] US military interventions, and America's support for Israel and some Arab dictators. 'A lot of thinking needs to be done,' wrote Sontag, '[…] about options available to American foreign policy, particularly in the Middle East.'[5]

The prevailing interpretation of those events among Western political elites was, however, a different one. In their eyes, although the attacks took place on American soil, America was not the real — or only — target. For them, the US represented not just a nation state, a geographical territory, or particular set of interests; it also (and more importantly) represented the values and ideas that define the West. The German writer Ralph Giordano described America as a 'code word' for liberal modernity.[6] The German social scientist Michael Ehrke added that this was particularly true of New York:

The attack on the World Trade Center was not a counterstrike by the Third World on the First World, but rather in fact an attack on […] the civilisation of the Enlightenment […] Hardly any city in the world comes as close to [embodying the Enlightenment] ideal as New York, the multicultural city par excellence […] It was not only White Anglo-Saxon Protestants who died in the World Trade Center; it was people of all nationalities, skin colours, religious beliefs and social classes.[7]

From this perspective, the idea that America had brought the attacks on itself, or that the attackers had particular aspects of America's foreign policy in their sights, was wrong, because the attacks were aimed not solely at America, but at *all* similarly constituted states and societies and those which espoused ideas such as personal freedom, human rights, and democracy. The pithiest expression of this was the headline that appeared in the French daily newspaper *Le Monde* two days after the attacks: '*Nous sommes tous Américains*' — 'We are all Americans'.[8]

That interpretation had considerable consequences for the 'War on Terror' which followed the attacks. Western political elites did not see the conflict as being about America's Middle East policy, but about the Western model of society itself. It was a challenge not only to Americans, but to all those who were committed to liberal, Western values. Viewed from this perspective, 9/11 was not simply a terrorist attack, but the beginning of a protracted confrontation in which the West — led by America — had to defeat a powerful ideological enemy. This is precisely the way President George

W. Bush framed it when he spoke to a joint session of Congress on 20 September: 'Enemies of freedom committed an act of war against our country. [...] The civilised world is rallying to America's side.'[9]

What at first glance appeared to contradict Fukuyama's 'end of history', actually fit the pattern he postulated rather easily. The new threat was not a caesura, but the logical continuation of the conflict between liberal modernity and its totalitarian foes. Indeed, just months after the attacks, the conservative writer Charles Krauthammer described the War on Terror as a new version of the Cold War:

> On September 11, our holiday from history came to an abrupt end [...] American foreign policy acquired seriousness. It also acquired a new organizing principle: We have an enemy, radical Islam; [...] and its defeat is our supreme national objective, as overriding a necessity as were the defeats of fascism and Soviet communism.[10]

It was this hubristic world view that was the cause of the most serious mistakes made in the subsequent years. After years of *under*estimating the threat posed by Al Qaida, Western political elites now grotesquely *over*estimated it. And rather than concentrating on fighting the jihadist movement, the War on Terror became about 'modernising' completely foreign societies as quickly — and with as little effort and cost — as possible. As shown in this and later chapters, that led to the West's becoming entangled in a long, expensive, and in many ways disastrous conflict which severely damaged the position and appeal of modern liberal ideas rather than increasing them.

(Over-)Reaction

Two main factors contributed to the overestimation of the jihadist threat after the 9/11 attacks. The first was the fact that neither President Bush nor any other Western politician defined precisely who the enemy in the great new conflict was. There were, at most, 2,000 fighters in bin Laden's immediate circle that had organised the US attacks, but the network of so-called Afghan veterans who bin Laden had fought with in the 1980s (out of which Al Qaeda eventually grew), numbered an estimated 10,000 to 20,000 fighters. In addition, there were a dozen local groups in countries such as Algeria, Egypt, and Yemen, which were either allied to Al Qaeda or were under the influence of former fighters in Afghanistan. Depending on how they were counted, Al Qaeda had between two thousand and a hundred thousand 'members' — a huge possible range.

This became more complicated if the enemy was defined not just as Al Qaeda, but as 'radical Islam' — or Islamism — in general, as it was by Charles Krauthammer. This definition meant the enemy also included groups like the Taliban and Palestinian Hamas, for example, which were militant and Islamist but did not carry out attacks on Western targets. Other groups were also radical but generally not militant, such as the fundamentalist Salafist movement or the Muslim Brotherhood, which boasted millions of followers in dozens of countries. And then there were of course the states with Islamist governments, such as Saudi Arabia and Iran, which propagated their respective religious convictions around the world, but at the same time presented themselves as allies in the fight against terrorism. So who was now a friend, and who a foe?

Unlike the Cold War, there was no central point like the Kremlin, from where the global movement was managed, and even if the War on Terror was interpreted as being a 'war on *Islamist* terror', the 'enemy' remained vague, ill-defined, and confusing. The US under secretary of defense for policy and prominent neoconservative, Douglas Feith, later admitted that the term was imprecise and that his government struggled to describe the new conflict. However, Feith believes this also had its advantages. In his memoirs, he writes that it 'allowed the Administration to defer naming the enemy while it considered these perplexing questions'.[11]

The second factor was the hysteria whipped up by the media and by experts. In *Inside Al Qaeda*, the first book on the group, which was published six months after the attacks, the Sri Lankan–born terrorism expert Rohan Gunaratna portrayed Al Qaeda as a global hydra spreading through every country in the world, adapting to local conditions and constantly working towards the destruction of Western civilisation. Readers of Gunaratna's book — which became required reading in many security services[12] — were left with the impression that Al Qaeda was unbeatable.[13]

Similar ideas were spread by the American criminologist Harvey Kushner, who appeared on many chat shows talking about the 'infiltration' of America by a 'secret Islamic terror network' and lost no opportunity to warn of 'sleeper cells' just waiting for the order to carry out more attacks. According to his book *Holy War on the Home Front*, virtually every Muslim organisation in America was part of a widespread conspiracy in which Al Qaeda coordinated its activities with those of the Muslim Brotherhood, the (largely secular) PLO, and the Abu Nidal Organisation (which had been inactive for years).[14]

Another such example is the journalist Paul Williams, who, like Kushner and Gunaratna, was employed by the FBI and other security agencies as a 'consultant' after the 9/11 attacks. In *Al Qaeda: brotherhood of terror*, Williams claimed that the group had a 'nuclear program' and was in possession of Russian-made tactical nuclear weapons, so-called suitcase bombs.[15] In a later book he even went so far as to claim that a high-ranking member of the group had gained access to a Canadian nuclear power plant and stolen more than 80 kilograms of nuclear material.[16]

None of this was true, but reports of this kind gave many people in both America and Europe the feeling that their existence was under threat. Although barely anyone had shown an interest in it before 9/11, bin Laden's group now suddenly seemed more powerful — and more fanatical — than the Soviet Union during the Cold War.

The threat matrix

The information among the security services was little better. Since Western secret services had long paid almost no attention to the jihadist movement, there was little knowledge immediately after the attacks of how the movement functioned, who belonged to Al Qaeda, and what relationship other Islamist groups had to bin Laden's network. John Evans, the former head of the British domestic intelligence service MI5, describes the phenomenon as an 'Islamist soup': 'We had a lot of Islamist groups in London — all with similar ideologies, but with different set-ups, regional interests, personalities, and connections. It was difficult to imagine Al Qaeda as a single structure.'[17]

Another factor at play was public pressure, as the secret services did not want to be accused of having missed the signs of an imminent attack once more. The former top CIA officer Michael Hurley remembers:

After the attacks we drew up a threat matrix which was presented to the president each day. It was a file containing everything that was intercepted by the NSA, the CIA, and the military. Of course, we wanted to prevent a repeat of the 9/11 disaster at all costs. But at the same time, many of my colleagues were concerned with covering their own asses. Nobody wanted to be the one who missed the next attack. And so we reported everything we heard — sometimes even unconfirmed or uncertain information.[18]

The author David Frum, who was a White House speechwriter at the time, recalls 'scary' presentations about possible planned attacks 'which would make 9/11 seem harmless by comparison'. By the end, Frum continues, 'everyone was as white as a sheet'.[19] Peter Bergen, a reporter for CNN who had interviewed bin Laden in Afghanistan in 1997, has a similar recollection of the mood: 'After 9/11 everyone thought another attack would happen soon.' His conclusion: 'They *over*estimated the danger because they had *under*estimated it before.'[20]

This near-hysterical view of the threat situation shaped the entire War on Terror and formed the basis for America's so-called One-Percent Doctrine, under which terrorist threats that were previously seen as improbable were now treated as if they were inevitable. That was particularly true of possible attacks using weapons of mass destruction, which bin Laden had declared in interviews it was a 'religious duty' to acquire. In the view of Vice President Dick Cheney, the most likely way for terrorists to get hold of such weapons was from 'rogue states' that already possessed them and would be willing to pass them on to terrorists for ideological or opportunistic reasons. The combination of terrorism, weapons of mass destruction, and 'rogue states' thus came to be seen as the worst-possible horror scenario, which American, and also other Western politicians such as Tony Blair in Britain and John Howard in Australia, were determined to prevent at any cost.[21]

An immediate consequence of this was that almost any means of fighting terrorism now seemed justified. When the West's very existence was at stake, Enlightenment values, which the War on Terror was in fact meant to defend, were suddenly not so important. 'The Constitution is not a suicide pact' was an often-quoted phrase, which meant in practice that the principles of the rule of law could be ignored in order to counter any threats. Cheney in particular believed America had been attacked only because it had signalled 'weakness' to its enemies — for example by hastily withdrawing its troops from Somalia, or by not retaliating after the attack on the warship USS *Cole*. 'Weakness is provocative,' the vice president said in a TV interview. 'It's encouraged people like Osama bin Laden […] to launch repeated strikes against the United States […] with the view that he could, in fact, do so with impunity.'[22]

Confusion over who were the real enemies in this war helped foster a situation in which America and its allies were prepared not only to accept serious human rights violations, but to actively promote them. The later Secretary of Defense Robert Gates said in an interview, 'A lot of the measures, including the renditions, Guantánamo, the enhanced interrogation techniques — all were out of a sense of desperation to get information because we had so little.'[23]

Imposed modernisation

Of course, 9/11 was followed by a search for the deeper causes — not least of all because President Bush had made it clear from the start that he wanted to fight not only terrorism, but also the 'roots' of terrorism. Explanations that branded either Islam or America's 'imperialist' foreign policy as the fundamental evil received much attention in the media, but carried relatively little influence. In the view of Western political elites, the important issue was that the Middle East,[24] the region which had produced the 9/11 attackers, lagged behind the rest of the world both politically and economically. For the American commentator Gary Schmitt, it was the only region where liberal modernity had failed to deliver on its 'promise'. So, the West's response to 9/11 should be neither a 'culture war', as pursued by the right, nor a 'retreat', as demanded by some on the left, but — on the contrary — it should be to 'export' modern, liberal ideas even more vigorously. The modernisation of Arab and Muslim-majority societies was the great 'unfinished business' that had become even more urgent due to the 9/11 attacks.[25]

The mainstream Western political elites readily accepted this argument. The Middle East's presumed 'backwardness' and the political and economic malaise it engendered were a constant topic of discussion at international conferences even before 9/11. In 2000, the United Nations Development Programme (UNDP) set up a working group made up of (mostly Arab) academics that produced several reports in the following years on the state of 'human development in the Arab Region'. Those reports, the first of which was published in 2002, became the bible of the modernisers. They described in great detail how the region had fallen behind the rest of the world since the 1960s: while economic productivity grew rapidly throughout the world, it shrank in the Arab Region; and, although literacy rates increased, education was slow to progress, schools were bad, and women were systematically disadvantaged. Reports indicated that the biggest problem was the political situation. The Middle East was the most 'unfree' region in the world, its citizens had few rights, political dissent was suppressed, and there was no media freedom. All that, together with high population growth and the 'surplus' of young men with few prospects for the future, created a 'powder keg' that was bound to explode sooner or later.[26]

In the view of the Western political class, the UNDP reports provided the perfect explanation for the fact that the Middle East had become a 'breeding ground' for extremist movements. Moreover, the recommendations for action made in the reports — for more education, women's rights, and political freedoms[27] — were in line

with the modern liberal agenda and bolstered the still boundless
optimism regarding the triumph of liberal democracy. Even a year
after the attacks had taken place, the liberal professor Michael
Mandelbaum wrote that the combination of democracy and the free
market were 'unbeatable', that they no longer had any rivals, and
that they would continue to spread under American leadership.[28]
His Harvard colleague Robert I. Rotberg even believed that the
War on Terror would provide fresh impetus to help weak or failed
states onto their feet: 'The new imperative of state building,' writes
Rotberg, '[...] trumps terror.'[29] Despite the dramatic geopolitical
situation, no task appeared too difficult for the liberal modernisers.
No problem that could not be solved with more market economy
and liberal democracy.

Against this background, the positions taken by the
neoconservatives were not as extraordinary as they seem in
retrospect. Their analysis of the problems in the Middle East was
for the most part identical to that of the UNDP reports. According
to people like the leading neoconservative Fouad Ajami, those
mainly responsible for the Middle East's problems were not foreign
powers but rather local rulers who oppressed their populations and
were incapable of providing them with jobs and adequate living
conditions. To distract from their own failures, these rulers tried to
deflect their people's frustration towards America or Israel, which,
in turn, benefitted the Islamists as it added extra authenticity to
their anti-Western narrative.[30] Thus the line of conflict that was
decisive for the 9/11 attacks did not run between America and 'the
Arabs', but within Arab societies. The root of the conflict was not
America but rather a lack of political freedom.

If America were guilty of anything, it was not recognising the situation sooner, and relying too long on a policy of supposed stability. Neoconservatives and liberals agreed that America's long-standing support for dictators and royal families who presented themselves as guarantors of American interest, but who were in reality inciting their populations against America, had contributed to the rise of Islamism. In this view, the cause of the widespread anti-American sentiment in the region was not that Arabs rejected Western values, or that Islam was incompatible with democracy, but that America was withholding from the Arabs the very thing its presidents spoke of in grand terms as 'America's mission' — namely, freedom. The American professor Michael Doran put it in a nutshell: 'They didn't support *us* because we didn't support *them*.'[31]

Europe vs. America

Europe also had intellectuals and politicians who espoused those positions. These included some on the left of the political spectrum who later vehemently opposed the Iraq War. A prominent example was Joschka Fischer, who was Germany's foreign minister at the time of the 9/11 attacks. In his book *The Return of History*, Fischer describes 9/11 as 'the most radical response' to the 'modernisation crisis' in the Middle East.[32] He claimed the states in the region were corrupt and lacking in innovative businesses, while the profits from selling oil and gas were wasted. For Fischer, the governance situation was even worse: 'Societies are usually ruled in an authoritarian or even dictatorial way, democracy, human rights, an independent judiciary, gender equality and a modern education system are broadly lacking in many states.'[33]

Fischer believed that it was not the Americans or the West that were to blame for this, but the region's authoritarian rulers who were keen to prevent any kind of progress for fear of losing their grip on power. Criticising Israel, America, or the West was mainly a way of 'detracting from the real reasons for the modernisation blockade in the region'.[34] Fischer held that radical change was necessary to destroy the 'roots' of terrorism:

> Stabilisation of the status quo will not enable it to absorb the dramatically growing pressure for change. From the West's point of view, it has been clear since 9/11, if not before, that continuing to cling on to the status quo in that region would also mean accepting very great and barely calculable risks.[35]

Fischer's analysis, his description of jihadism as a kind of 'totalitarianism',[36] and — not least of all — his call for a radical modernisation imposed from the outside, were almost perfectly in line with the framing of the situation by the American neoconservatives. He freely admitted this: 'When it comes down to it,' Fischer writes in his book, 'Europe shares the [US's] strategic interest in a democratic transformation of the entire region to prevent a future terrorist threat in the long term.'[37]

The difference between the neoconservatives and the rest of the Western political elites was not their objective, but the means by which they thought their aim should be achieved. International organisations had always been less important to America, as the hegemonic power, than they were to Europe, but the neoconservatives' stance was extreme even by American standards. As early as October 2001, one of the best-known proponents of that stance, Richard Perle, a key advisor to the secretary of defense, declared he did not care about international law and that America neither required nor sought international support for its War on Terror. He found even NATO's show of solidarity in the wake of the attacks uncomfortable: 'If it gives the impression that we [...] have to get NATO's approval, then it is more damaging than useful to us.'[38]

This was closely connected with a focus on the use of military means. As the neoconservatives saw it, there was no other way to remove the brutal dictators who were standing in the way of the modernisation of the Middle East. In their eyes, democratisation meant regime change, and regime change was only possible if America helped to 'liberate' the oppressed people from the oppressors. This was also Bush's view when he declared at the start of the war in Iraq: 'We believe the Iraqi people are deserving and capable of human liberty. And when the dictator has departed, they can set an example to all the Middle East of a vital and peaceful and self-governing nation.'[39]

What was Europe's response to that? People like Joschka Fischer didn't mince their words when it came to criticising the neoconservatives' approach. But neither Fischer nor any other European politician could come up with a workable alternative. None of the proposals put forward by the European political elites after the 9/11 attacks was likely to achieve their grandiosely stated aim of bringing about a 'democratic transformation in the entire region'. On the contrary, the Europeans too failed to 'modernise' a foreign society rapidly from the outside in, as the next chapter shows.

CHAPTER 7
The Good War

AFGHANISTAN WAS NOT A PLACE THE US PLANNED TO SPEND A LOT OF time. When it emerged that the 9/11 attacks were organised from there, and that Osama bin Laden had found refuge and set up his training camps there, the Bush administration saw no alternative but for America to take military action. However, no one in the administration had any grand plans for Afghanistan, nor did they see the country as a central pillar of the 'modernisation project' formulated by the liberal and neoconservative elites in Washington in the wake of the 9/11 attacks. Afghanistan was too far off the beaten track, too backward, too unimportant, and too complex. As George W. Bush told Tony Blair in a telephone call, Afghanistan was just a preliminary staging post — 'the first circle' in the War on Terror,[1] the main aim being to take out the terrorist networks that were responsible for 9/11. The Bush administration wanted to avoid anything that might give the impression of a permanent presence in the country, or of 'nation building'.[2] And they certainly wanted to avoid anything that might indicate they were prepared to stay as long as the Soviet Union had in the 1980s. If anything, the war was intended as a 'signal' of America's determination to deal ruthlessly with terrorists and their state backers in the future. The strategy was to 'hit them hard' and then retreat.[3]

This attitude was reflected in the fact that Afghanistan barely featured in discussions among the US leadership and the conservative elites in America, and planning the war was left almost completely in the hands of the military and the CIA. There was not even a clearly defined military goal when the US began bombing terrorist training camps and Taliban positions on 7 October 2001. Priority was given to destroying the training camps and killing or capturing Al Qaeda members. Closely connected to this was the aim of toppling the Taliban regime, which had harboured Al Qaeda. However, many questions remained unanswered. Were the Taliban also a threat? What kind of a government should they be replaced with? And who would be responsible for rebuilding and stabilising the country?[4] No one in Washington was keen to think about the future.

The military campaign culminated just one month later in the capture of the Afghan capital, Kabul. Rather than launching a complex and expensive invasion with ground troops, America had sent a small number of CIA officers and special forces into Afghanistan who allied themselves with anti-Taliban groups and coordinated the air strikes. The journalist Josef Joffe described this kind of warfare as 'so novel and effective' that it ushered in a new era in the history of military conflicts.[5]

However, it quickly became apparent that the low-level presence of American troops also had its drawbacks. America had to rely on local warlords and militia leaders, who had their own agendas and who were often just as unpopular with the public as the Taliban was. And when the CIA eventually located bin Laden — the most important military aim of the entire campaign[6] — and surrounded him in the cave complex at Tora Bora, there were too few troops to stop him escaping across the mountains to Pakistan. Alongside bin Laden, an estimated 1,500 other Al Qaeda members fled to the tribal areas of Pakistan in autumn 2001, where they set up new training camps in the following years.[7]

When the last major battle against Al Qaeda was won in March 2002, many American generals wanted to end the military campaign and leave the country.[8] That view was shared by the Bush administration, which had already tasked central command (Centcom) with preparing for the Iraq War in November 2001. Although Blair managed to persuade the Americans not to withdraw completely from Afghanistan,[9] they still reduced their troop presence in the summer and cut reconstruction funding by 90 per cent. They initially earmarked a mere one million dollars for the creation of a new Afghan army. Dov Zakheim, a neoconservative who was under secretary of defense in charge of finances, later referred to that amount as 'laughable' and described the policies of his government as 'tragic'.[10]

Thus, the 'modernisation' of Afghanistan was never an American project. As it turned out, it was mainly the political elites in Europe who from the outset saw the military engagement in Afghanistan not just as an anti-terrorism mission, but also as part of a comprehensive modernisation programme. After the preliminary end of the (American) military campaign, they pushed for a continued presence in Afghanistan, for the country to be rebuilt, for stable, democratic structures to be put in place, and for human rights — especially women's rights — to be enforced. The failure of that ambitious project was not due primarily to America, but far more to the completely unrealistic ideas pursued, though not nearly sufficiently funded, by European governments.

'True Believers'

Of course, security concerns were also important for the Europeans. Under Taliban rule, Afghanistan was believed to have become a safe haven for terrorists from all over the world, and European countries were also thought to be among their targets. As British Prime Minister Tony Blair argued, it was vital to 'ensure that Afghanistan ceases to harbour and sustain international terrorism'.[11] This was closely connected to the concept of 'solidarity among allies' and Europe's obligation to stand, in Blair's words, 'shoulder-to-shoulder' with America in the wake of the 9/11 attacks: 'We, like them, will not rest until this evil is driven from our world.'[12]

However, it soon became clear that security interests were not sufficient justification. For many in Europe, the terrorist threat from Afghanistan remained abstract, and reservations about 'unequivocal solidarity' with the American superpower caused unease even among many who were not part of the political left. So, rather than restricting their arguments to the security issue, European political elites increasingly began to argue that the military campaign in Afghanistan was a mission to promote peace, development, and human rights. As such, the aim was not merely to fight terrorism, but to 'liberate' Afghanistan from the 'brutality, inhumanity and, backwardness' of the Taliban. The military mission to Afghanistan was not only a necessary war, but also a 'just' one.

Those justifications were not mutually exclusive and there were many who, depending on the occasion or audience, linked the two. For example, the diplomat Christoph Heusgen, who worked with the EU foreign policy chief Javier Solana at the time, advocated for a 'broader approach' that went beyond America's objectives: 'We were convinced that the only way the fight against terrorism could succeed was if the state was on a reasonably stable footing, and so state building was also a necessary task.'[13]

But as the debate in the German parliament on 22 December 2001 showed, normative — i.e., moral — arguments were what mattered to left-wing politicians in particular.[14] At that session, lawmakers voted on whether Germany's armed forces should participate in the stabilisation mission established by the United Nations — known as the International Security Assistance Force (ISAF). In their speeches, members of the two parties of the governing coalition at the time (Social Democrats and Greens) consistently referred to it as a 'peace mission'. Rather than chasing terrorists, the Afghan government had to be assisted in establishing democratic institutions. ISAF would remain strictly separated from America's ongoing anti-terror operations — as if the two had nothing to do with one another.[15] It seemed Europe was only to be responsible for fighting the 'good' part of the war.

Women's rights were the most important issue for many parliamentarians. In their eyes, the Taliban, who advocated stoning women to death and forced them to wear the burqa, were an even worse enemy than bin Laden. Members of the government repeatedly stressed that 'the rights of women and girls in particular [...] would have continued to be suppressed' if the Taliban regime had not been overthrown.[16] The minister for development aid, Heidemarie Wieczorek-Zeul, proudly reported that women had 'removed the veil' after the liberation, and many girls were able to attend school for the first time. She promised that the women of Afghanistan could 'rely on our support'.[17]

In several speeches during the debate, parliamentarians also mentioned the principle of 'the responsibility to protect', according to which the international community has a duty to intervene in grave abuses of human rights and 'crimes against humanity'. Instead of retaliation for the 9/11 attacks or self-defence, these politicians' were concerned with enforcing universal values:[18] 'If we want to establish a fairer world order,' said Wieczorek-Zeul, 'in which human rights are respected and the international system of values applies, [...] then this is our moment.'[19]

The few parliamentarians who abstained in the December 2001 vote or voted against the deployment already suspected that those expectations were completely unrealistic. Helmut Rauber of the centre-right Christian Democrats pointed out that the number of troops allocated to the mission was far too small to guarantee peace in a country the size of Afghanistan. He also called attention to the fact that the new Afghan president, Hamid Karzai, was reliant on the support of warlords whose human rights records were as dismal as the Taliban's. Wolfgang Gehrcke, a former communist and member of the Left Party, was even more explicit, saying he had supported the 1979 Soviet intervention, 'with the same bad arguments you are using now'.[20]

'The bare minimum'

For a number of years, it seemed as if the European elites' plan was working. In mid-2005, the German Foreign Minister, Joschka Fischer, reported 'impressive progress' in stabilising Afghanistan: 'The completely democratically legitimate central government now controls most of the country, reconstruction efforts are progressing successfully, and the overall security situation has improved.'[21] In the spring of 2006, the British defence secretary reportedly declared that Western troops would be able to leave the country within three years 'without a shot being fired'.[22] However, the situation escalated within a few weeks. The Taliban, whose presence had until then been seen as limited or sporadic, were suddenly active once again all over the country. 'The Taliban gradually returned,' writes British journalist Ben Anderson, 'slipping back over the border from Pakistan as easily as they had left.' Beyond Kabul, Anderson adds, 'there was no one around to stop them'.[23] There were more than 130 suicide attacks before the year 2006 was out — many of them targeting Western troops and military facilities. After four years of relative calm, war had returned to Afghanistan.

The failures that led to the resurgence of the Taliban are now well documented. One of the biggest mistakes was made very early on. Fearing a total collapse of the country, the delegates at the December 2001 Petersberg peace conference in Bonn backed a strong, centralised system of government. But the position of president went to Hamid Karzai — an intellectual who came from a prominent Pashtun family but had no 'power base' and who, as Helmut Rauber had predicted, was dependent for every important decision on the support of warlords who were more interested in enriching themselves than creating democratic structures. This made Karzai a weak president who often had no choice but to leave corrupt governors in office if he didn't create alternative posts for them or bring them into his government. Although he himself may not have been corrupt, he presided over a system in which billions of dollars in aid just seeped away and in which the Afghan people — quite understandably — never placed their trust.[24]

This was compounded by the fact that the only party to unconditionally support Karzai and his project for a democratic Afghanistan — i.e., the 'international community' — completely failed to live up to expectations. The reconstruction aid promised by the West fell far short of expectations. Ten billion US dollars were pledged in the three years following 2001, with 14 billion promised in the subsequent six years. However, some of that money remained unpaid, some of it ended up in the coffers of corrupt officials and warlords, and as much as 40 per cent flowed back to the West in the form of corporate profits, consultant salaries, and wages for Western development aid workers.[25] A study by the RAND Corporation think tank calculated that during this period Afghanistan received only around half as much per-capita aid from the West as Mozambique, a quarter as much as Serbia, and only one twenty-fifth (!) of the amount spent on Kosovo.[26] The former president of Germany's Federal Intelligence Service (BND) August Hanning admits, 'We focused on the wrong things. We should have done far more to promote economic development.'[27]

The situation was similar when it came to security. The 5,000 troops initially provided by ISAF were too few to safeguard security in such a big country. When the conflict escalated, the number of troops was increased significantly (there were almost 20,000 non-US ISAF troops in Afghanistan in 2007; in 2010 that number stood at almost 40,000), but they never managed to gain control over the insurgency. One reason for this was that many European ISAF members lacked a political mandate and/or the necessary equipment to take on the Taliban, and many were engaged in securing supply lines, logistics, and protecting their own troops. Of the 50 nations present in Afghanistan, only America and a handful of other countries actually took part in combat missions in any practical sense.[28]

Even politically uncontentious tasks became mired in massive problems. For example, in spring 2002, Germany offered to train Afghanistan's new police force. This was an important task since, alongside the Afghan army, it was the police who symbolised the authority — and the monopoly on the use of force — of the new democratic government. The Afghan national police force was meant to number 40,000 officers within two years. But achieving that aim with the programme organised by Germany would probably have taken decades. The German government provided a total of just 17 trainers and planned to put recruits through a full three-year training course, as is the case in Germany, before they were deployed as police officers.[29] Germany's efforts were so inadequate that it was relieved of the task only a year later, in 2003. Even Chancellor Gerhard Schröder's security advisor at the time, Bernd Mützelburg, now takes a critical view of Germany's involvement.

'We didn't have a supply of police trainers we could just take out
of a cupboard somewhere and send to Afghanistan [...] It was a
very difficult learning curve.' His conclusion is rather telling: 'When
it comes down to it, we Germans only ever did enough to allow
us to sleep easy at night. That attitude coloured great phases of
our involvement in Afghanistan.'[30] Stefan Kornelius, chief foreign
policy editor at the *Süddeutsche Zeitung* newspaper, concurs with
that view: 'Fear about the public mood and about setting demands
for itself that it could not meet led Germany to keep its political
ambitions to a minimum.'[31]

This kind of Western reticence was also the reason why for
such a long time no one considered what the Taliban represented
and how they should be treated. One of the few positions on which
the Europeans, the Americans, and the Afghan government were
able to agree very quickly was that the Taliban must be defeated,
not negotiated with. The Europeans in particular saw the Taliban
as the 'bogeyman' to such an extent that for a long time any kind of
political engagement with them seemed impossible. Mützelburg,
who was appointed Germany's special envoy to Afghanistan at the
end of the decade, recalls:

> There was incomprehension all round when I said that
> peace must also — and indeed particularly — be made
> with the other side. That was especially the case among
> those who were very concerned about human rights. They
> always replied, 'Surely you're not seriously recommending
> that we should make peace with these people who are up
> to their ankles in blood?'[32]

Although the BND was already in contact with the Taliban at that time, it was not until the early 2010s that the Taliban were accepted as a political actor with deep roots in the Pashtun areas of southern Afghanistan.[33]

Culture warriors

If the Western political elites had paid attention earlier — and more intensively — to Afghanistan, they would have seen how far removed their ideas of modernising the country were from the realities of daily life for many Afghans. Europeans learned what the people of the country wanted for their future and that of their society mainly from the tiny minority of 'progressive' Afghans who lived in the capital Kabul, 'removed the veil' when Western politicians came to visit, spoke fluent English, and had well-paid jobs working for the international community. The European modernisers had little or no contact with the three quarters of the Afghan population who lived outside of the main cities, enjoyed little formal education, made their living from agriculture, and lived according to tribal traditions and their interpretations of Islam, as well as the rhythm of the seasons.

But these were precisely the people who had supported the Mujahidin back in the 1980s and who now sympathised with the Taliban twenty years later. Once again, their anger was directed towards foreigners and 'progressive' Afghans who were determined to 'liberate' the rest of the country from its supposed backwardness. And, just as they had before, the insurgents portrayed themselves as the defenders of religion and the traditional way of life. Without even realising it, the West became entangled in an inner-Afghan culture war that had been smouldering since the 1920s and had erupted in violent conflict multiple times.

Often, even the mere presence of foreign 'non-believers' supported the Taliban's narrative. As well as Western troops, an army of Western aid and reconstruction workers descended on Kabul and provincial capitals, often showing little regard for Afghan social norms, dressing in ways considered provocative, throwing rowdy parties, and drinking alcohol. The sight of heavily armed female soldiers patrolling the streets in tight T-shirts was equally shocking. Public events celebrated in the West as signs of 'progress' and 'modernisation' — such as concerts given by popstars or the first 'Miss Afghanistan' pageant after 2001 — were considered humiliating by conservative Afghans, or they were seen as proof of the decline of Afghan culture.[34] Rising prices and only very slow improvements in living standards led to resentment that played into the hands of those who opposed the Western intervention. 'See where your democracy gets you,' the mullahs preached, 'they want to kill our values.'[35]

The women's rights agenda also contributed to the mobilisation of the Taliban. None of the Western governments that insisted on 'equality' after the fall of the Taliban had seriously examined the situation and role of women in Afghanistan. Many of the extremely restrictive practices that the Taliban were accused of introducing before 2001 were in fact deeply rooted in large parts of the country. Even in liberal provinces, it was usual practice for male family members exclusively to communicate with outsiders. Only very close members of their own families saw women outside their own homes, and it was completely inconceivable that a stranger — no matter their gender — should meet alone with an Afghan woman.[36] The likelihood that such women would be reached by Western-financed projects was practically nil. Indeed, attempts by Western non-governmental organisations to help women in rural areas to assert their rights led to unrest and to a conservative backlash in many places.[37] This led Chris Johnson, a British development worker for Oxfam in Afghanistan, to argue that 'change for women is thus impossible unless there is a change first in the attitudes of men'.[38]

Some progress was made, of course. After the fall of the Taliban and with the aid of the West, the new government promoted the construction of schools, and many Afghan girls were given the chance to receive an education for the first time. By 2004, girls already made up a third of school students, and the Taliban even relaxed its opposition to compulsory education for girls. However, once again, there were great differences between 'modern' cities like Kabul and Herat where two thirds of girls went to school, and rural areas, especially in the south, where fewer than 5 per cent of girls received a school education. It was in such areas in particular that newly built schools were left standing empty because no teachers could be found to work there, and schools were attacked as 'anti-Islamic' or as symbols of Western influence.[39]

Rory Stewart, a British diplomat and later the secretary of state for international development, lived in Afghanistan for several years and set up a foundation there. In 2008, he wrote that the challenge went far beyond the Taliban: 'The rural areas of Afghanistan remain far more isolated, conservative and resistant to change than we publicly acknowledge.' According to Stewart, the ambition of creating a state based on democracy, respect for human rights, gender equality, and the rule of law could not be achieved with the means available: 'Many of these objectives are not simply difficult but dishonest and impossible.'[40] Hannah Neumann, a conflict researcher and Green Member of the European Parliament for Germany, takes a similar view today:

> There was a complete overestimation of what was possible for outsiders to achieve. The international community believed people in the mountains would be interested in the fact that we were building headquarters in Kabul. The narrative was, 'We'll go there and liberate the women.' I can appreciate the thinking behind that, and the idea in itself is not wrong, of course. But it's based on a concept of state-centralised democracy such as we have in Europe. [...] We should have been asking what resources we actually had available to us, how people were living before, and how we could make small changes for the better in three or four areas.[41]

It would be more than a decade before this view gained general acceptance among the European political elites. Even the more-than 130,000 Western troops (of which 90,000 were from the US) mobilised again by the West in 2011 and 2012 were unable to break the insurgency. The West — and Europe in particular — failed in Afghanistan, not only because of the Taliban, but above all also because of itself.

CHAPTER 8
Regime Change

UNLIKE AFGHANISTAN, THE IRAQ WAR THAT STARTED IN MARCH 2003 was a profoundly American project. According to the media at the time, the West was 'split', and the 'Western project' was in danger.[1] However, the rifts that opened up on the continent were geopolitical rather than ideological in nature. Those who backed America in 2002 and 2003 did so for pragmatic reasons. Neither Spain's prime minister, José María Aznar, nor the leader of the opposition in Germany at the time, Angela Merkel, or Australia's John Howard agreed with the central premise of this American war. They supported America's plans not because they actually believed in the 'liberation' of Iraq, but principally because they wanted to maintain the Western alliance.

Even Tony Blair, who was to become Bush's closest ally, was far from convinced at first. As the British inquiry into the Iraq War later showed, Britain did not see the Iraqi dictator Saddam Hussein as an imminent threat, and America's grandiose plans to transform the Middle East were received with concern in London. When Blair wrote to Bush in mid-2002 that Britain would stand by the US 'whatever', he and his closest advisors had already come to the conclusion that war with Iraq was 'inevitable'. Blair hoped a close partnership would give him more influence on America's actions. His objective was a profoundly 'European' one — namely the 'authorisation' of the war by means of a binding resolution from the UN Security Council.[2]

The idea that a Middle Eastern state such as Iraq could be conquered effortlessly by the West and then — practically through no action of its own — be transformed into a liberal democracy, was rooted in hubris and fed by the hysterical fear of threats following the 9/11 attacks. The problem was not a lack of planning or preparation, as claimed by those who defend the war, but the fundamental ideological assumptions that made transforming the country appear straightforward. The price paid by America and the West for that miscalculation was high. The Iraq War not only cost countless lives; it also increased the terrorist threat, undermined the credibility of modern liberal ideas, and severely damaged America's position as the only remaining superpower.

Threat scenarios

One of the myths surrounding the Iraq War is that it was planned far in advance.[3] It may be that 'rogue states' were a foreign policy priority for George W. Bush's new administration, and that several members of his cabinet signed an open letter in 1997 calling for Saddam to be overthrown,[4] but there was no talk of a war of aggression when the new administration assumed office in January 2001. According to his former speech writer David Frum, Bush had learned from his father's election defeat that foreign policy successes were not rewarded by voters. That was the reason he planned to concentrate on domestic issues during his first term as president. 'The attacks forced him to become a foreign policy president, but that was never the plan.'[5] This was consistent with the fact that those who viewed Saddam as being 'contained' and wanted to avoid an escalation of the conflict initially had the upper hand. Secretary of State Colin Powell called for 'smart' sanctions, not war, and his position prevailed during the summer of 2001. William Kristol and Lawrence Kaplan, two of the most influential neoconservatives, complained at the time that Powell had 'watered down' the strategy of containment and that the government was now further removed than ever from a policy of 'regime change'.[6]

The change in favour of war was due in large part to the dramatically altered perception of threats after 9/11. As previously mentioned, the combination of terrorism and weapons of mass destruction was suddenly seen as the greatest possible threat, and Saddam was the leader under whom that combination would be most likely to become a reality. The belief that Iraq possessed weapons of mass destruction was widespread, not only among supporters of the war, but also beyond the Bush administration — not least because Saddam had repeatedly obstructed international weapons inspections. Even the intelligence services of France and Germany, countries that opposed the war, considered it possible that the Iraqi dictator was still in possession of such weapons.[7] However, in contrast to those rather cautious assessments, Vice

President Dick Cheney in particular shut down any doubt after the 9/11 attacks. On the basis of the theory that the mere *possibility* that Saddam was in possession of weapons of mass destruction constituted an unacceptable risk, he dismissed all objections, presented rumours as facts, and interpreted everything that fitted his narrative as conclusive evidence.[8] The result was a complete distortion of the situation that made the existence of Iraqi weapons of mass destruction appear to be a fact — and a growing threat.

It was a similar story when it came to the assumption that Saddam was cooperating with the jihadists. Advocates of the war knew full well that there was no significant — or state-tolerated — presence of jihadist groups in Iraq, and that Saddam was a secular dictator who had had jihadists in his country tortured and executed because he considered them difficult to control. Nonetheless, the war's supporters focused on the danger that this might change. The former CIA officer Kenneth Pollack argued that the Iraqi dictator was far more irrational and unpredictable than those who supported the strategy of confinement claimed. Saddam saw himself as an enemy of America, maintained relations with a variety of mostly nationalist and anti-imperialist terrorist groups, and had openly welcomed the 9/11 attacks. Pollack believed it was only a question of time before he would drop his reservations towards jihadists:

> Although there is no evidence that [Saddam and Al Qaeda] have [cooperated], there is always a first time. Especially if Saddam and Al Qaeda both find themselves desperate [...] they might put aside their differences to make common cause against their common American enemy.[9]

The connection between the 9/11 attacks and the Iraq War, which was always contested by opponents of the war, was seen by war advocates as not only obvious, but also compelling: what was theoretically possible — even with only 1 per cent probability — became a 100 per cent certainty after 9/11.

'Cakewalk'

Against this backdrop, neoconservative ideas that had enjoyed little currency until then — even within the Bush administration — suddenly became popular. They enabled precisely what the Bush administration was looking for in this new situation — a policy combining an aggressive approach oriented towards America's security interests with a modernisation agenda that had an air of universalism. And indeed, in the eyes of the neoconservatives, Saddam was not only a security risk and a threat to America, but also a brutal dictator who had had hundreds of thousands of political dissidents killed, and left the entire region in a state of shock and paralysis with his warmongering and constant threats, rendering all political and economic development impossible. Therefore, overthrowing him would not only solve the problem of Iraqi weapons of mass destruction and end Iraq's support for terrorism, but would also remove one of the most important root causes for the backwardness of the entire region.[10] 'Regime change', wrote the leading neoconservative Paul Wolfowitz, would not be a destabilising factor, as opponents of the war claimed, but the beginning of the end of instability.[11]

Neoconservatives hoped regime change in Iraq would trigger

some kind of chain reaction. If it were possible to turn one of the most brutally run states in the region into a peaceful, modern democracy in a short space of time, people in other Arab states would start to wonder if that could happen in their countries, too. Furthermore, America's determination to support democratic change, by military force if necessary, would impel the rulers of those states to initiate the change America wanted. Each successful transformation would reduce America's military effort. The neoconservatives imagined Saddam would be the first domino that would start the rest toppling.[12] At the end of that process, the region would be not only more democratic, but also more secure, and there would no longer be any place there for weapons of mass destruction or terrorism. Even peace with Israel would then be possible, according to Wolfowitz.[13]

The seductive thing about the neoconservatives' ideas was not only their ambitious, modernist vision, but also the way they made everything seem so simple. After the rapid victory in Afghanistan, there was a belief that no country in the world could now withstand the combination of America's technological and military clout. The former diplomat Ken Adelman was of this view:

I believe demolishing Hussein's military power and liberating Iraq would be a cakewalk. Let me give simple, responsible reasons: (1) It was a cakewalk last time [the 1991 Gulf War]; (2) they've become much weaker; (3) we've become much stronger; and (4) now we're playing for keeps.[14]

This self-confidence also applied to assessments of the political situation. For the neoconservatives, the only obstacle on the path to democracy was Saddam Hussein himself. He was a blockage that simply needed to be removed so the democratic forces in Iraq could break through. As soon as that happened, Iraq's enormous oil reserves would quickly lead to prosperity for the country and its population.

The fact that Iraq was a complex, multi-ethnic society interested the neoconservatives little, as did the point that Saddam's own ethnic group, Sunni Arabs, would have to forfeit their power and privilege in a new, democratic Iraq. No one considered the fact that decades of dictatorship had created a situation in which civil society was virtually non-existent outside of the mosques, and so there was no foundation on which democratic structures could be built. Also ignored was the fact that Iraq's neighbours, such as Iran, were ready and waiting to exploit the power vacuum left by removing Saddam for their own aims. Any scepticism from experts who had spent decades studying Iraq and its society was systematically ignored or dismissed as 'part of the problem'.[15] As if to say, 'If it doesn't fit the narrative, it can't be true.'

The biggest miscalculation was the idea that Iraqis would welcome the Americans as liberators and be eternally grateful to them. As is often the case among Western modernisers, the neoconservatives lacked any sense that other nations do not always see the West — and especially the superpower America — as being as benevolent and altruistic as it sees itself, and that there is always a loser when regime change happens. Michael Doran, an American professor of Middle Eastern studies who supported the neoconservatives at the time, is now critical of his own attitude in retrospect:

> We Americans have a very naïve belief that if there is a dictatorship somewhere, and that dictatorship is removed, democracy will flourish. That was the American experience [after World War II] in Germany and Japan. It strengthened our belief that it would work the same way everywhere and that it is our mission to drive that project forward. The neoconservatives did not deliberately deceive people. They really believed what they said.[16]

Aside from the issue of whether the war was legally justified or not, the above point was the main one on which the European elites disagreed with their American counterparts. Despite having their own, profoundly European illusions about the universal validity of liberal ideas, barely anyone in Europe believed in the possibility that an American-imposed democratisation process would be a 'cakewalk', or that American troops in the very heart of the Middle East would be seen as 'liberators' for very long.

Revolt of the 'losers'

Toppling Saddam actually turned out to be relatively easy. It was barely three weeks from the launch of the invasion on 19 March 2003 to the capture of the capital, Baghdad, by American troops. The Iraqi army offered almost no resistance, and fewer than 200 Western troops were killed in the combat. However, within the space of just a few weeks, any delight over the rapid victory was gone. The forced 'liberation' had not caused an outbreak of democracy, but rather its initial result was anarchy, which developed within months into a bloody civil war costing hundreds of thousands of lives. While it's true that Iraq now no longer poses any danger to the rest of the world, the instability the country still emanates is one of the reasons for the region's continued failure to find peace.

Just like in Afghanistan, the Americans never intended to help with state building over the long term in Iraq. The Bush administration believed that while the situation was stabilising, the occupying authority would work together with representatives of Iraqi groups and then quickly hand over responsibility for running the country to a provisional government. The United Nations would then be responsible for rebuilding the country. For that reason, America did not consider it necessary to draw up a detailed plan of action.[17] Emma Sky, a British representative in the occupying administration, recalls how the Americans believed their work was done once Saddam had been ousted:

> There was an incredible amount of optimism. All the Americans I worked with were convinced that they had delivered democracy to the Iraqis. That their job was the same as it had been in Japan or Germany [...] That was a combination of idealism and incredible naivety — the idea that we could solve any problem; and that America was a benevolent power and not an imperialist one [...] I remember Paul Bremer [the American head of the occupying authority] telling me that America would not

undertake any major infrastructure projects as Britain had
done during its time as a colonial power. He said, 'Our
legacy is democracy'.[18]

This attitude was one of the reasons not only for the war, but
also for the major mistakes made in its aftermath. In the belief
that democracy and freedom would just fix it somehow, no one
considered how the Sunni Arabs, who enjoyed privileges under
Saddam and occupied important state, military, and secret service
positions, were to be integrated into the new country. The simple
fact that they made up only a quarter of the population meant
it was clear that they would enjoy less power and influence in a
democratic system. However, rather than including them in the new
political system, the occupying authority took every opportunity to
show it had no interest in any kind of Sunni participation. Even
before the insurgency against the American 'occupiers' began, Paul
Bremer rejected several offers from Sunni tribal leaders to support
the Americans in setting up security structures. As the Australian
military expert David Kilcullen writes, tribal leaders did not fit into
Bremer's concept of a 'modern', democratic Iraq.[19]

The policy with the greatest consequences was the so-called de-
Baathification of Iraq. The neoconservatives saw Saddam's Baath
Party as the Iraqi equivalent of the German Nazi Party, and wanted
neither its members nor the Baath-dominated security authorities
to have any influence in the 'new' Iraq.[20] For this reason, Bremer
issued two decrees just a month after Saddam was overthrown,
firing all Baathists in higher civil service positions and dismantling
the Iraqi army, police, and secret services with immediate effect.

In this way, the occupying authority not only destroyed Iraq's state administration almost overnight, but also got rid of all Iraqis whose job it was to maintain security in an already chaotic situation. And to make matters worse, of the approximately 700,000 soldiers and policemen who lost their jobs, livelihoods, and status in this way, an overly large proportion were Sunnis.[21] For them, there was no longer any reason to show loyalty to the state,[22] and so, rather than opposing the insurgency, many of them joined it within a few months.

Even though there were already more than a thousand attacks against military and civilian targets per month by the autumn of 2003, it was to be almost a year before the Americans admitted to themselves — and the public — that they were involved in a insurgency. Until then, the American military had consistently described the insurgents as 'losers', 'fanatics', 'Saddam loyalists', or 'bandits', even internally. No one could understand why America's 'gift' — the liberation of Iraq — was met with so much resistance from the liberated. No one wanted to admit how organised and tenacious the resistance had become in such a short space of time. 'We were prepared for chemical weapons,' says Emma Sky, 'but not for that.'[23]

Just two years later, at the peak of the civil war, the idea of a united, democratic Iraq had receded into the far distance. There was little mention of liberation anymore. In fact, the only thing the vast majority of Iraqis could agree on was their rejection of America as the liberator. In a survey carried out in 2005, almost 80 per cent of respondents said they rejected 'American influence' in their country, and more than 60 per cent approved of attacks on American troops.[24]

Defeat

By the end of the decade, it was obvious that America had been unable to achieve any of its strategic goals in the Iraq War. Although peace was able to be established for a few years with a new American strategy starting in 2007, including sending 30,000 extra troops, and a further escalation of the civil war was averted, the overall result was bleak. At least 100,000 Iraqis died in attacks and combat between the invasion in 2003 and the withdrawal of American troops in 2011. Up to a million more died as a consequence of the war, for example due to the lack of a properly functioning healthcare system.[25] By the end of the decade, rather than becoming a stable, 'modern' democracy, Iraq was a deeply divided nation, in which Shi'ites, Sunnis, and Kurds all saw their relationship as a zero-sum game and in which the existence of the state itself was routinely questioned. The American intervention did not leave behind a strong state, but a weakened or 'failed' one, which was held together mainly by the fear of yet more war and chaos.

The chain reaction that the neoconservatives had hoped for in the region also failed to materialise. Rather than initiating a democratic transformation, the states that America wanted to 'liberate' next[26] did everything in their power to avoid precisely that. The Syrian president, Bashar al-Assad, for example, opened his country's border with Iraq, creating a 'pipeline' for the insurgency. There is also now proof that Assad allowed hundreds of Lebanese and Syrian Islamists to travel to Iraq to join the fight against the American occupation. The insurgents' links to Syria became such a problem for the Americans that the US grew increasingly reliant on

Assad's cooperation.[27] With that, the issue of 'regime change' was closed.

There was a similar reaction in Iraq's neighbour to the east, Iran, which gained access to Iraq and its majority Shi'ite population after the ousting of Saddam. Relations between Iraqi Shi'ites and the Iranian government were complex, but no one doubts that Tehran held sway over important parties and politicians in the 'new' Iraq, and that Iran was involved in the development of Shi'ite militias which later carried out attacks on American troops. Thus, the Iraq War not only led to an increase in Iran's influence in the region, but also provided its government with another 'screw' with which to increase the political and military pressure on America. This was surprising for the neoconservatives: 'We had totally suppressed the issue of Iran,' says Michael Doran. 'For me, it was a shock that we had strengthened Iran's position with the war.'[28]

The record was particularly disastrous when it came to terrorism. The neoconservatives had presented the conflict as being part of the War on Terror, not least because they believed that modernising the country would mean it was no longer a 'breeding ground' for terrorism. In fact, Iraq became the birthplace of a new, more aggressive kind of jihadism. The presence of American troops in the heart of the Middle East helped the movement renew itself after its defeat in Afghanistan. Iraq became a magnet for jihadists from all over the world even as early as 2003, albeit not to the great extent that was later to be the case during the Syrian conflict (see chapter 12). The Jordanian jihadist Abu Musab al-Zarqawi founded the so-called Islamic State of Iraq there, which later migrated to Syria and renamed itself simply Islamic State (IS).[29]

The war in Iraq also resulted in a marked increase in the terrorist threat in the West, and numerous attacks, such as those in Madrid (2004) and London (2005). According to Jonathan Evans, former head of the British domestic intelligence service MI5, the war provided jihadists with 'useful propaganda' and confirmed their assertion that 'the West was hostile towards Islam'.[30] Evans' predecessor, Eliza Manningham-Buller, even went so far as to say that Britain's participation in the war 'radicalised a whole generation of young people'.[31] A similar development was clear in Germany, which had distanced itself from the war. The terrorism expert Guido Steinberg, who worked at the Federal Chancellery at the time, reported the 'massive radicalisation' of young Muslims. Many of them were previously marginalised, says Steinberg, 'but there had to be a trigger, and the Iraq War was the most important trigger of all'.[32] Even in Australia, the terrorist threat was said to have increased as a consequence of the Iraq war.

The damage done to the ideological project of liberal modernity was equally severe. After 9/11, Western modernisers believed that the 'promise' of liberal modernity must be delivered on in the Middle East. However, both the War on Terror and the attempt to impose democracy from the outside — including by force — achieved the precise opposite. Even after President Barack Obama took office — that is to say, more than six years after the invasion — polls showed that nine out of ten Arabs had a negative view of America. Almost half believed that America's priorities in the Middle East were primarily connected to oil and protecting Israel. Only one in 20 believed that America was sincerely interested in promoting democracy and human rights.[33] There was still a high level of approval for democracy as such, but almost 90 per cent wanted democratic reforms to be brought in cautiously rather than suddenly. A third feared that democracy would lead to chaos. And up to a quarter expressed a wish for a 'strong leader' to prevent a civil war with a 'strong hand'.[34] The neoconservative fantasy that people in the Middle East were just waiting for America to give them democracy was shown to be completely and utterly false. If anything, scepticism of democracy and Western calls for democratic transformation had increased rather than decreased.

The Iraq War also left deep scars in America itself. Most significant were the fact that almost 5,000 American soldiers lost their lives in the war, and the astronomical financial cost of the war, which the Nobel Prize–winning economist Joseph Stiglitz estimated at $3 trillion.[35] Just as important was the time and enormous effort the war cost America over many years. While China was focusing on economic growth and increasing its influence in Asia and Africa almost unnoticed, American presidents had to grapple with the situation in Iraq, which, from 2004, was no longer a question of gaining a geopolitical advantage, but pure damage limitation. From a strategic point of view, the ten years following the Iraq War was a 'lost decade' not only for the Middle East, but also for America.[36]

This was compounded by the deep sense of insecurity among the American people due to the loss of the war. The neoconservatives were convinced that America had a historic mission to spread modern liberal values throughout the world — and with them, its own social model. Yet it was precisely this mission that more and more Americans questioned after the Iraq War. As shown by the support given to the isolationist Ron Paul in the 2008 Republican presidential primaries — and to a much larger extent later to Donald Trump — many Americans wanted to step back after their country's experience in Iraq and have nothing more to do with wars and conflict in other parts of the world. They wanted America to be a superpower, but without the responsibility and obligations that come with that role. The intractability of that contradictory stance was to become clear during Obama's presidency.

CHAPTER 9
Market Excesses

No examination of the first decade of this century would be complete without a consideration of the economic changes that took place. In no other period in recent economic history did so many people escape poverty and poorer countries' economies grow so quickly. In the five years up to and including 2008, the global economy grew by an average of 4.6 per cent a year. The strongest growth was in Asia, home to half the world's population, where annual economic output increased by an average of 9.5 per cent. In Africa and the Middle East, growth rates exceeded 6 per cent, while the highly industrialised countries of the OECD expanded by an average of 2.5 per cent a year.[1] The 'global South' — and China in particular — was catching up in leaps and bounds.

So, had Thomas Friedman, the prolific *New York Times* columnist, been proven right? Did globalisation and economic liberalisation result in prosperity for all, with no losers? The answer was both yes and no. Yes, because the changes to the global economy were momentous; and because virtually every national economy in the world benefited from those changes, especially the economies of the global South; and because they really were caused by the opening up and closer integration of global markets. But at the same time, no, because the 'neoliberal ideas' propagated by people like Friedman created a highly unstable system, the collapse of which caused enormous financial and social harm from 2007 onwards. The answer was also no because, while the economic changes reduced the gap between the 'North' and the 'South', it also increased economic inequality *within* societies. One of the immediate consequences of this was the rise of the right-wing populist Tea Party in America, which cleverly intertwined economic developments with political and cultural changes, attacking not just globalisation and specific economic developments, but liberal modernity as a whole.

Turbo-liberalisation

The ideas behind the enormous economic changes of the first decade of this century were not new. A quarter of a century before the end of the Cold War, Milton Friedman and his colleagues at the University of Chicago developed the basics of the theory that was later to become economic orthodoxy in the 1980s under the governments of Ronald Reagan in America and Margaret Thatcher in Britain. They were: lowering government involvement in the economy to a minimum, reducing taxation and state regulation, and liberalising the markets. The collapse of Eastern Europe's planned economies appeared to prove that those ideas were right and, although some states resisted the 'neoliberal diktat', the measures which Thomas Friedman later referred to as the 'Golden Straitjacket' became the global 'consensus' in the 1990s.[2]

The spread of neoliberal ideas not only continued in the early 2000s, but also intensified dramatically. Liberalisation of the labour market was accompanied in Western states by a far-reaching liberalisation of the finance markets, which accounted for a steadily increasing share of economic output until the financial crisis of 2007. Western political elites generally took a positive view of that development, and in the Anglo-Saxon world especially, the belief prevailed that regulating the financial markets was not just unnecessary, but harmful. As the former chairman of Britain's Financial Services Authority, Adair Turner, explains, the view was that the markets should be left to police themselves:

> The approach assumed that: markets were generally self-correcting; [...] the primary responsibility for managing risk lay with senior management, not regulators [...]; and consumers were best protected through unfettered and transparent markets, not product regulation or direct intervention.[3]

This philosophy was based on a theory of financial economics known as the efficient-market hypothesis, which postulates that, in a free market, prices always reflect all information available at a given time. In other words, prices are in a sense a perfect reflection of the goods or services behind them. Consequently, no political intervention is able to ascribe value as efficiently as the market, and any attempt to do so is not only doomed to failure, but also leads to market distortions and financial losses. For libertarian-minded regulators, such as the long-standing chairman of the US Federal Reserve, Alan Greenspan, a devotee of the libertarian philosopher Ayn Rand, the best course of action during that period was therefore to do nothing.[4]

Internationally, the main concern was to increase free trade. The European Union's enlargement to the east played a part in achieving that: ten new members joined the EU in 2004, followed by two more in 2007, creating the world's largest single market, in which goods, services, capital, and people could move freely. The 'game changer' that completely altered the dynamics of world trade, however, was China's accession to the World Trade Organisation in 2001. Western political elites expected that that would bring China into the international regulatory system, forcing it to open up both economically and politically to the rest of the world.

Economically at least, that did indeed happen — and with dramatic consequences. Between 2001 and 2007, the value of China's exports increased fivefold, from just under $300 billion to $1.5 trillion, and in 2009, China overtook Germany for the first time as the world's biggest exporter. During the 2000s, the Chinese economy grew annually by around 10 per cent, and the proportion of the population living in poverty according to international definitions fell from almost 50 per cent to below 20 per cent.[5] Although political reforms failed to materialise, capitalism, the 'Golden Straitjacket', and the 'neoliberal ideology' of free trade had lifted more Chinese people out of poverty than decades of development aid and state programmes. In 2005, Thomas Friedman predicted that China could become an 'Asian version of the United States'. 'If [...] China move[s] in that direction, the world will not only become flatter than ever, but also [...] more prosperous than ever.'[6]

Another important factor was technological innovation, including improvements in transportation technologies, especially in shipping and air transport, which made it easier to move goods across entire continents and so integrate countries like China and India into global supply chains. Even more consequential was the 'information revolution', which not only made communication much faster and connected people all over the world, but also — quite incidentally — created an entire new industry that generated trillions in revenue and in which the value of the companies involved came to exceed that of the oil and industrial giants of the 20th century in the space of just a few years.

Western political elites took this as an inspiration. In their view, the information revolution was confirmation of their basic modern, liberal belief that the necessary condition for growth and innovation was the greatest possible freedom for individuals. It set in motion a process of 'creative destruction', which was to renew the economic systems of the West. This also nurtured the hope that scientific progress would sooner or later lead to social progress. The British finance journalist Martin Wolf was convinced that 'Modern computer and telecommunications technology liberates rather than imprisons.'[7]

Thus, the years preceding the global financial crisis were a period of great optimism, despite the wars in the Middle East. Another economic downturn, let alone a depression, was inconceivable. The American Robert Lucas Jr, winner of the Nobel Prize in economics, wrote that 'the central [macroeconomic] problem of depression prevention has been solved';[8] and the British chancellor of the exchequer, Gordon Brown, promised the end of economic cycles ('no more boom and bust').[9] Western political elites were unanimous in their conviction that these massive changes would lead to a new, better, more global economic system to the benefit of all, as long as governments restrained themselves and gave free rein to the forces of economics and technology.

Redistribution

Of course, Western countries benefited from those changes, but the wealth they generated was not as evenly distributed as their proponents liked to suggest. Free trade created an international division of labour, in which the production of consumer goods was increasingly relocated to low-wage countries like China. This was beneficial for Western consumers because it made products cheaper to buy. The US National Bureau of Economic Research estimates that American consumers saved more than $340 billion in the first five years after China's accession to the WTO.[10] But the price for this benefit was paid by low-skilled workers, who suddenly had to compete with their counterparts on the other side of the globe when it came to pay and non-wage benefits. The advent of new technologies had a similar effect. Initially, this development created millions of new jobs for medium- and highly skilled workers, which principally benefited Western countries, especially the United States. However, it also led to less-qualified workers being replaced by machines, often in the same countries. This is at least partly responsible for the fact that the number of people working in manufacturing in the United States fell by more than a third — from 17 to 11 million — in the course of the first decade of this century.[11]

Although Western economies showed sustained growth until the financial crisis of 2007, there were not only winners. This was particularly evident in the increase in economic inequality. In most industrialised Western nations, the poor did not necessarily get poorer, but middle incomes fell slightly, while lower incomes stagnated, and the rich made significant gains.[12] In almost every major industrialised country, there was a rise in the so-called Gini coefficient, which is a measurement of income distribution, and an ever-increasing concentration of assets in the hands of an ever-smaller group of elites.[13] The economist Thomas Piketty believes that there has been no period in history with greater inequality, with the exception of the years leading up to the French Revolution.[14]

There were also geographical consequences to this trend. While regions where many high-tech companies had settled boomed, traditional industrial areas such as in the Midwest of the United States or the North of England fell further and further behind.[15] It was in those areas that the negative social consequences of this economic change were felt particularly keenly.

These developments barely featured in the public debate. Even social democrat politicians distanced themselves from the 'class-war rhetoric' of their predecessors and fancied themselves as 'comrades of the bosses'.[16] Peter Mandelson, a close advisor to Tony Blair, told business people: 'We are intensely relaxed about people getting filthy rich.'[17] Thomas Friedman considered it to be a 'transition phase', in which workers and lower-skilled employees in Western industrialised countries should be retrained so that they are 'one step ahead' of their competitors in China and elsewhere. Rather than slowing the pace of globalisation, says Friedman, the aim should be to increase the overall size of the 'global [economic] pie' as quickly as possible.[18]

Martin Wolf went even further. For him, globalisation was not only a practical imperative, but also a moral one. The West had dominated the production of consumer goods for centuries, he argued, and it was only fair that this should now change:

> It would be immoral for rich countries to deprive the poor
> of the world of so large an opportunity for betterment
> merely because they are unable to handle sensibly and
> justly the distribution of the internal costs of a change
> certain to be highly beneficial overall [...] Only the most
> selfish Westerners can complain about a transformation
> that has brought so much to so many so quickly.[19]

But, beyond training opportunities and transfer incomes, Wolf had little to offer those supposedly 'selfish' workers. Like Friedman, he believed the transformation process was unstoppable, and the losers would do well to accept the consequences without complaint — or even with gratitude.

Financial collapse

The main reason it took so long for those economic inequalities to become obvious was the gigantic financial bubble that had developed over the course of the decade. The causes of that bubble were many, and are still disputed today. Among the most commonly cited culprits are the US Federal Reserve's low interest rate policy in the wake of the 9/11 attacks, a global surplus in savings accumulated in major banks in London and New York, and a financial sector which had — unnoticed by politicians and regulators — spiralled completely out of control.[20] The consequence of this was that gaining credit became easier than ever before and many households in America, Britain, and parts of continental Europe took on debts, some of which were so large they would never be able to repay them. Even people without jobs or assets had no problem getting six-figure mortgages to buy houses that then served as collateral for even more loans.[21] As the American political scientist Michael Barkun wrote, everything seemed fine as long as income inequality was 'masked [...] by rising home values [...] that allowed people to use their houses as ATMs.'[22]

By the middle of the decade, it was considered an open secret that house prices in America were unrealistically high. However, almost no one suspected that when the bubble burst, it would be only a few weeks before the entire financial market would collapse, leading to the worst financial crisis since the Great Depression of the 1930s. The financial sector had become so complicated that everything seemed to be tangled up with everything else, and no one could really tell how high any given bank or business partner's investment in the worthless mortgages was. So the bursting of the housing bubble gradually laid bare how dysfunctional the entire sector had become, with over-reliance on highly complex mathematical risk models, complete disconnection from the activity of the real economy, corruption at the rating agencies, and — not least of all — the ideologically and politically sanctioned absence of any kind of control.[23]

The consequences were dramatic. In 2007 and 2008, economic activity came to a temporary standstill. Global economic output fell by $2 trillion; and in many Western countries, the unemployment rate doubled. It took almost four years for the US economy to recover from the 'shock' of the financial crisis, and — once again — it was middle- and low-income earners who paid the highest price in the form of foreclosures, job losses, and financial insecurity.[24]

More even than the greed of bankers or the incompetence of regulators, the global financial crisis exposed the total inadequacy of Western political elites. Their admission of economic failure took the form of the bank bailouts that involved Western governments using taxpayers' money and state guarantees to save the financial system from total ruin. This was unavoidable, as banks are the circulatory system of any national economy,[25] and letting them collapse would probably have worsened the damage to growth and employment even further. However, the fact that the sector of the economy that was supposed to be the most competitive and in which performance was supposed to be the only thing that counts had to be saved from the consequences of its own decisions with huge state subsidies was — not least of all — an intellectual declaration of bankruptcy. What became clear was that the system that hails bankers as 'heroes'[26] and sees the market as the ultimate authority on all decisions had failed spectacularly. Even Josef Ackermann, the controversial chief executive of Deutsche Bank, remarked at the time, 'I no longer believe in the market's self-healing power.'[27]

Loss of control

It might be expected that the natural response to this crisis would be a shift to the political left. However, to the surprise of Western political elites, the strongest — and most vociferous — new force on the US political spectrum sprang up not on the left, but on the far right. Calling itself the Tea Party, it articulated people's economic, and also political and cultural fears, and gained much popularity in 2009 and 2010 especially. Its supporters were opposed to free trade, and were anti-immigration. They blamed the crisis not only on bankers, but also on the 'liberal elites'. Put simply, their anger was directed at not just certain economic aspects of globalisation and liberal modernity, but at the whole package. Although it lost much of its influence in the decade that followed, the Tea Party was an early sign of the backlash that modern liberalism was about to face from *within* Western societies.

The Tea Party movement began in February 2009 after an angry rant on television by correspondent Rick Santelli, who demanded a 'new Tea Party' — a reference to the anti-taxation protest by American merchants in 18th-century Boston. The first demonstrations of 2009 took place less than a month after Santelli's TV appearance, to protest against state aid for homeowners. Later, the Tea Party focused on the Obama administration's healthcare reform plans, which — like the bank bailouts — were portrayed as being part of a 'socialist takeover'. At its height, the movement had more than half a million active supporters.[28] They were often white, mostly middle-aged, male Republicans, who were generally neither poor nor unemployed, typically members of the (lower) middle class, who were disproportionately likely to come from areas of the US which had been particularly hard-hit by the structural changes of the 1990s and the early 2000s.[29] In the run-up to the midterm elections of 2010, their political influence was so strong that a dozen Republican Congress members who were considered 'too lax' lost their nominations to more radical candidates. Of the 233 Republicans who won seats in November 2010, 60 — more than a quarter — were active supporters of the Tea Party.

Historically, this was nothing new. Many times in its past, America has seen extreme right-wing and right-wing populist movements gain a lot of support, particularly during periods of economic uncertainty or rapid social change.[30] The most prominent example of this is the Ku-Klux-Klan, which saw a rise in its popularity particularly among white people in the South of the country during three such periods: immediately after the American Civil War, during the Great Depression, and during the time of the civil rights movement in the 1960s.[31] Just like its predecessor movements, the Tea Party agitated against 'elites' and 'newcomers', and once again, just as in the past, conspiracy theories played an important part.[32] The most insidious of these was that Obama was not a 'real' American, as he was supposedly not born in America, which would make him ineligible to be president under the US Constitution. This claim cleverly combined both political and cultural grudges and was believed by 45 per cent — i.e., almost half — of Tea Party supporters, according to one poll.[33] One of its most enthusiastic promoters was Donald Trump.[34]

From the start, the ideological spectrum of Tea Party supporters was far broader than just the financial crisis. Their outrage was not just reserved for greedy bankers, but also covered the state rescue packages, as well as any attempt to cushion the consequences of individuals' misconduct with state interventions. Why should the general public pay for the bad decisions taken by some individuals? With its emphasis on individual responsibility, the Tea Party articulated the frustrations of those Americans who, while not particularly wealthy, were in a slightly better position than those reliant on government assistance. In their opinion, those who had taken out a mortgage during the boom years and were now no longer able to make the payments, only had themselves to blame. As Rick Santelli succinctly put it: No help for losers![35]

Economic fears were often coupled with cultural resentment. The proportion of Americans who were of 'European origin' — in other words, white — had been steadily shrinking since the 1990s, while the number of immigrants, mostly from Latin America, rose rapidly. The 2010 national census showed that almost half of Americans below the age of 18 were from so-called ethnic minorities, and that white Americans were destined to become 'a minority in their own country' in just a few decades' time.[36] What is more, with Obama, the US now had an African-American president, who spoke constantly about diversity, and some worried he would impose his 'elitist' ideas concerning the country's gun laws or gay marriage for example, on the rest of society.

It was therefore no coincidence that Tea Party supporters were vehemently opposed to the state programmes propagated by 'liberal elites', that primarily benefited immigrants and people from minorities.[37] As the American historian Ronald Formisano explains, the Tea Party supporters' economic and cultural fears were an expression of the same, seemingly all-pervasive feeling of powerlessness among members of the white middle class, who believed there was no place for them in the 'more colourful', globalised America propagated by the 'liberal elites':

> Millions of [white] Americans [...] sense that, from family to neighborhood to nation, the moral fabric of our community is unravelling around us [...] They are losing control over their lives and [fear] that vast impersonal forces, some global in character, exert too much influence over their ability to live as they wish.[38]

Thus, a decade that began with boundless optimism ended with deep insecurities. The 9/11 attacks showed that the West was vulnerable; the wars in the Middle East exposed the limits of its military power, and the collapse of the financial markets revealed the contradictions inherent in its economic model. As the rise of the Tea Party made clear, there was resistance to the spread of modern liberal ideas, not only abroad, but also within the West's own societies, often stemming from those who, despite all the optimistic rhetoric, counted themselves among the 'losers'. White, often Islamophobic Americans who railed against Obama therefore had more in common with the Islamist Sunnis of Iraq than generally supposed.

PART III
DISILLUSIONMENT:
2011-2015

CHAPTER 10
Arab Spring?

THE START OF THE SECOND DECADE OF THE 21ST CENTURY WAS MORE optimistic than the end the first. The most important political event of global significance came right at the start. The Arab Spring began with nationwide protests in Tunisia, which led to the ousting of the country's long-standing president Ben Ali in January 2011. In the weeks that followed, demonstrations were held in almost every country in the region, calling for freedom and human dignity, an end to corruption and repression, and the resignation of each nation's respective ruler. However, what looked like a democratic wave, ended just a few years later in chaos, war and, an authoritarian revival — not least of all because of the West's hesitant reaction.

The structural causes of the Arab Spring were the same as those that had already been outlined in the UNDP's Arab Human Development Reports in the early years of the decade: a lack of economic and business opportunities coupled with corrupt and repressive regimes that offered their citizens neither security nor prospects for the future. If anything, the trends identified at that time had grown worse. Population growth had continued and even accelerated, so that by the start of the new decade, two thirds of the Arab population were under the age of 25. Unemployment rates stood at between 20 and 40 per cent depending on the country. Joblessness affected young people and the well-educated most severely. This was compounded by a drastic increase in food prices starting in 2007, creating a situation where households had to spend between one third (in Lebanon) and two thirds (in Morocco) of their monthly income on food.[1]

The autocratic governments in the region did not know how to respond. In the previous decade, many had followed a policy of neoliberal reform, cutting social spending and privatising state-owned companies. This led to economic growth in Egypt and Syria, but it was far too little to make up for the escalating socio-economic problems. What is more, cuts to social services and — most importantly — the way in which state-owned companies were privatised (essentially by being sold off to the families and friends of those in power) increased the people's hatred of their corrupt rulers. Towards the end of the decade, all that was left of many Arab governments was their apparatus of repression.[2]

The sudden eruption of that resentment, leading to protests in virtually every Arab state, was also closely connected to the power — and possibilities — of global communication networks. While fewer than 20 per cent of the population had an internet connection of their own,[3] more people than ever in the Arab world were now literate, the majority of them were social media users (mostly Facebook), 80 per cent were mobile phone owners, and almost everyone got their news from satellite television channels, especially Al Jazeera.[4] In contrast to earlier times, Arab governments were unable to prevent their citizens from gaining access to information critical of them, while government critics had far more ways of communicating with each other and organising themselves.

News of the protests and state abuses spread across the region via the internet and Al Jazeera. The fact that protesters in the Bahraini capital Manama were chanting the same slogans as those heard just days earlier at demonstrations in Cairo and Tunis would have been inconceivable without social media and satellite television. In this respect, Facebook and Al Jazeera were not the *cause* of the Arab Spring, but they created a 'new [pan-]Arab public sphere' that made it possible to challenge the authoritarian status quo in every part of the region.[5]

The initial reaction among Western political elites was one of naïve, almost blind enthusiasm. From the Western perspective, the Arab Spring promised not only an end to jihadist terrorism, but also a revival of 'liberal optimism', and with it the hope that the whole world would sooner or later join the project of liberal modernism. But beyond that, it was less clear what the response should be: torn between enthusiasm and a fear of being dragged into new conflicts, Western governments reacted with a range of fainthearted and contradictory strategies that failed to live up to the West's leadership claims, contributed to the chaos and instability, and gave impetus to those who opposed liberal modernity. Rather than learning from its mistakes as demanded by the historian Heinrich August Winkler,[6] the West fell into a kind of shock-induced paralysis.

Liberal optimism 2.0

The defining moment of the Arab Spring came with the demonstrations on Cairo's Tahrir Square, beginning on 25 January 2011. They were started by left-wing and liberal youths, who were later joined by traditional opposition groups — first and foremost the Muslim Brotherhood. The demonstrations resulted in a largely peaceful popular uprising, uniting completely disparate groups in the fight against repression and for a new, freer Egypt, and eventually leading to the resignation of President Hosni Mubarak. The success of the protests sent a signal to the entire region: if a couple of thousand young people could succeed in toppling the dictator of one of the most important and most populous Arab states, then democratic transformation was possible anywhere. 'Egyptians have finally won a chance at creating a free and just society,' wrote *The New York Times*. 'The Egyptian protesters inspire us all.'[7]

No sooner were the demonstrations in Cairo over, than talk spread of a 'domino effect' or a 'new wave of democracy'.[8] Observers compared the events to those of the March Revolutions in Germany and other European countries in 1848,[9] the Prague Spring of 1968,[10] or the peaceful revolutions in Eastern Europe in 1989.[11] Almost no one, on either side of the Atlantic, doubted that this was a historic moment, or that the events in Tunis and Cairo would lead to democratic transformation across the entire region. The Middle East expert Daniel Gerlach recognised 'very strong sympathies' among German politicians based on the idea that 'all the world's nations somehow aspire to democracy and the Western republican system' and that — despite all the problems — 'there is a young, enlightened, modern population'.[12] The sociologist Bernard Rougier described a similar mood in France: 'Anyone who expressed doubt faced accusations of racism or [anti-Arab sentiments]. Almost everyone was drunk on the idea that the Arab states would now become democracies.'[13] Scepticism and opposition were equally thin on the ground in America.[14] As usual, Francis Fukuyama went even further: in a guest column for *The Wall Street Journal*, he asked 'Is China Next?'[15]

However, the notion of a new democratic wave was based on two false assumptions. The first was that the revolutions were led by a new generation oriented towards the West. In the eyes of Western observers, it appeared as if the deeply divided, politically antagonistic societies of the Middle East had suddenly — and out of nowhere — given rise to a young, liberal middle class made up of people who used social media, spoke fluent English, had no interest in religion, and pursued the same aims and ambitions as their peers in New York or Paris. 'The revolutions, from Tunisia and Egypt to Libya, show us that the Arab world is far more modern than we thought,' wrote the French historian Emmanuel Todd, for example. 'Muslim countries are full of young, highly motivated people. They fight for Western values, progress and self-determination.'[16]

The reason for that impression was the way the events were covered by Al Jazeera and Western television broadcasters, focusing on Tahrir Square where the protests were dominated by groups with a left-wing or liberal leaning, in the initial days at least. The most prominent figure among them was Wael Ghonim, a computer engineer who was 29 years old at the time. While working for Google in Dubai, he launched a Facebook campaign against police violence. He returned to his native Egypt in mid-January 2011, but was arrested by the police just two days after the demonstrations began. His detention made him a global symbol of the new Arab 'millennials' and their 'new age revolution'.[17] Even President Obama had heard of him. He reportedly told one of his aides, 'What I want is for the kids on the street to win and for the Google guy to become president.'[18]

In truth, however, those millennials accounted for only a small part of the revolution. As the American Middle East scholar Marc Lynch explains, although the protests were initiated by young, liberal Egyptians, their movement did not become a revolution until it gained support from more traditional layers of society: 'Articulate liberals,' he writes, 'may not speak for the Arab world any more than does al-Qaeda.'[19] That support came a few days after the start of the protests when Egypt's oldest and most powerful Islamist organisation, the Muslim Brotherhood, allied itself with the 'millennials'. The Muslim Brotherhood continued to let the 'millennials' take the limelight, but played an important part in defending Tahrir Square against attacks from Mubarak supporters.[20] John Sawers, head of Britain's foreign intelligence service, MI6, at the time, remembers:

> The Muslim Brotherhood was in the background at the beginning. But there were pivotal moments during the protests when it rallied its strength and supporters. It was particularly active during the clashes in Tahrir Square in the last week of January. It had far more discipline [...] than the liberal students and middle-class protesters, giving them the strength needed to prevail.[21]

The strength of the Islamists was reflected a short time later at the ballot box. The Muslim Brotherhood gained almost 40 per cent of the votes in the November 2011 to January 2012 parliamentary elections, making it the strongest political force, and in the following summer, it won the presidential election with a narrow majority. By that time, little remained of the dream of a 'liberal revolution'.

The second mistake on the part of Western elites was their assumption that the problem of jihadist terrorism was over. One of the most prominent advocates of that theory was the French Middle East expert Jean-Pierre Filiu, who claimed in countless articles and interviews that fear of the 'Islamist threat' was nothing but a fantasy of the authoritarian rulers. The revolutions in Tunisia and Egypt, he said, proved that oppression could be ended and dictators removed without the need for violence. 'The jihadists have no fall-back option,' according to Filiu, 'The millions of Arab demonstrators are defying the ruling cliques and their security forces, not to demand a "caliphate" or an "Islamic emirate", [...] but to get free and fair elections, a decent administration and transparent and representative institutions.'[22]

Even terrorism experts agreed with this interpretation. Fawaz Gerges, a Middle East expert at the London School of Economics, believed that 'only a miracle' could save jihadism from its demise.[23] The logic behind such statements was always the same: the more modern and democratic the Arab states became, the fewer reasons people would have for joining groups like Al Qaeda.

Events were to prove them wrong. Although jihadists played no part in the protest movement, they were quick to seize the opportunities it offered. Anwar al-Awlaki, a Yemeni imam and

Al Qaeda member, wrote as early as spring 2011 that it was not important whether the new governments were 'democratic or Islamic': 'Whatever the outcome, our [...] brothers [...] will get a chance to breathe again after [...] decades.'[24] And indeed, within the space of a few months, thousands of jihadists were released from jail, the pressure of persecution by the police and secret services eased, and, for the first time in decades, Islamist, Salafist, and jihadist groups could organise themselves openly.[25] When the Arab Spring turned to 'winter', democratic transformation failed and supposedly long-settled antagonisms returned, the 'jihad movement' became stronger than ever.

'Intentional impotence'

The enthusiasm of Western political elites for the Arab Spring had much to do with the contradictory nature of Western policy. For decades, European governments had declared their commitment to strengthening democracy in the Middle East in countless resolutions and speeches, but had done little to achieve that in practice. They always saw authoritarian rulers as the 'lesser evil' compared to Islamists, and European governments mostly 'turned two blind eyes' to Arab states' failure to implement the reforms required of them.[26] America's reaction was similar. In a prominent speech in June 2009, President Obama committed himself to the spread of democracy in the Middle East. He declared that freedom of opinion, the rule of law, and representative governments were 'not just American ideas; they are human rights. And that is why we will support them everywhere.'[27] But in reality, America continued cooperating with the very rulers who were responsible for suppressing those rights. In short, nowhere was the contradiction between liberal rhetoric and real political practice more glaring than in the Middle East, and Western politicians and experts — who were well aware of this — were happy and relieved when the Arab Spring promised to resolve that contradiction.

However, that was dampened by a second aspect that was at least equally as important for the fate of the Arab Spring. At the time the protests began, the West was in a state of both political and psychological exhaustion.[28] The interventions in Afghanistan and Iraq had not only failed to bring democracy or stability to those countries, but they had also sparked civil wars, run up astronomical costs, and deepened the rift between the West and 'the Muslim world'. Furthermore, they had led to a crisis of confidence. The opinion that interventions of any kind are always doomed to failure was often voiced, even among Western political elites. Also, it was often said that the West should keep out of the region, and that there were enough other problems which were more worthy of the West's attention than the Middle East. Obama was aware of that sentiment and promised to end the seemingly interminable wars in the Middle East. At the highpoint of the Arab Spring in June 2011, he made it clear that his priority was 'nation-building here at home'.[29]

That is why the belief expressed by the journalist Michael Lüders — that America used the Arab Spring as a pretext to instigate more wars in the Middle East — is absurd.[30] Although they had catastrophic consequences, America's intentions were precisely the opposite: to promote democratic change without getting even more bogged down in the Middle East. The result was a fainthearted, often contradictory policy described by the Arab American journalist and scholar Hussein Ibish as 'intentional impotence'.[31] Its main driving force was the fear that Western interference might create a dynamic which could get out of hand and become unmanageable at some point, and possibly lead to yet another seemingly interminable conflict. This was coupled with the belief that the success of the Arab Spring was due to the fact that, unlike in Iraq, it had not been initiated from the outside, and that any kind of intervention would be damaging to the democratic forces at work. Both beliefs pointed towards the same policy for the West: avoid all risks and keep as low a profile as possible.[32]

By May — a mere three months after the fall of Mubarak — America had abandoned any thoughts of a coherent strategy. In a speech at the US State Department, Obama praised the courage of the protesters and repeated his assertion that he would support the enforcement of civil liberties and human rights. At the same time, however, he stressed the fact that America should meet the developments with 'a sense of humility' and allow the people of the Middle East to determine their own future. He said there was no overall doctrine for America's response to the protest movements in the Middle East. Obama pointed out that 'each country is different', and America would decide its position on a case-by-case basis.[33] For the Middle East analyst Emile Hokayem at the International Institute for Strategic Studies in London, it was clear that:

> The Americans were struggling with the situation.
> Their hearts were on the side of the demonstrators. But

politically, they didn't know how to deal with it. And strategically, they were afraid of the whole thing. And I think that resulted in a very disorganised, ambivalent reaction.[34]

With the exception of the conflict in Libya (see chapter 11), Europe also adopted this hesitant and mostly reactive policy. That was most evident in the case of Egypt. When it looked as if the 'millennials' would take power, there was broad support for liberal reforms and a hope of democratic transformation. However, as soon as it became clear that the 'millennials' were not going to be the strongest political force in the country, but rather the Islamists, the policy changed. Within a very short space of time, the Muslim Brotherhood came to be seen as the 'Islamic new centre' in Egypt,[35] and the German government 'rolled out the red carpet' for the country's highly dogmatic president Mohamed Morsi.[36] When Morsi also got into political hot water, the West's position changed again. In summer 2013, America and Europe supported the coup led by the commander-in-chief of the armed forces, Abdel Fattah el-Sisi, who established an authoritarian regime that not only resembled Mubarak's dictatorship, but even surpassed it in brutality. So the West had thrown its support behind every politically relevant force in Egypt within the space of less than three years, only to end up back at square one: with an authoritarian dictatorship.

The only consistent policy to be boosted by the Arab Spring was the Internet Freedom Program. As early as January 2010, the American secretary of state, Hillary Clinton, announced the US government's plan to do much more to promote fundamental

freedoms and the internet. The idea originated during the so-
called Green Movement in Iran in summer 2009, when Clinton's
aides noticed that young Iranians were using Twitter to organise
demonstrations. The idea that the internet — and especially
social media — played a key part in democratic revolutions was
confirmed by the events of the Arab Spring. In the following years,
the American government supported a variety of initiatives and
programmes aimed at providing opposition activists with access to
the internet and the latest technology.[37]

The Internet Freedom Program fitted in well with America's
techno-optimism, which saw the internet as an instrument of
political liberation and democratic change. Furthermore, it cost
relatively little and was less likely to provoke domestic political
controversy than military interventions were. But most importantly,
it did not entail a risk for America of becoming entangled in more
wars. 'Tweet [your] way to freedom'[38] became the credo of the
Obama administration and a substitute for the global political
leadership role from which America had withdrawn out of fear of a
new, seemingly endless war.

Counter-revolution

Five years after the start of the Arab Spring, the protest movements
and democratic transformations had failed in every country except
Tunisia. In most countries, old antagonisms re-erupted, leading to
polarisation, conflict, and war. This was not down to the protests
themselves, or to the demands for freedom and democracy, but to
the fact that authoritarian rulers had either swept those conflicts

under the carpet for years, or had stoked them for power-political reasons. The West's — and especially America's — mistake was not its enthusiasm for the democratic protest movements, but its naïve belief that the antagonisms and lines of conflict which had characterised the Middle East for decades had been suddenly swept away by the Arab Spring, and that dysfunctional societies would transform into peaceful, stable, and democratic states without the need for active support. The Middle East was left to its own devices, creating a vacuum and leaving the West surprised and annoyed that it was not the forces of liberalism which profited from the historic situation, but the enemies of liberal modernism: Islamists and autocrats.

Not all conflicts ended as brutally as those in Libya and Syria, where the lack of Western leadership and engagement had catastrophic consequences. However, almost everywhere, the protest movements resulted in instability, insecurity, and — in some cases — chaos. The biggest beneficiary was initially the Muslim Brotherhood, which had built up political parties, networks, and charitable organisations all over the Middle East and enjoyed broad support. This was also the assessment of the president of Germany's Federal Intelligence Service (BND) Gerhard Schindler:

When we looked at who the main players in all those areas were, the Muslim Brotherhood kept cropping up: in Tunisia, in Egypt, in the entire Near and Middle East. We could see how smart they were being. How quickly they filled positions: in the media, in the administrative systems, in the courts, and so on. We were concerned at the time that they were heading towards a largescale Islamisation process.[39]

More dangerous, even, was the rise of Salafist and jihadist groups that explicitly rejected democracy, preached religious intolerance, and — in the case of the jihadists — legitimised the use of violence. As previously mentioned, it was only after the Arab Spring that the Salafists and jihadists were able to organise themselves, spread their message, and recruit members publicly for the first time in many Arab states. This grew into an ecosystem of many organisations that deepened the religious and sectarian fault lines and led to terrorist attacks — not only in the Middle East, but also in Europe (see chapters 11 and 12).[40]

As the Islamists and jihadists continued to gain in strength, the autocrats saw a new chance. With the support of Saudi Arabia and the United Arab Emirates, there was a revival of monarchical and authoritarian rulers, who promised stability as an alternative to chaos and theocracy. Their narrative fell on fertile ground, and state repression increased, not just in Egypt but almost everywhere in the region. A type of ruler seen as problematic before the Arab Spring had now, just a few years later, come to be seen as the solution again.

Even beyond the region itself, the Arab Spring gave autocrats an opportunity to raise their own profile. Vladimir Putin supported the Syrian dictator Bashar al-Assad with a military intervention. In Putin's view, it was not Assad who was to blame for the civil war that had been raging for four years in his country, but rather the West's 'promotion of democracy'. Putin presented his intervention as an 'anti-terror operation' aimed at restoring law and order. Although it did not put an end to the conflict, Russia's intervention stabilised Assad's position, and Russia became a powerbroker in the Middle East again for the first time since the end of the Cold War (see chapter 12).

And what of the internet? As it turned out, the opponents of liberal modernism understood the importance of the internet just as well as the West. This was most obvious in the case of IS. The jihadist militia was present on virtually all Western internet platforms in 2014 and 2015. That enabled it to mobilise tens of thousands of foreign fighters, who headed for the self-styled caliphate.[41] At the highpoint of its power, IS followers were estimated to be posting two hundred thousand propaganda messages *per day*[42] — disproving the claim that the internet always and inevitably has a democracy-building effect.

The autocrats also began using the internet for their own ends. Since the Green Movement, if not before, says the author Evgeny Morozov, the rulers in Tehran, Moscow, and Beijing regarded the internet as an instrument of Western interference. What American political elites portrayed as promoting democracy, was in their eyes a form of hybrid warfare, with which America sought to destabilise its geopolitical adversaries.[43] The immediate consequences were therefore not just new censorship measures, firewalls, and surveillance, but also the development of offensive strategies aimed at influencing, and dividing, popular opinion in Western countries. The US government's Internet Freedom Program had unwittingly sparked a kind of virtual arms race which — probably — did more to damage democratic discourse in the West than it did to promote it abroad.

However, the consequences of Western policy were far more severe in two key countries of the Arab Spring, which are covered in the following chapters of this book.

CHAPTER 11
France's Adventure

When Muammar al-Gaddafi was killed on 20 October 2011, many observers were surprised that the Libyan dictator had survived for so long. Unlike Mubarak or Ben Ali, Gaddafi was not the kind of dictator to wear grey suits and spend most of his time ensconced in his palaces. Furnished with petro-dollars and an eccentric personality, Gaddafi developed a philosophy of his own, which he wrote down in his so-called *The Green Book* of 1975. He saw himself as a pan-Arab nationalist, as a champion of Islam, and as the 'King of Africa'. While on foreign visits, he slept in his own Bedouin tents flown in from Libya, and was accompanied by an elite unit of female bodyguards.[1] He annoyed many with such antics, while others just assumed he was crazy.

Gaddafi's eccentric nature was not the only reason he had so many enemies. Inside his own country, he destroyed state institutions and civil society, seized the assets of entrepreneurs and real estate owners, and replaced political structures with 'revolutionary councils', all in the name of his home-grown philosophy. Anyone who resisted Gaddafi or his ideas was tortured, shot, or jailed indefinitely. From the mid-nineties onward, Gaddafi used these methods to fight a jihadist uprising, killing or jailing tens of thousands of fighters, their family members, and sympathisers in the process.[2]

Gaddafi also ignored the rules when it came to international relations. For decades, he supported so-called liberation groups and was considered one of the world's major sponsors of terrorism. He saw not only other rulers in the Middle East as his enemies, but also — and especially — the 'imperialist' West. He was responsible for an attack on a disco in West Berlin in 1986, in which a US soldier was killed. President Ronald Reagan responded with air strikes on the Libyan capital, Tripoli. Gaddafi in turn brought down a Pan Am passenger jet over the Scottish village of Lockerbie. At the time, Reagan branded Gaddafi 'the mad dog of the Middle East'.[3]

All this meant there was no direct communication between Gaddafi and the West for decades. Tensions finally eased when Gaddafi handed the mastermind of the Lockerbie attack over to an international court and — as a result of the Iraq War — agreed to scrap his chemical and nuclear weapons programmes. Although relations never became warm, or even cordial, sanctions in Libya were lifted in the 2000s and cooperation improved — whether in the oil industry or on issues like illegal migration and terrorism. Gaddafi sent his son Saif al-Islam to study at the London School of Economics, where he wrote his doctoral thesis on the (non-existent) civil society in Libya.

This opening up to the West did little to alter Gaddafi's

absolutist style of leadership, and the Arab Spring sparked protests in Libya, too. Initially, they were largely confined to the coastal city of Benghazi, which had been particularly affected by the crackdown on the Islamist uprising in the 1990s and 2000s. On 22 February 2011, Gaddafi gave a speech in which he denounced his opponents as 'cowards and traitors' and threatened to go 'house by house, street by street, person by person, until the country is clean of dirt and impurities'.[4] Just two days earlier, his son had warned of 'rivers of blood'.[5] In Western capitals, such threats were interpreted as an announcement of a planned genocide. This led to a military intervention, which resulted in the end of Gaddafi's regime in August 2011 and his gruesome death two months later.[6]

The West's intervention was a French initiative, with which the then president, Nicolas Sarkozy, wanted to go down in history and give his country a decisive role in the Arab Spring's democratic wave. Although Sarkozy was bolder and more ambitious than America in intervening actively and reinterpreting the protection mandate as a mandate for regime change, France and its main ally, Great Britain, shared America's fear of new and seemingly interminable wars. Shortly after Gaddafi was toppled, the two countries surprisingly withdrew, leaving Libya, which had no political structures or institutions after forty years of absolutist rule, to its own devices. The consequences of this were not only chaos and a brutal civil war in Libya, but also conflicts in other parts of Africa and instability and terrorism in Europe.

'Like the French Resistance'

No one could have predicted that, of all countries, it would be France that would be at the vanguard of the intervention in Libya. The French government did not have a clear position at the start of the Arab Spring. When the protests were already in full swing in Tunisia, the French foreign minister, Michèle Alliot-Marie, offered to support the Tunisian government in quashing them.[7] At the same time, a group of French diplomats published an open letter criticising Sarkozy's foreign policy and accusing the president of 'amateurism' and a lack of a coherent plan. 'France's voice has disappeared in the world,' the signatories of the letter concluded.[8]

France's reticent, not to say negative, stance changed after Gaddafi's threat to annihilate the insurgents. United Nations reports of mass graves and shootings appeared to confirm that the Libyan dictator's intentions were serious,[9] and by the end of February, a military intervention was not just conceivable in the eyes of the French, but imperative. Once again, the doctrine of the 'responsibility to protect' was cited as justification. It states that the international community has a duty to intervene when governments threaten the security or existence of their own populations. According to Sarkozy, the events unfolding in Libya were similar to the Rwandan genocide or the massacres of Muslim civilians during the civil wars in former Yugoslavia. The failure of the international community, which stood idly by as hundreds of thousands of innocent civilians were murdered, should not be repeated. According to Mark Hecker of the French Institute of International Relations (IFRI), the conclusion was: *'plus jamais ça'* — 'never again'.[10]

From the outset, Sarkozy's rhetoric was connected to a more ambitious agenda. In the French president's view, it was not just Gaddafi's announcement of his intention to annihilate his political opponents that was the problem, but the dictator himself. Even if Gaddafi had *not* threatened genocide, he would still be a symbol of the old, autocratic Middle East, which the Arab Spring had rendered obsolete. For Sarkozy, this was a chance to redress his government's failings and position himself on the crest of the 'democratic wave'. The Middle East expert Bernard Rougier believes Sarkozy wanted not only to gain geopolitical influence in a new, more democratic Middle East, but also to boost his prestige and popularity at home. 'He wanted to be able to say to the public: "Look! We didn't miss the Arab Spring. We're on the side of the democrats. We are part of a universal democratic agenda."'[11] This is why Sarkozy mentioned France's 'mission' at least as often as he mentioned the 'responsibility to protect' — as well as speaking of the idea that France is always present 'wherever the freedom of people and nations is threatened'.[12] His aim was to protect the protesters in Benghazi from being killed, but also to drive out the dictator who was threatening their lives. 'We will bring him to his knees,' Sarkozy is reported to have said, 'We will make him bite the dust.'[13]

The fact that this was thought possible was connected to the almost exuberant idealism that had spread among the French political elites. 'It was all very emotional, very morally based. The inner circle Sarkozy surrounded himself with had their own truth and brooked no dissent. Nobody gave a serious thought to the dangers and risks.'[14] A significant portion of the responsibility for that mindset goes to the philosopher and intellectual Bernard-Henri Lévy, who was in close contact with Sarkozy during this period. Despite knowing virtually nothing about Libya, Lévy had travelled to Benghazi when the protests began and met with opposition representatives, whom he brought back to Paris and introduced not just to Sarkozy, but also other Western politicians — including Secretary of State Clinton.[15] Lévy convinced Sarkozy that it was right to pursue a strategy of regime change in Libya, that a 'reasonable', Western-oriented opposition already existed there, and that Libya could become a democracy, despite its almost total lack of institutions, structures, and a civil society. Lévy saw the Libyan insurgents as equivalent to the French Resistance and, just as millions of French collaborators had become supporters of the democratic president Charles de Gaulle after the end of the German occupation in World War II, Lévy believed millions of Libyans would turn into sincere democrats after the end of Gaddafi's regime.[16] As late as November 2011, Lévy dramatically declared that the 'reconciliation' between Islam and democracy unfolding in Libya was a global political event 'of outstanding importance'.[17]

Britain and America supported the French intervention, but the enthusiasm was more muted in London and Washington. The British Prime Minister, David Cameron, shared the concerns about a possible genocide and spoke of a duty to protect the threatened citizens. But his second argument was more pragmatic. For him, the focus was not on the global struggle for freedom and democracy, but on the negative consequences if Gaddafi continued to rule Libya. According to Cameron, if the West failed to intervene, Libya would descend into a brutal civil war that could bring instability to North Africa and lead to more terrorism and uncontrolled immigration in nearby Europe. 'Just because we cannot do the right thing *everywhere*,' Cameron told the House of Commons, 'does not mean we should *not* do it when we have clear permission for and a national interest in doing so.'[18] Seen in this light, Britain's agenda was far less idealistic than France's, although Cameron's aims also ultimately made regime change a necessity.

In America, there was initial resistance to the intervention. Vice President Joe Biden believed Sarkozy's plans were an example of the kind of intervention that could quickly escalate into an unmanageable war. At the same time, however, a group of passionate supporters of the intervention was forming. As well as Clinton, that group included the former journalist and human rights activist, Samantha Power, who had written an entire book on liberal interventions,[19] and the US ambassador to the United Nations, Susan Rice, who had worked for the National Security Council during the Rwandan genocide and witnessed the failure of the international community at first hand.[20] Obama's 'compromise' between the two camps was for America to support a limited intervention, but only under the condition that France and Britain take the lead, bear the cost, and assume full responsibility for it. Thus, America was on board, but wanted to make it clear to all that this was a 'European war'.[21]

Breach of trust

The intervention began on 19 March 2011 and was inconsistent from the outset. UN Security Council resolution 1973 authorised only measures 'to protect civilians [...] under threat', and not 'regime change'. In the early days of the conflict, meticulous care was therefore taken to make sure only such targets came under fire as were really instrumental in the killing of civilians.[22] On 28 March, President Obama declared that the strategy of pursuing regime change 'would be a mistake'.[23] And at the same time, a high-ranking NATO officer who was responsible for coordinating the campaign pointed out, 'We are not [the Libyan opposition's] air force.'[24] However, the intervention conceived in this way was sluggish and made little progress for weeks. Frederic Wehrey, a Libya expert with the Carnegie Foundation, says NATO had almost no reliable information, and it often took days for air strikes to be authorised.[25]

That changed when France and Britain sent special forces to Libya to support the insurgents on the ground. The intelligence provided by these 'military advisors' became the most important source of information for the air strikes and was instrumental in stopping Gaddafi's advance on Benghazi.[26] The problem was that this turned NATO into a military 'service provider' for the opposition, and it became increasingly difficult to differentiate between operations to protect civilians and those that were also — or exclusively — aimed at overthrowing Gaddafi. By mid-April at the latest, it had become clear that the objective was now not just to prevent genocide, but also to bring about regime change. This was made clearest in a guest article in *The New York Times* published on 14 April, written jointly by Sarkozy, Cameron, and Obama, in which the three leaders pledged to uphold Security Council Resolution 1973 and stressed that the aim was 'not to remove Gaddafi by force', but added that 'It is impossible to imagine a future for Libya with Gaddafi in power.'[27]

So, had Sarkozy and Cameron hoodwinked the international community? Bernard Rougier and the secret service chief John Sawers, who both took a sceptical view of the intervention, don't believe there was any deliberate deceit at play. Sawers believes the two objectives 'merged with one another' over the course of the campaign, eventually making it impossible to differentiate between 'protecting civilians' and 'regime change'.[28] According to Rougier, another important factor was military success: 'The idea [of regime change] was there from the start, but it did not become an objective of war until there were military successes and some momentum developed from that.'[29]

However, it is also true that both leaders had formed a notion from the outset which effectively ruled out the possibility of Gaddafi remaining in power. It was also true that there was never a ceasefire, a 'pause in hostilities', or a serious offer of peace negotiations made to Gaddafi (or his son).[30] Whether it was planned from the start or not, Russia and China, which had made it possible for the UN Security Council to pass the 'protection mandate' by abstaining in the vote, were now left with the impression that they had been duped by the two Western powers and that their 'good will' had been abused. As events would soon show, this breach of trust was to have considerable consequences — far beyond the borders of Libya.

Rapid retreat

A further inconsistency was that while Sarkozy and Cameron constantly spoke of a 'stable' Libya, at no point were their countries willing to support the new government in stabilising the situation. Rougier reports that Sarkozy and his advisors wanted to hear nothing of any problems and had 'zero interest' in a 'deeper understanding of Libyan society, the tribal system, or the potential consequences for neighbouring states in the Sahel and West Africa'.[31] As they saw it, Gaddafi was the obstacle to a breakthrough of democracy and as soon as he was overthrown, the Western-oriented opposition groups would prevail.[32] In other words, there were no plans for the post-war period, because they were not considered necessary.

There was less optimism in Britain. Learning from the experiences of the Iraq War, a special unit of the British Foreign Office set to work relatively early drawing up extensive plans for a new, democratic Libya. The problem was that it lacked the necessary information.[33] The British intelligence services, as John Sawers explains, had until then concentrated on Libya's nuclear programme and the terrorist threat, and knew relatively little about Libyan society and its social and power structures.[34] Even the then Foreign Secretary William Hague later admitted that while it was 'not fair to say that there was a lack of planning,' the government 'relied on plans that were incapable of implementation'.[35]

There was, though, agreement concerning what was seen as the central lesson of the Iraq War: that a long-term presence in a liberated country sparked more conflicts than it solved. That was why the plan included a rapid transfer of responsibility to other countries, regional organisations, or the United Nations. Those who defended the intervention later argued that this policy was right in principle, since the Libyan opposition had declined a Western-dominated peace mission.[36] But in truth, there was never any question of an occupation lasting years. It was not French or British troops that were lacking, but Western money and expertise to help with state-building.[37] Even a small presence, says the Middle East analyst Emile Hokayem, would have made 'a great difference'.[38] But the Western lead nations not only refused to provide a presence themselves, but also made absolutely no effort to get a multilateral mission off the ground, although they themselves had called for just such a mission. The French conflict researcher Olivier Schmitt wrote that it was surprising 'that the United Kingdom or France did not even try to get the Arab League or the African Union to deploy an assistance mission to Libya'.[39] The former British diplomat Arthur Snell is more cynical: 'Maintaining and building peace is just not as interesting as fighting a war, particularly if you are the leader of a medium-sized country [such as Britain] that is desperate to show the world that it is still militarily virile.'

Obama later commented that he had had 'more faith in the Europeans [...] being invested in the follow-up'.[40] Instead of that, the two lead nations left the country to its own devices, with no significant political or civil structures and institutions after 42 years of brutal dictatorship. Florence Gaub of the EU Institute for Security Studies says the attitude was one of 'Let them do it on their own now. Everything will be fine!'[41]

Disintegration

On their first — and only — visit to the 'free Libya' on 15 September 2011, Sarkozy and Cameron received a hero's welcome. After a short stay in the capital Tripoli, which had been captured by the insurgents only days before, they travelled on to Benghazi, where the revolution had begun and where hundreds of people were waiting to wave French and British flags outside the city courthouse. Sarkozy congratulated Libyans on their decision in favour of 'peace, freedom, and economic progress'. And he promised that France, Britain, and Europe would 'always be at the side of the Libyan people'.[42]

In summer 2012, there was still great optimism. 'Everyone was euphoric,' says the Middle East scholar Daniel Gerlach. 'Many people believed that everything had passed off smoothly.'[43] The then president of the BND, Gerhard Schindler, recalls how the American services also saw the situation as positive: Gaddafi was gone, oil production was resuming, and the opposition group favoured by the West — the National Transitional Council (NTC) — had organised free elections. 'The impression was that Libya was on an excellent track.'[44]

However, just a year later, that opinion had flipped. The mood was gloomy in all the capitals of Europe. Washington also now took a more critical view of the situation. A report published by the US State Department in September 2013 highlighted a long list of problems:

A central government with weak institutions and only tenuous control over its expansive territory; the ubiquity of uncontrolled weapons and ammunition; porous and inaccessible borders; heavily armed militias and tribes with varying loyalties and agendas; high unemployment among young males along with slow-moving economic improvement; divisions between the country's regions, towns, and tribes; political paralysis due to infighting and distrust among and between Libya's political actors; and the absence of a functioning police force or national army.[45]

What had happened? Many of the problems did not just arise in 2013, but had existed even before the West's intervention. The fact that they had become so volatile, however, was down to the course chosen by both Libyan and foreign stakeholders in the first few months following the liberation.

Perhaps the most disastrous decision was that taken in December 2011 by the National Transitional Council (NTC): to pay militia members a state wage. The intention was to gain control over the countless private armies that had formed during the intervention. But the NTC — originally a 50-strong group of opposition intellectuals, entrepreneurs, and former civil servants — had no means of disbanding or disarming the militias. So the decision failed to create a national army under the control of the transitional government, instead producing even more militias, funded by the state but unwilling to submit to its authority. Frederic Wehrey called this 'probably the most ruinous decision made by Libyans' after Gaddafi's fall.[46] Rather than ending the state of war, this policy institutionalised it.

In addition to this, the NTC was deeply divided. For many who joined the organisation after the victory, its leadership was too secular, too liberal, and too tolerant of former supporters of the Gaddafi regime. Just months after the takeover, fierce clashes broke out between the more Western-oriented founders and the 'Islamic current' made up of representatives from the Libyan Muslim Brotherhood and veterans of the jihadist revolts in the 1990s. The disputes were not just over the future direction of the country, but also — and mainly — about its past. In May 2013, the now dominant 'Islamic current' passed a law prohibiting former supporters or civil servants of the Gaddafi regime from holding political office for ten years. That included the founding member of the NTC, Mahmoud Jibril, whom Bernard-Henri Lévy had brought to Europe at the start of the conflict.[47]

In short: the vacuum left by the sudden withdrawal of the West created a messy and increasingly volatile situation in which political, ideological, and regional tensions were all combined. Civil war eventually broke out in May 2014, when the hostile regional powers Qatar and the United Arab Emirates forged two coalitions out of the many different interests, and provided them with weapons and funds. The resulting conflict lasted six years and turned Libya into a failed state in every regard.

Pandora's Box

The consequences of the instability in Libya were manifold and went far beyond the borders of the country. Even before 2011 was out, members of the Tuareg nomadic ethnic group plundered local weapons caches and set out for Mali, where their fellow Tuaregs were fighting for independence. The result was that Malian separatists suddenly had access to mortars, high-tech anti-tank weapons, and heavy machine guns. When they began to bear down on the capital Bamako a few months later, France had to come to

the aid of the Malian government with a military mission, which —
in various iterations — has continued to this day.[48]

The same smuggling routes were subsequently used — albeit
in the opposite direction — by West African migrants heading for
Europe. The south-west of Libya — and specifically the town of
Ghat on the Algerian border — became a hub for the so-called
central Mediterranean route, used by the more than 100,000
Africans who made their way to Europe every year in the middle of
the decade.[49]

Another consequence was the spread of terrorism. Libya had
supported militant groups all over the world during the Gaddafi
era while always cracking down hard on any form of rebellion on
its own territory. But after the intervention, the country developed
into a kind of terrorist breeding ground where terrorist groups could
settle, free of any central government control. This was particularly
true of jihadist groups, which in many places could count on
being tolerated — if not actively supported — by Salafists, Islamic
militias, and other representatives of the 'Islamic current'.[50] From
2014 onwards, Libya thus developed into one of the most important
provinces of the so-called Islamic State.[51] It was used as a base
from which the group planned numerous attacks in neighbouring
Tunisia and even the attack on a Christmas market in Berlin in
December 2016.[52] This is confirmed by the then EU Anti-Terrorism
Coordinator, Gilles de Kerchove:

> Libya descended into chaos and began exporting
> terrorism. That had consequences for its neighbouring
> countries and the entire Sahel region initially, but also for

us in Europe a little later. In the middle of the last decade, Libya, alongside Syria and Iraq, became one of the main foreign 'sources' of terrorist recruits, inspiration, and the training for jihadist terrorism in Europe.

Nonetheless, this was not seen by Western governments as a reason to engage constructively with Libya. Many states had completely withdrawn after the attack on the American consulate in Benghazi in September 2012. Instead of addressing the causes of the conflict, they tackled only its symptoms — weapons proliferation, migration, terrorism — and in doing so, contributed to the further division and dysfunction in the country.[53]

The saddest example of this was France. From 2015, Paris sponsored the Libyan central government, as well as various United Nations peace efforts, while at the same time backing the accused war criminal and self-appointed military commander Khalifa Haftar, who promised his foreign 'backers' he would fight the Islamists and govern Libya with 'a firm hand'. The country that had set out with much fanfare in 2011 to liberate Libya from its authoritarian ruler, was supporting another ruler of the same ilk within four years.

CHAPTER 12
The Syrian Disaster

When the Arab Spring began, the Syrian President Bashar al-Assad felt he was in a secure position. Since taking office ten years earlier, he had liberalised the country's rigid, socialist-style planned economy with some minor successes.[1] He and his glamorous wife Asma were young, close to the people, and lived in a relatively normal apartment on the outskirts of Damascus rather than in the presidential palace. More important, however, was the fact that, unlike Tunisia and Egypt, Syria was not dependent on the West, had opposed America in the Iraq War, and took its own independent position when it came to the Arab–Israeli conflict. Even in late January 2011, when the protests on Tahrir Square were in full swing, Assad still appeared to be confident that his country would remain unaffected by the Arab Spring. When asked by *The Wall Street Journal* about the mistakes made by Mubarak and Ben Ali, his answer was philosophical: 'You have to be very closely linked to the beliefs of the people. [...] When there is divergence between your policy and the people's beliefs and interests, you will have this vacuum that creates disturbance.'[2]

But less than six weeks later, the Arab Spring arrived in Syria, triggered by the detention and torture of a group of teenagers in the provincial city of Daraa. Within a few days, people all over Syria were taking to the streets. With the fates of Ben Ali and Mubarak in mind, it seemed clear to Assad that tolerance and an offer of political reforms would not pay off. He assumed that if Mubarak had moved to quell the protests more promptly and decisively, the situation would never have become critical.[3] With this in mind, he decided to quash the demonstrations in his country. The level of brutality shown by the Syrian authorities shocked even the supporters of the regime. The British historian John McHugo believes the only plausible explanation for this was that the Syrian president wanted to 'teach the people a lesson'.[4] The plan failed, however, and the protests soon spiralled into violent conflict. By the end of July, the fighting had escalated to such a degree that the Red Cross spoke of 'civil war'.

The disaster that played out in the years that followed, and continues to this day, is difficult to put into words. The following figures give an initial idea. According to official United Nations estimates, 2 per cent of the Syrian population — i.e., at least 350,000 people — have died as a direct consequence of the ten-year conflict. Other estimates put the number of dead at more than 600,000.[5] More than half the Syrian population has been forced to leave their homes; almost 7 million people fled abroad, with 50 per cent of the remaining population dependent on food aid.[6] The World Bank calculates that it will take the country 20 years to reach the level of economic performance it achieved before the conflict, i.e., in the year 2010.[7]

The question is: how did it come to this? The journalist Michael Lüders believes the answer is simple. In his opinion, what happened in Syria was 'not about "values", but about [Western] interests'.[8] The blame did not lie primarily with Assad, he writes, but with America and the rest of the West, which continued the 'policy of regime change' that it had 'pursued, and still pursues, in Iraq, in Libya and, covertly, in Yemen in recent years'.[9] America, Lüders claims, was determined from the outset to get rid of Assad, and even allied with jihadists to achieve that aim. In the light of that, he argues, the terror attacks in Paris, Brussels, and London are the logical consequence of Western policies: 'Those who systematically and deliberately set out to destroy other countries,' writes Lüders, 'should not be surprised when bombs go off in their own front yard.'[10]

Almost nothing about this narrative is consistent or empirically correct. Of course, the American government was never a friend of Assad's, but, despite rhetorical avowals, there was never at any point a truly consistent 'policy of regime change'. As in all the countries of the Arab Spring, America was afraid of being dragged into another incalculable conflict in Syria that might end as it did in Iraq. The Obama administration therefore pursued a series of 'avoidance strategies', which allowed the conflict to grow ever more chaotic and extreme while doing nothing to help bring about a solution. So, America certainly is guilty in connection with the Syrian disaster — not, as Lüders claims, because it pursued its own economic of geopolitical interests there at the expense of the Syrian people, but, on the contrary, because it refused to live up to its role as a geopolitical leader.

Rapprochement

What Lüders and his fellow believers in the regime-change theory like to leave unmentioned is that there was a systematic process of rapprochement between Syria and the West in the years leading up to the Arab Spring. In the early 2000s, Syria was one of the countries on the list of regimes to be toppled, but any such plans were abandoned after the Iraq War. The Bush administration was already cooperating with the Assad regime when it came to the torture of suspected terrorists.[11] When Obama took office, all the signs pointed towards a definitive easing of tensions. As late as 2009, the American president sent intelligence officials to Syria to discuss counterterrorism. At the same time, Sarkozy hosted Assad in Paris, Tony Blair travelled to Damascus, and both French and American companies received special authorisations to intensify economic cooperation.[12] The common view at the time was that Assad was a reformer who was fighting an old guard of corrupt businessmen, military leaders, and secret service chiefs, and that he deserved support in that endeavour.

Initially, the West's attitude changed little after the demonstrations began. In contrast to Tunisia or Egypt, where America had declared itself to be on the side of the 'democratic revolution', within days, the US was tight-lipped with its official statements on Syria. The view was that there were already enough 'open fronts', with Egypt, Tunisia, Libya, Jordan, Bahrain, and

Yemen, for the developments to be controllable. Behind the scenes, America and its allies tried to have a moderating influence on Assad. Throughout the spring, representatives of Western governments met with Syrian ministers, while European financial aid was discussed in Brussels.[13] Almost everyone wanted Assad to remain in office and seize the opportunity to counter supposed hardliners. Emile Hokayem believes the West's policy towards Syria was built on the premise that the president would stage 'a coup against his own regime'.[14]

This did not change until Assad started cracking down on the protests. The turning point came when the demonstrations reached the provincial city of Hama and Syrian troops killed almost 200 protesters.[15] In the days that followed, many articles appeared, criticising the West's political hesitancy over Assad. The harshest was a leader in *The Washington Post* which asked: 'Is it any wonder that Mr Assad thinks he can slaughter the people of Hama with impunity?'[16] Obama spoke with President Sarkozy, Prime Minister Cameron, and Chancellor Merkel just a few days later. They all agreed that Assad had lost his legitimacy and should make way for a successor more willing to compromise. On 18 August, Obama appeared before journalists and told them that 'President Assad must step aside'.[17]

Those words had a huge impact inside Syria. Haid Haid, a researcher with the British think tank Chatham House who was among the demonstrators himself, recounts how the news spread like wildfire: 'Everyone was excited. We were convinced that Obama had a plan and that other countries would follow America's example.'[18] The British conflict researcher Christopher Phillips goes a step further. He argues that from that day on, the entire strategy of the opposition was based on a belief that America would come to the aid of Assad's opponents at the crucial time:

> Most Syrians, and indeed Middle Easterners, had long been encouraged to believe the US to be an all-powerful state that can achieve whatever it sets its mind to. [...] As the President had come out in open opposition to Assad, it was not unreasonable for the Syrian opposition and their regional supporters to rejoice and expect future help.[19]

But America didn't have a plan. Instead, the hope was that Obama's statement would accelerate a process that was already underway. No one reckoned with Syria's president resisting the pressure from the streets for very much longer.[20] Western intelligence services, including Germany's BND, predicted an imminent coup.[21] Turkish ministers said Assad would be gone within six months at most,[22] and even the Iranian government, which was allied with Assad's regime, established contact with the opposition, just as a precaution.[23] For the West, Assad was the last domino of the Arab Spring[24] — and all America needed to do was to wait for it to fall.

Avoidance strategies

When Assad's resignation failed to materialise, America had a problem. Obama was committed to 'regime change' but had no strategy to bring it about. Furthermore, his administration wanted to avoid a larger-scale engagement in Syria at all costs. In internal discussions, the president warned, 'we can't fool ourselves into thinking we can fix the Middle East.'[25]

The first 'avoidance strategy' to be implemented was to attempt to reach a multilateral solution. Once it became clear that Obama's words alone would not drive Assad out of office, America advocated for international mediation and invested time and political capital in the United Nations–backed Geneva Process. There were two rounds of talks, which failed for various reasons: because Assad was unwilling to step down; because the opposition believed it could win a military conflict; and because key stakeholders, such as the Kurds or Islamic militias, were not even present at the negotiating table.[26]

One unintended consequence of this multilateralisation was that major powers that so far had relatively little to do with the conflict now began to play a bigger part. That was a problem in the case of Russia especially because Moscow, which had taken a sceptical view of America's agenda of 'regime change' for many years, was allied with Assad, and had never forgiven the West for the 'breach of trust' in Libya.[27] In the years that followed, Russia blocked all Western initiatives and used its veto on the UN Security Council to block even Western resolutions that were reasonable. 'The Russians were very annoyed about Libya,' says the Middle East expert Rougier, 'and Syria paid the price.'[28]

Another avoidance strategy involved outsourcing. Instead of America, states with a better understanding of the region and a greater proximity to the conflict, and therefore greater interest in its resolution, were expected to take the leadership role. Although this sounded sensible in theory, in practice it led to tensions because those states prioritised their own national or ideological interests. Turkey is a prime example in this respect. Although Turkey's then Prime Minister, Recep Tayyip Erdoğan, assured America of his support, the Turkish government promoted Islamists and Salafist militias in Syria, did everything in its power to weaken the position of the (US-allied) Kurds, and, until 2014, turned two blind eyes to the thousands of foreign jihadist fighters crossing its territory on their way to the Syrian border.[29]

This was compounded by the fact that some of America's allies were at odds with each other. Like Turkey, Qatar, Saudi Arabia, and the United Arab Emirates were on America's side, but their aspirations and pretentions to power were often mutually exclusive. In the absence of American leadership holding the tensions among those allies in check, Syria became another arena for regional power conflicts — in a similar development to that which was underway in Libya at the same time but more extreme and chaotic.

The third avoidance strategy was simply to refuse to honour previous agreements. This was evident in the summer of 2013, when Syrian helicopters attacked a suburb of Damascus with chemical weapons, killing almost 1,500 people. A year earlier, Obama had declared the use of chemical weapons to be a 'red line' for him, which should never be crossed under any circumstances. He mobilised his troops and for a few days it looked as if there would be a retaliatory strike, but at the last minute, Obama called off the attack, instead agreeing to a proposal from Putin that Assad should voluntarily surrender his (remaining) arsenal of chemical weapons.[30]

The Middle East expert Emile Hokayem believes Obama's

climb-down was 'the biggest strategic error of the entire Syria conflict. If there was ever a point at which America had the moral, political, and strategic arguments on its side, that was it'. Hokayem adds, 'America raised huge expectations, but just left the people hanging at the crucial moment.'[31] The former head of the BND, Gerhard Schindler, concurs:

> The West simply looked on. Everyone agreed: Assad was a dinosaur, a relic of times gone by, and that's not what we wanted as a global community. We should have taken the next step then. We should have said: 'Okay, we'll support the rebels then.' But what the rebels received was anything but support. It was half-hearted at best.

Schindler's British counterpart Sawers goes a step further. In his view, it was always clear that America's reticence did nothing to improve the situation, and, indeed, made it worse.

> I remember we did a big review of the conflict in Syria. Our conclusion was that the low level of support offered by the West to the opposition was not making a strategic difference. It was enough to keep [the] fighting going and prevent opposition forces from being crushed. But it wasn't enough to change the direction of the conflict or bring about a decisive breakthrough [...] So you could say that what we did in Syria in a way only prolonged the suffering of the people.[32]

And indeed, in two years the conflict had escalated and damaged America's geopolitical authority — while President Assad's position was more secure than at the beginning.

Jihadisation

Within Syria itself, America's half-hearted strategy and the political and military vacuum it created were part of the reason that the conflict grew increasingly complex, that the number of people involved increased, and that the ideological aspects became more and more extreme. In the space of just a few years, Syria became a playground for extremist groups, of which the so-called Islamic State was only the most successful.

This fragmentation became apparent early in the conflict. In August 2013, the US organisation the Carter Center, counted more than 1,000 so-called brigades and 3,250 battalions on the side of the opposition.[33] Even the so-called Free Syrian Army (FSA), which played an important role in the early part of the conflict, was in reality little more than a very loose coalition of local units that had little in common beyond their opposition to Assad, and which were rarely able to agree on a common course of action.[34]

The conflict researcher Samer Abboud illustrates how convoluted the situation was using the example of the Al Tawhid Brigade, a well-known militia from Aleppo. When the conflict began, the group was part of the FSA, but as early as 2012, it formed a new, Islamist-oriented umbrella organisation named the Syrian Islamic Liberation Front (SILF), which in turn became the Islamic Liberation Front (ILF) a short time later, and in 2014 became part of the alliance called the Syrian Revolutionary Command Council (SRCC). At the same time, commanders of the group formed the Levant Front, which split once again in 2015, with most of its members going over to the organisation calling itself the Nour al-Din al-Zenki Movement.[35]

Such situations are exemplary of the conflict as a whole. The more it escalated, and the more foreign sponsors became involved, the more splintered the opposition became. And the more violent the disputes became, the bigger was the role played by Islamist and jihadist groups, which were considered the best fighters due to their level of experience, discipline, and resolve.[36] Armed groups that had initially been relatively secular split from the FSA, adopted Islamic logos, grew their beards, and posted bellicose videos on YouTube to gain the attention of foreign backers.[37] This developed a momentum that led to the 'jihadisation' of the opposition.[38]

Not only was it almost impossible for anyone to fathom which group belonged where, it also became ever more difficult to trace the increasingly blurred lines between non-religious, Islamist, Salafist, and jihadist groups. The simple distinction between 'moderate' and 'extremist' rebels made by Western politicians sitting at their desks often lacked any connection to reality, since commanders who might be fighting for a 'moderate' militia one day would often turn up the next day — along with their weapons and men — fighting for an Islamist militia.

The extent to which foreign sponsors were willing to accept jihadist tendencies changed over time and depending on the prevailing mood. As late as December 2012, the Qatari foreign minister said, 'I am very much against excluding anyone [from the opposition] at this stage.'[39] And even Obama's foreign policy advisor Ben Rhodes resisted applying the terrorist label to the jihadist Al Nusra Front — out of which the Islamic State later developed.

> Al Nusra was probably the strongest fighting force within the opposition, and while there were extremist elements in the group, it was also clear that the more moderate opposition was fighting side by side with Al Nusra. I argued that labelling Al Nusra as terrorists would alienate the same people we want to help.[40]

Although there is no evidence that America, Turkey, or allied Gulf States ever deliberately supported the Islamic State, the above attitude meant considerable resources ended up in the hands of Salafist and jihadist groups with ideologies that were scarcely less alarming than that of IS — or which later even joined the Islamic State.

Beneficiaries

The 'Syrian Spring' started with demonstrations demanding more respect for human dignity and democracy. But within three years, the confrontation between Assad and his opponents had developed into one of the most brutal civil wars of modern times. Rather than bringing freedom and a new democratic wave, the revolutions in the Middle East resulted in destruction, misery, and a mass exodus that also presented Europe with huge challenges.

The main 'beneficiaries' of the Syrian disaster were not liberal democrats but those who opposed them, such as the Islamic State. Contrary to the popular perception, the jihadist group had not sprung up out of nowhere. Its growth had been fed by the fertile ground of a society that was deeply divided along ethnic and religious lines, and in which violent, sectarian conflict became the defining logic.[41] When the group split from Al Qaeda in spring 2013, the move initially attracted little attention. However, only a year later, IS was spreading fear and terror throughout the entire region. Operating from its base in eastern Syria, within a few months it had captured several provinces in western Iraq, including the major city of Mosul. In summer 2014, the territory it controlled stretched over several thousand kilometres, with 8 to 10 million inhabitants, and had advanced to within just a stone's throw of Islam's holiest sites — Mecca, Medina, and Jerusalem. Its military victories were so astonishing that Western observers grew concerned about the safety of the Iraqi capital Baghdad, as well as that of Jordan and even Saudi Arabia.[42]

However, the Islamic State's sights were never set on just Syria, Iraq, or the Middle East region. From the outset, IS saw itself as the alternative to both other currents within Islam and secular modernity. The rules, laws, and societal norms it imposed in its 'state' were explicitly aimed at countering supposed Western ideas such as equality and individual liberty. The aim was to create a society that would not just oppose Western modernism, but replace it. It was this 'utopian' vision that enticed the more-than 40,000 foreign fighters — including 6,000 Western Europeans and 230 Australians — to flock to the IS caliphate.[43]

Europe was to feel the consequences of this within less than 12

months. The first terrorist attack carried out by the Islamic State
on European soil came on 24 May 2014. It targeted the Jewish
Museum in Brussels, and the attacker was a French jihadist who
had fought in Syria just a year before. That marked the start of
the deadliest wave of jihadist terrorism in Europe to date, which
reached a peak in the middle of the decade with attacks in Paris,
Nice, London, Manchester, Berlin, Barcelona, and Stockholm.
Some of the terrorists had fought in Syria themselves, others had
tried unsuccessfully to travel there. Yet others were inspired by the
gruesome videos produced by the Islamic State in its caliphate
and posted on the internet.[44] The wave of attacks did not end
until America and the West set aside their 'intentional impotence',
intervened militarily in Syria, and destroyed the group's operational
base in Syria and Iraq.[45]

Other 'beneficiaries' included Vladimir Putin's Russia, which
rose up to oppose America increasingly openly in this period. Putin
had reached the conclusion during the first decade of this century
that the West's 'missionary zeal' had become a destructive force. So,
whenever Western leaders spoke of 'regime change', he spoke of
'stability', insisted that state sovereignty be respected, and portrayed
himself as a defender of traditional values.[46]

It was therefore no surprise that Russia sided with Assad from
the beginning of the conflict, and intervened militarily starting in
September 2015. At that time, the opinion in America was that
Russia would become embroiled in an endless war and would end
up with a 'bloody nose'.[47] However, with a limited mission precisely
targeting Assad's opponents, Putin succeeded in rapidly turning the
conflict in the Syrian president's favour. Russia not only achieved

its political and strategic goals, but had also earned itself a kind of veto that made it impossible for the conflict to be resolved without Russia's aid and agreement.[48]

This was an embarrassment for the US, exposing as it did America's insecurity about its own role in the world. As John Sawers put it, 'In Putin's eyes this was yet another example that the West was relatively weak, and of Russia's ability to push back against America when it wanted.'[49] This also became evident in Europe, where Putin had opened another front in his war on liberal modernity.

CHAPTER 13
German-Russian Illusions

WHEN VLADIMIR PUTIN BECAME RUSSIAN PRESIDENT AT THE BEGINNING of 2000, expectations were not very high. After the turbulent Yeltsin years, when the Russian state practically collapsed, a sober, efficient bureaucrat — not to mention a former KGB officer and deputy mayor of St Petersburg — was seen as a modest hope by the West. The top priority for Western states and for Russia itself was stability: (re)building a functioning state system, creating order in domestic affairs, and reliability in international policy. The Russia expert Mark Galeotti remembers: 'Putin seemed to be a safe pair of hands. Boring, dry, but at least he came from within the system; he knew his way around and no one had a hold on him.'[1]

In the first few years of his presidency, Putin fulfilled the hopes placed in him. The rising price of oil helped stabilise the Russian economy, and for the first time for years, incomes also rose. On the international stage, Putin strove to reduce hostilities and consolidate the positive relations with the West that had developed under Yeltsin.

When he was welcomed by the German Bundestag with a standing ovation on 25 September 2001 — less than two weeks after the terrorist attacks in America — Putin evoked Russia's partnership with the West, distanced himself from Stalinism, promised that 'no one can ever take Russia back to the past', and pledged to 'build a democratic society and a market economy'.[2] Wolfgang Ischinger, who was Germany's ambassador to Washington at the time, recalls: 'At first Putin was incredibly easy to work with. We understood each other, everything worked.'[3]

However, by the second half of the decade it was clear that Putin's attitude towards the West was changing. At the Munich Security Conference in 2007, he made a now-famous speech in which he struck an explicitly confrontational tone. A 'unipolar world' in which there is only 'one master and sovereign', Putin told the conference, was 'dangerous'. America's aggressive behaviour was harmful to world peace and destroyed trust in international law. He argued that the unipolar system must be replaced by one of multipolarity, in which various centres of power were counterbalanced by each other.[4] Ischinger, who was in the audience at the time, recalls: 'His message was clear: Enough is enough!'[5]

Although Putin's interim successor Dmitri Medvedev signalled something of a relaxation in relations, the situation came to a head in 2012 when Putin returned to office as president. He and his government now no longer portrayed themselves as just the geopolitical rival to an — in their opinion — over-powerful America; Russia now also presented itself as an alternative to liberal democracy. Putin's speeches no longer exclusively dealt with nationalist ideas such as defending Russia's sovereignty, Russian minorities, or Russia's sphere of influence. They also focused on an ideological project to create a patriotic, conservative-Christian society to fight against the supposedly decadent, godless West.[6] In just 12 years, Putin, the supposedly boring bureaucrat, had mutated into the leader of an anti-liberal movement who was doing his best to propagate his ideas throughout the world.[7]

How could that happen? If the American political scientist John Mearsheimer is to be believed, most of the blame for Putin's 'radicalisation' lies with the West, which increasingly 'surrounded' Russia and disregarded its 'legitimate security interests'. And at first sight, that did indeed appear to be the case: four Central European states joined NATO in the late 1990s, and the former Soviet Baltic States followed in 2004. Four years later, there was also talk of Georgia and Ukraine joining the Alliance (which was blocked by Germany and France, however). All this happened against the backdrop of the EU's enlargement to the east, America's 'regime change' rhetoric, popular uprisings in Ukraine and Georgia, the Arab Spring, and the 'abuse' of the Security Council resolution to topple Gaddafi in Libya. Thus, it was not surprising that Putin felt threatened, says Mearsheimer. The West seemed hell-bent on exporting its system to the entire world, and the institutions that most clearly embodied its ideas — the EU and NATO — were creeping ever closer towards Russia.[8] Ukraine was a particular 'red line' for Moscow, due to its historical ties with Russia, which were so close that Putin would often call the two countries 'sister nations', or even refer to Russians and Ukrainians as 'one people'.[9]

But Mearsheimer's argumentation was not completely correct. He was right to say that America's 'regime change' agenda caused paranoia among authoritarian leaders all over the world. He was also correct to point out that NATO's eastward enlargement took place without sufficient regard for Russian sensibilities. 'The Americans showed little tact,' says Ischinger. 'They should have applied the brakes more.'[10] What Mearsheimer ignored, however, were the facts that Russia had explicitly agreed to NATO's eastward expansion in 1997,[11] that supposed 'assurances' had been left unmentioned for a long time,[12] that candidate countries strove for membership of Western institutions of their own free will, and that one of the important reasons for this was not primarily the economic incentive, but a fear of Russian irredentism. That was particularly true of Ukraine, which had consistently professed its wish to join NATO and the EU since the late 1990s — even under supposedly pro-Russian presidents.[13]

Russia's domestic politics were just as important, although Mearsheimer shows no interest in them. By the time Putin re-ran for president in 2012, the decade of economic revival had come to an end. Oil and gas prices had fallen, and the Russian state had hardly any money with which to buy the loyalty of its citizens. Putin's party suffered bitter losses in the elections in autumn 2011, and he himself was booed when he appeared at a martial arts event.[14] As Obama's former advisor and Russia expert Michael McFaul writes, 'Putin needed a new enemy'. From spring 2012 onward, the former (and future) president began to portray himself as a fighter against the liberal idea.[15] Medvedev's modernisation agenda was quickly forgotten. Instead, all talk was suddenly of a Russian 'renaissance' and resistance to Western influences. One of the people from whom Putin drew his ideological inspiration for this was Alexander Dugin, a mastermind of national revolutionary thinking, whose philosophy combines Eurasianist power fantasies with theories of the New Right.[16] This went down well with voters: Putin's approval rating stood at 86 per cent after the annexation of Crimea in 2014.[17]

The fact that Russians were so receptive to an ultranationalist narrative points to the depth of the scars left by their experience of the transformations of the 1990s. Russia was no longer a superpower but still wanted to be treated as one — including having its own sphere of influence and a veto over the major political decisions made by (sovereign) states that used to be part of the Soviet Union. Arguably, the anti-Western dynamic was due less to the aggressive advance of Western ideas and institutions than to Russian feelings of humiliation and weakness after the collapse of the Soviet Union in the nineties, and the loss of its status as a world power. Russia had become 'a hostage to its own claim to be a superpower'[18] and Putin skilfully took advantage of that to secure his own grip on power. He was a populist imperialist.

The West's mistake was to fail to recognise this early enough. By 2012, if not before, confrontation with the West was no longer just an impulse or an occasional tactic for Putin, but a deliberate strategy on which the preservation of his political system depended. Rather than curbing this development, the West reacted with insecurity, division, and self-recrimination. Even after the annexation of Crimea, the political elites, in Germany particularly, clung on to the totally illusory idea that the conflict could be overcome by means of a gradual rapprochement and economic interdependence. This approach had fatal consequences. It not only led to countries like

Germany becoming politically and economically dependent on Russia, but also encouraged Putin to be increasingly brazen in the pursuit of his own interests.

The 'new(est) Ostpolitik'

The annexation of Crimea in spring 2014, and the 'hybrid war' waged by Russia in eastern Ukraine since, were an attack on Ukraine's territorial integrity. Yet the sanctions imposed and measures introduced as a result were relatively moderate: the West punished some Russian officials and companies, redeployed troops to eastern NATO countries, and gave extra financial aid to Ukraine.[19] One of the main reasons for the West's restrained reaction was the attitude of German elites, who ignored Putin's radicalisation and focused on trying to bring about political change through dialogue and economic ties rather than a show of strength.

It was often said that this policy was inspired by the 'neue Ostpolitik' ('new policy towards the East') introduced in the sixties by the Social Democratic West German chancellor Willy Brandt and his minister for special affairs, Egon Bahr. The aim of the policy was to end the hostility that characterised East–West relations. Rather than prioritising confrontation and the victory of one side over the other, it sought rapprochement and mutual acceptance. The idea was that dialogue, personal meetings, and 'a thousand small steps' would lead to a less hostile view of each other and an increase in mutual trust, which could in turn open the way to political progress. Brandt and Bahr put those ideas into practice when they came to power in 1969. That resulted in the recognition of international borders, in new trade agreements, and in a general easing of tensions in East–West relations, which also led to improvements on the humanitarian level. The trust engendered by the *neue Ostpolitik* defused numerous crises and helped bring about a peaceful end to the Cold War.[20]

Closer inspection reveals that the *neue Ostpolitik* was far more complex and multi-faceted than its proponents suggest. From the outset, Brandt and Bahr were not just concerned with improving relations with the Soviet Union, but also with Poland and Czechoslovakia, which were Warsaw Pact members at the time. Any agreement with Moscow that ignored or ran contrary to the interests of central European states would have been inconceivable for Brandt and Bahr. And, contrary to some claims, it was not in conflict with US policy at the time. Indeed, it came about with the active support of the United States. Bahr usually informed the government in Washington even before he informed the Bundestag, since 'Germany's policy of détente would never have existed without American backing'.[21] At least as importantly, the *neue Ostpolitik* also had a military component. Even as Brandt and Bahr were opening up channels of communication, the defence budget rose to a level never before seen in post-war West German history.[22]

Almost none of this found mention later in the narrative of the Putin apologists. The version of *neue Ostpolitik* identified by German elites as a model for solving the problem with Putin was so heavily truncated and romanticised that it bore little relation to the historical facts. What remained were mainly empty slogans. The first was 'change through rapprochement', which in practice meant dialogue on all levels with no preconditions. In the eyes of its elites, Germany bore a special responsibility because, on the one hand, the Nazis were responsible for the death of 25 million Soviet citizens,[23] and on the other hand, Germany had Russia to thank for reunification and therefore owed it a great debt.[24] The hope was that talks between decision-makers and representatives from civil society would again help to break down perceived hostilities, uncover common ground, and settle differences. The condition for such talks was that the Russian dialogue partners, as well as their views and interests, should be accepted without question.[25] In the opinion of the Bavarian conservative politician, Peter Gauweiler, anything else would lead to confrontation, would be seen as lecturing by Russia, and would drive the country even deeper into 'political isolation'.[26]

The dialogue that followed this approach resulted in little more than empty phrases and assertions of friendship, however. This was most apparent in the case of the 'Petersburg Dialogue' — an annual conference that was supposed to bring together the civil societies of Germany and Russia, but which mutated over the years into a purely economic forum because the organisers excluded controversial issues, and an ever-decreasing number of representatives from Russia's civil society were willing (or allowed) to take part. It became even more problematic when, rather than bringing about change, the dialogue resulted in identification with the Russian rulership. This criticism had previously been levelled at the *neue Ostpolitik*, which by the 1980s had developed such an acceptance of the communist powers that civil rights activists came to be perceived as 'troublemakers'.[27] There was a similar tendency among supporters of the new(est) iteration of *Ostpolitik*, who spoke of openness and dialogue, while downplaying political repression in Russia by referring to it with phrases like 'normative differences'.[28]

The second slogan was 'change through trade'. In the same vein as relations with China, closer ties with Putin's regime were principally justified by the idea that closer economic relations would lead to liberalisation and that violent conflict would be rendered less likely by more economic interdependence. One of the main proponents of this idea was Saxony's state premier, Michael Kretschmer, who visited Russia to promote investment. In interviews he said, 'Political differences are far more easily settled when you have close economic ties and you're in constant communication.'[29] Although there is no evidence that he regularly raised such differences with his Russian partners, Kretschmer was convinced that 'Mutual economic relations are a protection against aspirations to absolute power.'[30] German industry's Eastern Committee, an initiative of 350 companies that saw itself as the spearhead of German–Russian détente politics, held the same view — true to the motto: what's good for business might also be good for politics.[31]

In this way, the idea of 'change through trade' united liberal believers, who saw economic relations as a kind of peace project,[32] and cynical business folk who wanted to see a decoupling of economics and politics. Both groups believed the sanctions imposed on Russia by the West in reaction to the annexation of Crimea to be damaging. And both firmly supported the Nord Stream 2 pipeline project, spearheaded by the former chancellor, Gerhard Schröder, to transport natural gas from Russia to Germany beneath the Baltic Sea. From the point of view of *Ostpolitik*, this was a ground-breaking idea, as it promised to interconnect the two countries even further. But as it turned out, the project raised tensions all over Europe and even with America, as it would have made Germany (even) more dependent on Russian energy and would have rendered Ukraine (even) more vulnerable to blackmail.[33] Germany's then foreign minister Frank-Walter Steinmeier at least admitted later that his long-standing support for the project had been wrong. 'My adherence to Nord Stream 2 [...] was clearly a mistake,' said the now-president in April 2022. 'We kept clinging on to bridges that Russia no longer believed in and that our partners had warned us about.'[34]

Putin's (long) war on the West

In practice, the 'Ostpolitik daydreams'[35] of the German elites had no democracy-promoting or peace-making effects, simply serving to encourage Putin to pursue his anti-liberal agenda even more aggressively. His long war on the West began many years before Russia's invasion of Ukraine in February 2022, and was waged on many fronts with a wide range of means.

This first manifested itself inside Russia. Putin's election losses in 2011 and the demonstrations that followed had convinced the Russian president that the West was out to topple him using the same scenario as that which played out during the so-called colour revolutions in Ukraine (2004) and Georgia (2008), as well as the Arab Spring.[36] The Russian government therefore banned numerous civil society organisations, closed down the few remaining free media outlets, and restricted access to the internet. It came down hardest on the opposition politician Alexei Navalny, who had become a national figure thanks to the 2011 protests. Putin clearly found the anti-corruption campaigner so threatening that he repeatedly had him arrested and tried on trumped-up charges, and even had him poisoned in 2020.[37] Other Putin opponents 'fell out of the window' or were shot openly on the street — in several cases even in Western foreign countries.[38]

Within Russia's supposed sphere of influence — the states of the former Soviet Union — Putin made sure any orientation towards the West was impossible. The tools he used to achieve this ranged from propaganda and corruption to active destabilisation, for example by mobilising Russian minorities, or 'stoking' ethnic conflicts. Russia supported separatists in the Donbas region in eastern Ukraine, and for years sabotaged efforts to reach a peaceful solution under the French- and German-mediated Minsk Agreements. As a result, Ukraine never came to rest and was prevented from taking any further steps towards integration with the West.[39]

However, Putin's war on the West went far beyond such 'defensive' measures. Wherever the West had a military presence, Russia positioned itself on the opposing side. In Syria, Putin supported Assad; in Libya he allied himself with the army commander Haftar; and in Afghanistan he reportedly supplied arms to the Taliban.[40] While he was genuinely convinced that any attempt to 'export' Western concepts of democracy and human rights to other cultures would lead to 'chaos and violence',[41] he also realised that such attempts would create opportunities to weaken the West's position and strengthen his own. As the former head of Germany's BND, Gerhard Schindler explains, 'Putin created several "fronts" which he could use as bargaining chips. The idea behind it was: if he was needed in Syria, he could possibly demand concessions in Ukraine in return.'[42]

A further front in Putin's war was digital rather than military in nature. Contrary to the idea that the internet was one of the 'weapons' of liberal modernity and that it would help democracy conquer the world, Russia recognised the potential of digital warfare earlier than the West did. Russian hackers, working with the government, attacked Western institutions and leaked confidential data. At the same time, tens of thousands of Russian accounts swarmed social media platforms in an attempt to manipulate public opinion. This was most obvious during the Brexit referendum in Britain and the US presidential elections in 2016 (see chapters 15 and 16). The aim of such interventions was to deepen divisions in Western societies and increase polarisation — which explains why Russian propaganda often supported radical positions at both ends of the political spectrum, fuelling the culture wars in Western societies.

This does not mean that Russia had no ideological preference. Probably the most significant part played by Moscow in European politics in recent years was its role in the birth of the 'anti-liberal front'. After Putin 'came out' as a defender of conservative Christian values in 2011 and 2012, kindred groups created a Europe-wide network through which Russia supported right-wing populist parties all over the continent. This included invitations to Moscow, meetings with Putin's advisors, and even financial support such as donations to the Lega Party in Italy or a €10 million loan granted to France's Front National.[43] This earned the Russian leadership

allies in the West who not only actively contributed to destabilising
their own societies, but also voiced genuine and very enthusiastic
support for Putin, his policies, and his world view. An example of
this was the completely open declaration by the leader of France's
Front National, Marine le Pen, in 2017 that 'the politics I represent
[…] is the politics of Mr Putin'.[44]

Thus, Putin had already been waging war against the West for
years without his apologists in Germany (and elsewhere) noticing.
As was to be expected from a former KGB officer, he did not use
exclusively military means, but cleverly combined those with
political, propagandist, and psychological methods that usually
remained below the threshold of open conflict. The effectiveness
of such 'hybrid warfare' became apparent in the mid 2010s, when
the liberal idea of Europe threatened to shatter in the face of
the financial and refugee crises, while the anti-liberal alternative
promoted by Putin gained a lot of popular support.

PART IV
CRISIS:
2016 to the present

CHAPTER 14
Europe Under Pressure

FRANCIS FUKUYAMA WAS OFTEN ACCUSED OF WANTING TO TURN THE entire world into a carbon copy of America. But in fact, his theory of 'the end of history' prophesied a very different future. According to Fukuyama, it was not America that was left facing the end of history when all ideological enemies of liberal modernity were vanquished, but the 'flabby, prosperous, self-satisfied, inward-looking, weak-willed states [of Western Europe] whose grandest project was nothing more heroic than the creation of a Common Market'.[1] America's aggressive, often militaristic universalism is no longer appropriate for the times under such circumstances, says Fukuyama. All that's left at the end of history is trade, exchange, peaceful coexistence — and 'centuries of boredom'.[2]

The American political scientist and neoconservative Robert Kagan presented a similar analysis almost 15 years later. In his 2003 work *Of Paradise and Power*, he compared Europe to an 'island of the blessed' where power and violence have been replaced by international law and negotiation. Europeans, says Kagan, no longer believe in *Realpolitik*, but in a world where reason, the power of persuasion, and universally binding rules can resolve any conflict. He suggested the continent had entered a 'post-historical paradise of peace and relative prosperity, the realisation of Immanuel Kant's "perpetual peace"'.[3]

Although Kagan and Fukuyama's analyses were massively oversimplified, the two political scientists were not entirely wrong. They were simply explaining to their (American) audience in an exaggerated way something that was generally accepted in Europe — namely, that European unification was conceived as a liberal peace project following the devastation of World War II. Europe was to be a continent where enemies found reconciliation and traded with each other, and where a new, common identity would gradually grow out of the mutual exchange of ideas, common rules, and the knowledge that they had a 'shared destiny'.

The founding fathers of modern Europe, the German Chancellor Konrad Adenauer and the French Foreign Minister Robert Schuman, took the same view of this as their political grandsons such as Helmut Kohl or the long-standing European Commission president, Jacques Delors. Although Europe and European unification have been more politically controversial since the signing of the Maastricht Treaty in 1992,[4] the political elites of today still support the idea of Europe as a liberal peace project with great conviction. Nathalie Tocci, the senior advisor to the former EU foreign policy chief Federica Mogherini, explains:

The EU is a liberal project which is not possible any other way. Imagine if all the member states of the EU had far-right governments: would the European Union exist? The answer is no! And the reason for that is because nationalist government would be unable to agree on anything, because nobody would make concessions, and because compromise would be inconceivable. The values on which the European Union is built are profoundly liberal and democratic.[5]

Nothing about this vision of Europe is wrong or undesirable. However, it turned out that it confused the *idea* of a united, liberal Europe with the far more complex reality. And it led to a policy that overestimated people's acceptance and underestimated the often enduring cultural, economic, and political differences in Europe.

This became particularly apparent during the two great crises of the 2010s. The currency crisis, which began in the first half of the decade, was the result of a process in which European politicians prioritised their vision of a united Europe over economic and financial imperatives. Although many of the problems the eurozone struggled with were foreseeable, they were ignored because they stood in the way of realising that liberal vision. The same is true of the so-called refugee crisis, which reached its peak in 2015 and 2016. Here, too, ambitious elites took a step towards further integration — in this case, by creating the Schengen area — without making the necessary changes to asylum legislation. This resulted in growing divisions and the development of a reactionary alternative to the modern liberal idea of Europe.

Euro-vision

Monetary union, which came into effect in two stages in 1999 and 2002,[6] was not principally an economic project, but a political one. That does not mean that there was no economic justification for the euro. After the single market became a reality in 1992 and goods, services, capital, and people could move freely within the Union, currency differences were the only remaining 'trade barrier'. Jacques Delors had warned as early as the late 1980s that this would cause tensions.[7] And indeed, the European Exchange Rate Mechanism to coordinate the exchange rates between the currencies of its members, did break down several times in the 1990s. A common currency promised to put an end to such problems — it eliminated exchange rate risks and also created an international anchor currency, which benefitted European companies even when doing business outside of the single market.[8]

However, it was the political justification for introducing the common currency that was pivotal. Helmut Kohl made no secret of that. In countless interviews, he said the common currency was a 'pre-requisite for peace and freedom in the 21st century' that would make the process of European unification 'irreversible' and, that it created a joint sense of identity into the bargain. 'Currencies are more than a mere means of payment,' wrote the former German chancellor, adding that after the introduction of the euro 'a sense of community emerges completely naturally'.[9] Ruprecht Polenz, the long-time chairman of the German Bundestag's foreign affairs committee, still sees it that way today: 'The common currency is something that binds us together and that will create a shared European consciousness in the course of time.'[10]

This is why the construction of the currency union mainly followed political rather than economic imperatives. The very diverse national economies of Europe were forced into the corset of the common currency, which robbed them of the opportunity to devalue their currency, change interest rates, or increase their money supply, while at the same time no new mechanisms were created to hedge the debts of member states or reduce imbalances. From the outset, the low interest rates that had been available to everyone for years came with the risk that trade deficits in the so-called southern countries, such as Greece, Italy, Spain, and Portugal, would further increase. And the so-called 'stability criteria', which were supposed to guarantee a sound financial and economic policy based on comparable principles, were already so weakened at the start of the currency union that they played virtually no role at all.[11]

Even the champions of European integration knew that such a currency union could never work. Nonetheless, there were no serious attempts to correct the euro's obvious design flaws until the crisis broke out. This was because such a move would have required measures that would have met with opposition in Germany — the eurozone's most important member. Charles Grant, Director of the Centre for European Reform think tank, explains:

> Shared debt liability in particular would have set alarm bells ringing in Germany. The Germans would have thought, 'We're the largest country in Europe and we'll end up having to pay off the debts of the Greeks and Italians.' That would have further increased scepticism in

Germany about monetary union. And without Germany, there would have been no monetary union.[12]

So, the fact that the necessary financial tools were not created was not down to a mistake or a lack of economic competence. In the eyes of the European elites, a faulty euro was better than no euro at all. The economics professor and EU commission president at the time, Romano Prodi, even openly admitted this. In 2001, he said, 'I am sure the euro will oblige us to introduce a new set of economic policy instruments. It is politically impossible to propose that now.'[13] And he continued, 'But someday there will be a crisis and new instruments will be created.'[14]

Euro crisis

The crisis evoked by Prodi began in Greece and led to the first 'aid package' in spring 2010, in which the eurozone members and the International Monetary Fund provided a total of €110 billion in loans. Greece's problems had many causes, including the country's chronically weak economy, irresponsible economic management, and the dramatically weakening effect of the American banking crisis on the international financial system.[15] However, the more basic cause lay in the structure of the currency union, which did nothing to compensate for the loss of countries' sovereignty in monetary policy. This was also the reason for the further crises experienced by Portugal, Spain, Italy, and Cyprus in the subsequent years. Their respective triggers were different, but they all ultimately came down to the same problem, namely the lack of a guarantee for the sovereign debt of member states that — for whatever reason — had got into difficulties.

The situation did not begin to calm until the then president of the European Central Bank, Mario Draghi, created what the financial markets saw as the necessary mechanism to guarantee the continued existence of the currency union. In September 2012, he announced that the ECB would do 'whatever is necessary' to buy government bonds from the countries in crisis. In essence, he signalled that the central bank would 'print' money on a large scale to finance the debt of troubled member states.[16]

The political price for this was that it was no longer possible to uphold the illusion of a joint currency *without* joint liability. As Prodi had predicted, in the years that followed, European politicians created a series of instruments and mechanisms, each of which was a response to a different aspect of the crisis, but which were all based on the idea that the community as a whole was responsible for the financial and economic problems of its members, and, as an ultimate consequence of this, must also bear the associated costs. The European Stability Mechanism (ESM) was set up to provide loans to states in financial difficulty, the Fiscal Pact was signed, committing such states to economic and budgetary coordination, and the so-called banking union was initiated, which socialised the costs of bank bailouts.[17]

All this helped stabilise the euro, but some of the economic consequences were catastrophic. In return for receiving European loans, the 'southern countries' had to commit to harsh 'reform programmes' that included radically cutting their state spending and far-reaching structural reforms — for example of their pension systems. Combined with the loss of sovereignty over their monetary policy, this meant that countries like Greece, Spain, and Italy were left with absolutely no economic or fiscal leverage to boost their economies. This was most apparent in Greece, where the economy crashed, and did not return to annual growth of more than 1 per cent again until 2017. Even in Spain and Italy, it took until the middle of the decade for economic performance to pick up again. In short, membership in the common currency condemned those countries to years of stagnation. Even the Organisation for Economic Cooperation and Development in Europe (OECD) described the situation as a 'trap' with no easy means of escape.[18]

Loss of trust

The negative effects of the euro crisis were not limited to economic performance; it also damaged confidence in Europe's institutions. This was most palpable in Italy, the eurozone's third-largest economy. While in 2007 almost 60 per cent of the population said the European Union was 'trustworthy', five years later that figure had fallen to just over 20 per cent.[19] For many Italians at that time, Europe was the scapegoat not just for the hated austerity policy, but also for all manner of problems, many of which were 'domestic'.[20] From the middle of the decade, this began to be reflected at the ballot box. In the parliamentary elections of 2018, the anti-European Lega Party led by Matteo Salvini gained 17.4 per cent of the vote and became part of a governing coalition; and the party won no less than 34 per cent of the vote in the elections to the European Parliament in 2019. Its share of the vote has fallen since then — but only because it has been overtaken by the equally populist 'Brothers of Italy'. The sad conclusion is that the euro crisis turned what was once one of the most pro-European countries in Europe into one of the most anti-European.

Even in the 'northern countries', which benefitted enormously from the introduction of the euro and did not suffer greatly in the crisis, there was a surge in Euro-scepticism. Many people felt cheated because they had been assured that the euro would not involve any socialisation of debt. The huge sums of money announced for each rescue package gave the impression that the supposedly more reliable states in the north were paying for the financial mismanagement of the south.[21] In Finland, the True Finns party upped its share of the vote from 4 to 19 per cent; in the Netherlands, the vote share of the Party for Freedom rose from 6 to 15 per cent, and in Germany, a completely new party emerged, the Alternative for Germany (AfD), which claimed to offer an alternative to the old parties' euro policy, to which people had been told there was no alternative.

The dream of the liberal euro-visionaries had turned into the exact opposite. Instead of increasing enthusiasm for Europe and creating a strong sense of community, the inadequately planned and dishonestly presented monetary union project resulted in divisions and a loss of trust in European institutions.[22] The liberal elites who had insisted on introducing monetary union could not understand that most citizens' sense of European identity was less strong than their own, and that most people did not see transferring money from Germany to Greece the same way as, for example, the financial transfers between the different federal states of Germany. In other words, the European elites' modern liberal vision did not correspond to the actual reality in Europe, and their attempt to impose it on Europeans through deception did not lead to acceptance, but to rejection.

From Schengen to Dublin

The second great European crisis started in summer 2015, when ever-increasing numbers of refugees began to arrive in the countries of the European Union via various routes from Syria, Iraq, Afghanistan, and West Africa. By March 2016, an estimated 2 million people had made it to Europe in this way, most of whom were taken in by Germany, Austria, and Sweden.[23] This was the biggest refugee wave in Europe since the end of World War II, and it presented the destination countries with great practical and political challenges. However, although the exact timing and scale were a surprise, the crisis had been looming for a long time and was ultimately a result of Europe's flawed asylum policy.

The starting point was the Schengen Agreement, which resulted in the gradual dismantling of border controls between EU states in the 1990s. Of course, this was supported by economic arguments (border controls take time and interrupt supply chains), but even more than in the case of monetary union, the motive was the realisation of a vision of a Europe without borders. Waldemar Schreckenberger, who negotiated the agreement on behalf of Helmut Kohl, was later quoted as saying it was 'one of the most important works of my life' because, 'For centuries, the states of Europe have been hostile to each other, but today there are twenty-five states in the Schengen area.'[24]

However, just as was the case with the introduction of the euro, the positive, supposedly identity-forming aspects of the agreement were implemented without considering the politically challenging repercussions. It was not only protecting the external borders and cooperation between security services that were urgently required, but also, and most importantly, a unified asylum policy. As Charles Grant points out, 'The Schengen area cannot work without [...] some kind of common system for dealing with asylum seekers. Otherwise, they will all make for Germany and Sweden. And that's not fair.'[25]

The Dublin Regulation was agreed by the Schengen states in 1997 and it stipulates that asylum seekers may only apply for status as such in one Schengen country. That must also be the country in which they first entered the Schengen area. This was particularly advantageous for Germany because it is surrounded by other Schengen states and was therefore seldom the country of arrival for asylum seekers. The only problem was that the procedure never worked in practice. Most refugees did not want to stay in the country they first arrived in, and most countries of first arrival had no interest in keeping them there. Even long before the refugee crisis, there was a culture of 'waving them through', which resulted in many refugees finding their way to Germany and the other northern states. Furthermore, Greece and Italy treated asylum seekers so badly that those who were returned there from Germany under the Dublin Regulation quickly made their way back to the northern states. Germany's Federal Constitutional Court supported this by declaring it illegal to deport asylum seekers back to Italy and Greece due to the living conditions they were kept in there. As a result, even before the refugee crisis and despite the Dublin

Regulation, Germany kept most asylum seekers.[26] Still, Germany did everything it could to uphold the system and, as late as the year 2013, still resisted the introduction of a European quota system.[27] Ruprecht Polenz remembers:

> Whenever I broached the subject [in Berlin], colleagues responsible for home affairs would just point out that we had Dublin and that the whole thing was the problem of the countries with external borders. And that was that. At that time, Germany consistently blocked any move towards a common EU asylum and refugee policy. That's simply the truth.[28]

By 2011 at the latest, it had become clear that several crises beyond Europe's borders would increase migratory pressures. After the fall of Gaddafi, Italy could no longer rely on Libya holding refugees back in Africa, while the conflict in Syria was increasing pressure on Turkey. The situation in all states neighbouring Syria was worsening dramatically. According to the United Nations' refugee agency, the UNHCR, 85 per cent of refugees had insufficient access to necessary supplies at the beginning of 2015, and almost 40 per cent had no access to clean drinking water.[29] However, rather than seeking a solution pre-emptively and concluding agreements with non-European neighbouring countries, the European states cut their funding to the UNHCR. In short, although Europe had created a common migration area by creating Schengen, it made absolutely no effort to prevent the imminent wave of refugees from crossing its borders.[30]

Refugee crisis

The consequences of this negligent policy became clear in late summer 2015. The number of refugees arriving in the European Union had been rising throughout the year and by autumn and winter it often exceeded 10,000 a day. No European government was prepared for this, and no effective system existed for identifying the refugees, distributing them, or stemming the stream of arrivals. An advisor to the then European Council President Donald Tusk compared the situation to a tropical storm — 'a natural disaster [that leads] to a frightening breakdown in law and order. [...] Now [people are] waking up to Europe's powerlessness.'[31] It was not until March 2016 — after seven long months — that the number of arrivals started to decline significantly.

It is still debated today whether Germany should simply have closed its borders. This appears to have been the plan, for a few days at least. The journalist Robin Alexander claims that the order already existed but it was changed at the last minute to remove the closing of the borders.[32] The migration researcher Gerald Knaus believes it would never have been possible to close the borders anyway. Almost all the refugees who entered Germany did so across the Austrian border, and any deportations back to another Schengen country require that country's consent. Also, effectively closing Germany's borders would have required the deployment of the country's entire national police force; such a move would have created chaos on the Austrian side of the border; and most refugees would have kept retrying to cross the border anyway. 'It would have gone well for eight days at the most,' says Knaus.[33]

The former head of the BND, Gerhard Schindler, takes a

different view. He admits that a long-term closure of Germany's border would not have been possible, but he is convinced that closing it even for a few days would have had a dramatic psychological effect, deterring other refugees from making the journey to Europe:

> The important thing in this kind of approach would have been the message it sent out. As if to say, 'Guys, we've got to stop this now. You'll have to find a different way, use a different procedure. But you won't be crossing this border anymore. You've seen the images. It's over.'[34]

It is difficult to judge whether that would have worked either, as the German government changed tack in September of that year. It now backed the so-called European solution — precisely the system of distribution and quotas that it had blocked for years. As early as the summer, the German government had begun to solicit support for this in other countries, but was met with resistance, particularly from parts of Eastern Europe where there was only a very small migrant population and where opposition to immigration from outside Europe was strong.[35] Ignoring such concerns, the German interior minister, Thomas de Maizière, spoke of a 'fairer sharing of the burden' within Europe and reminded the sceptical Eastern Europeans that they would face a cut to their grants from the European Structural Fund if they refused to join in with Germany's new-found enthusiasm for a European quota system.[36]

The (at that time still) liberal government in Poland eventually gave in to German pressure and Germany's proposal gained the necessary majority at the end of September. But it was a Pyrrhic victory: not only was the plan never implemented, it also caused the long-simmering conflicts between Western and Eastern Europeans to erupt. Herbert Reul, a member of the European Parliament at the time, recalls:

> At first, we all celebrated [the acceptance of the distribution of refugees]. It was a major breakthrough. It was not until later that we realised that the reaction in Eastern Europe was very different, and that it was seen as a diktat from Brussels and Berlin. They felt reminded of the old 'instructions from Moscow'. For Viktor Orbán, this was his big chance. He portrayed himself the leader from that point on.[37]

In the months that followed, Orbán and the Austrian foreign minister, Sebastian Kurz, closed the borders along the so-called Balkan route, while the 'Western Europeans', led by Angela Merkel and Dutch Prime Minister Mark Rutte, negotiated an agreement with Turkey. This was a reflection of the two different philosophies at play: Kurz and Orbán wanted to deter potential refugees by closing the borders, while Rutte and Merkel pursued diplomacy and cooperation with Turkey. Both approaches had their strengths and weaknesses. A deal with Turkey *without* the threat of border closures would have failed due to Greek resistance. And closing the Balkan route *without* a deal with Turkey would have transformed Greece into a 'gigantic refugee camp', as refugees heading for Germany and Sweden would have ended up stuck there.[38] Thus, the interpretation that is most generous to all sides is that it was a combination of both approaches that led to a significant decrease in the flow of refugees seven months after the crisis began.

Reactionary revival

The refugee crisis had more far-reaching repercussions for the liberal idea of Europe than even the currency crisis did. While the euro crisis caused people to lose trust in European institutions in many states, the refugee crisis spawned a reactionary counter-project with the Hungarian prime minister, Viktor Orbán, as its champion. His most important speech in this regard took place as early as September 2015. It began with a scathing criticism of 'liberal ideology':

> Why should we be surprised [by the wave of refugees]? Well, Ladies and Gentlemen, for years we have taught [people in other parts of the world] and told them that in fact this world is a global village [...] We told them that there are universal human rights which apply equally to everyone, whatever corner of the Earth they may be in. We forced on them our ideology [...] Then, whoever would not accept this ideology, we bombed [...] We created the World Wide Web, announcing freedom of information to the world, and we said that every human being must have access. Immediately! [...] Now we are surprised that they are knocking on our door.[39]

Orbán contrasted all this with his idea of an 'identitarian' Europe, which was virtually indistinguishable from Vladimir Putin's ideology.

He called for a Europe that was conservative and nationalist, which preserved its ethnic composition, protected its borders, and acted as a bulwark against 'Islamisation' and 'invasions' by other cultures. Orbán saw the refugee crisis as a 'huge opportunity' to achieve this vision.[40]

Although the Hungarian head of government was rejected by the liberal mainstream across Europe, his ideas proved popular in many places. This view became the quasi-official orthodoxy in the countries of the Visegrád Group — Hungary, Poland, Slovakia, and the Czech Republic. And even in 'old' Western Europe, increasing numbers of parties and political movements sprang up that shared Orbán's world view. This was not only the case in France and Austria, where right-wing populist parties had been successful for years, but also — and most importantly — in countries that were most affected by the refugee crisis, namely Germany and traditionally liberal Sweden.[41] After the end of the crisis, these parties consolidated their success and in some countries, such as France, increased it. For the first time in the modern history of the European project, a reactionary right-wing fundamental opposition was hounding the liberal parties virtually everywhere in Europe.

In other words, the way these two great liberal dreams of the European visionaries were implemented did nothing to further the liberal idea of Europe, but instead damaged it. The result was not a 'stronger sense of community', but fresh conflicts and the shattering of the idea that a united Europe must also necessarily be a liberal one. As of the middle of the 2010s, Europe was neither an 'island of the blessed', as claimed by Kagan, nor Fukuyama's

CHAPTER 15

The Brexit Revolt

ONE OF THE MOST DRAMATIC AND SURPRISING CONSEQUENCES OF THE European crisis was Brexit. Even on the eve of the vote on 23 June 2016, no one could have predicted that the opponents to Britain's membership of the EU would win. The first exit polls predicted a narrow, 52-to-48-per-cent victory for Remain — but the actual result was precisely the other way around. Early in the evening, Nigel Farage, the leader of the right-wing populist party UKIP, told reporters that 'it looks like Remain will edge it'.[1] Boris Johnson, a key figurehead of the Vote Leave campaign, even admitted that the Remain camp 'had the better arguments'.[2] But when the first counts began to be announced around midnight, the mood started to change. The Leave campaign gained far bigger majorities than expected, particularly in the former industrial heartlands of the North of England. There were strongholds of Remain support in places like London, the university cities of Oxford and Cambridge, and Scotland, but turnout in such places was often lower. Early the next morning, Prime Minister David Cameron, who had been re-elected only a year earlier, announced his resignation. Alarm bells rang out all over Europe: so soon after the monetary and refugee crises, was this the beginning of the end of the European unification project?

Defenders of a liberal Europe rationalised Brexit as a purely British trauma that had nothing to do with developments in the rest of Europe and therefore had no further repercussions for the continent. Great Britain, they argued, had been damaged by decades of negative press in the British media, had never identified with the vision of an ever-closer union, and was still smarting from the loss of its empire. As Natalie Tocci argues, Britain's decision to leave the EU 'was not necessarily a bad result [...] and perhaps the best result from Europe's point of view'.[3]

However, this interpretation was not entirely true. Of course, Britain had had a reputation as a 'blocker' for many years, and approval rates for steps towards increased integration were always below the European average. But the country's membership of the European Union was never previously up for much discussion. Surveys carried out between 2000 and 2015 show that the proportion of those who wanted Britain to leave the EU completely was never more than one third.[4] And a survey of 600 British journalists, academics, and opinion pollsters carried out during the referendum campaign showed that 87 per cent of them believed Remain would win.[5] Neither the country's traditional Euroscepticism nor nostalgia for the lost empire — or, for that matter, the activities of Russian 'bots' on social media[6] — can explain how it could have come to such an exceptionally high — even by British standards — level of rejection.

The deeper reason was that the Brexit vote was never just about Britain or its relationship with the EU. David Goodhart, a conservative British commentator, admits:

> In a way, leaving the European Union was collateral damage. For 20 or 30 years — or perhaps even longer — voters had had no opportunity to express their opinion on the general direction society was taking, because none of the main parties deviated from the liberal, pro-market, pro-EU consensus. Anyone who didn't like the direction society was going voted against the European Union. As they saw it, they were one and the same thing.[7]

Just like the supporters of the Tea Party in America and the other right-wing populist parties in Western Europe, Brexit voters were more likely to be older, less educated, male, and white than the general population. Many were lower middle class and came from parts of the country that had suffered from the consequences of structural change. Most importantly, almost all of them were deeply unsettled by the political, economic, and cultural changes they saw occurring around them, leaving them with the feeling that they had no place in a hyper-modern, hyper-diverse, and hyper-globalised world. Such people were often described in the media as 'left-behinds'.[8]

So, the complex of political causes that led to Brexit was anything but purely British. Almost every Western European society experienced its own revolt against liberal democracy from the middle of the 2010s onwards, albeit with varying degrees of intensity and not always with such serious consequences as Brexit.[9] Brexit shows the power such revolts had to mobilise opinion, and how difficult it was for the political elites to understand them; but it also shows how little such revolts ultimately did to solve the problems that had caused them in the first place.

'Take Back Control'

This campaign slogan shows what Leave supporters cared about: 'Take Back Control' not only sounded more reasonable and more moderate than some populist battle cry, it also powerfully articulated the sense of loss of control felt by many voters.

The most important issue was undoubtedly migration. In the eyes of Leave supporters, the loss of control had begun with the accession of Central and East European states to the EU in 2004, since, unlike most other EU states, the British government had chosen not to make use of a transitional regulation, and immediately granted citizens from the new EU countries full freedom of movement. This resulted in the arrival of almost half a million Poles in the UK within less than three years, rather than the 30,000 predicted by the British authorities.

That was a boon for Britain's economy, as the newcomers filled the very great need at the time for skilled tradespeople, healthcare, and construction workers, as well as other low or medium-skilled workers. However, at the same time, the Eastern European migrants competed with the local population who worked in those sectors, driving wages down and suddenly increasing the demand for housing and public services in the often economically underdeveloped peripheral areas where they settled.[10] This was a typical example of a development that benefitted the economy as a whole but simultaneously created 'losers' — although this did not appear to concern the political class for a long time.[11]

Another important aspect was the European refugee crisis, which ended only three months before the referendum took place. Although Britain itself took in almost no refugees, the political impact of the events on the continent was disastrous from the point of view of the Remain supporters. The British Europe expert Mark Leonard explains:

> Firstly, the headlines were completely dominated by the issue of immigration throughout the entire referendum campaign. Secondly, the images that appeared every day on the television created the feeling that the situation was completely out of control. And thirdly, they reinforced the impression that the EU was a failed project that was on the brink of collapse.[12]

The refugee crisis gave Leave supporters an opportunity to escalate the issue of migration in the crucial weeks leading up to the referendum. They repeatedly brought up the possibility of Turkey joining the EU, supposedly allowing almost 80 million people to move to Britain and also 'opening the floodgates to Syria and Iraq'.[13] This was closely associated with warnings that terrorists could enter Europe — disguised as refugees — and then find some way to travel to Britain.[14] Despite the fact that many such arguments were flawed, because there was no prospect of Turkey joining the EU any time soon and because Britain was not a member of Schengen and so could stop refugees from entering anytime it wanted, pro-EU campaigners had a hard time making their more nuanced arguments heard.

The second issue was legislative control. On a superficial level, this was mainly about the so-called single market directives, which are issued by the EU Commission in Brussels and must be implemented by national parliaments. There had been resistance to this in Britain for decades, often on the grounds that it was neither transparent nor democratic. The fact that the rulings of the European Court of Justice took precedence over national legislation and could override it was also regularly criticised. However, in the course of the referendum campaign, such traditional demands for a restoration of national sovereignty were mixed up with general criticism of the establishment, which, in the view of Leave supporters, had not only sold out British interests, but also imposed an elitist interpretation of political correctness on the rest of the country. The British journalist Tim Shipman believes the EU became a symbol of the liberal-modern project and rejecting it was — above all — 'a revolt of the provincial classes [...] against the cosy metropolitan consensus'.[15]

The third issue was financial control. For decades, Britain had been a 'net contributor', meaning it paid more into the EU's budget, after the deduction of all financial returns, than it got back in grants and subsidies. In the 1980s, Prime Minister Margaret Thatcher had successfully negotiated a 'rebate', reducing the country's contributions but not making it a net receiver. Of course, Britain benefitted from being part of the EU's internal market, as it enabled British companies to export goods, capital, and services to the biggest common economic area in the world — the European Union — free of any customs duties, taxes, or restrictions. (For many American companies, this was precisely the reason they chose London as the location for their European headquarters.) But such financial benefits were far more difficult to quantify than the contributions paid to the EU, and so the annual 'membership fee' transferred by the British government to the European institutions became one of the arguments used by the Leave campaign. Put provocatively, the idea that British taxpayers should be subsidising olive trees in Greece while the country lacked the necessary funds for its national health services was absurd in the eyes of many voters. Just as it did on the issues of migration and sovereignty, the Leave campaign promised the people of Britain that they would win back control over their own fate by putting their cross in the right place on the ballot paper.

More than just money

The Remain campaign had trouble countering such attacks. Its central argument was that Brexit was a leap into the unknown that would endanger jobs and prosperity. They hoped the 'economic argument' would be the deciding one, and that most people would vote conservatively in the referendum, meaning that they would ultimately vote for the status quo — despite all their doubts.

However, those assumptions were wrong. As all exit polls showed, the economic arguments of the Remain campaign had indeed got through to people (meaning most voters thought leaving the EU was economically risky), but the general feeling of alienation and dissatisfaction with the current system was so great that many were prepared to ignore such concerns. It also did not turn out to be the case that most people tended towards preserving the status quo. Although the Remain camp did make up a few points towards the end of the campaign, Leave supporters were more highly motivated and turned out in greater numbers to vote. To Remain supporters, it seemed a contradiction that economically deprived areas in particular, like Wales and the North of England, voted by a large majority to leave the EU depite receiving billions in EU funding. But the reality was that Brexit was never just about money — the main issue was the perceived loss of control.

Although Remain supporters didn't realise it, many of their actions contributed to their rivals' success. For example, they calculated that leaving the EU would make every British household poorer by £4,300 pounds a year. But that seemed like an abstract amount and one that was so high that most people — especially low earners — didn't find it credible. Rather than winning it new supporters, such assertions simply exposed the Remain campaign to charges of scaremongering.

Even more damage was caused by statements from important people or institutions warning of the negative economic consequences of leaving. This included not only statements by Cameron and his Chancellor of the Exchequer, cautions from the heads of major banks and global companies, the International Monetary Fund (IMF), the Organisation for Economic Cooperation and Development (OECD), the finance ministers of the G7, and President Obama, who made it clear on a visit to London that Britain could not expect a quick trade deal with the US if it should leave the EU. The aim of such interventions was to underscore the seriousness of the situation, but for many voters, they were simply further confirmation of the fact that the EU was an elitist project which scarcely benefitted 'ordinary citizens'. According to Shipman, this was also the impression gained by Phil Wilson, the Labour MP who was Tony Blair's successor in the north-east England constituency of Sedgefield. 'Many voters thought: What's the IMF? What's that got to do with my life? What's the OECD? What's that got to do with me?'[16]

The Remain campaign was at its clumsiest when it came to the issue of migration. It tried to ignore the matter until four weeks before the referendum. When it finally became unavoidable, the Remain campaign presented a plan that was far too complicated for anyone outside the campaign to understand.[17] The Remain supporters therefore had no plausible answer to the Leave campaign's arguments, and there was no serious attempt to explain the system of free movement. Shortly before the day of the vote, one of the leaders of the Remain campaign suggested, 'Why doesn't the government just say we would end free movement?' To which his colleague answered, 'Well, that would mean leaving the EU.'[18]

'It's fabulous!'

Brexit was an enormous blow for supporters of a liberal vision of Europe. Although no other countries have so far followed Britain's lead, it was the first time in the history of European integration that a member state had left the 'European project' and refuted the mantra of an ever increasing, ever closer European peace zone.

However, that does not mean that Brexit was a success, or that its supporters succeeded in realising their vision of taking back control and national sovereignty. On the contrary, the events of recent years have shown that in practice Brexit brought no advantages, and many of the problems that caused it have only grown worse.

Many of those difficulties stemmed from the fact that the Leave campaign never had to formulate a realistic post-Brexit plan, and so it remained completely unclear what kind of a relationship Britain would have with the European Union after it left. Had people voted for a 'hard' or 'soft' Brexit?[19] Should there be a trade deal with the EU, and if so, based on what model? The former British foreign secretary, David Miliband, sees that lack of definition as one of the main reasons why Brexit happened in the first place:

> They [Leave supporters] had a huge structural advantage because they never had to put a concrete proposal on the table, which their opponents could then have attacked. Up until the vote, Brexit was an empty vessel into which anyone could project whatever they liked.[20]

The consequence of this was that the process of defining what Brexit meant in practice did not come until *after* the referendum, and other issues, which were more pressing for most voters, such as education, pensions, and healthcare, fell by the wayside for years.[21]

Internally, Brexit did not lead to new strengths, but to division. The longer the process took, the more the debate strayed from the real matter at hand and descended into recriminations. And instead of the opposing camps putting their differences aside, it deepened social divides. Various studies show that a person's stance on Brexit became a social identity, according to which people in Britain chose their friends and even their romantic partners.[22] Leaving the EU reignited the conflict between Catholics and Protestants in Northern Ireland. And in Scotland, where 62 per cent of the population voted against leaving, it gave the independence movement reason to call for another referendum on Scotland leaving the United Kingdom.

The same was true when it came to Britain's role on the world stage. Many Brexit supporters believed Britain would be able to play a more independent role if it were outside the EU, and that relations specifically with America and other English-speaking countries such as Canada and Australia were anyway more important, closer, and less fraught than its relations with Europe. But in fact, it was Britain's membership and role in the EU that made it such an influential partner. The American government especially had seen Britain as a 'bridge' to Europe for decades.[23] That's why David Miliband believes Brexit was a 'deliberate act of self-harm':

> It not only raised trade barriers, Britain also withdrew needlessly from its biggest, closest, most valuable and most enduring group of allies — at a time when the values and interests of those countries were under greater attack than at any time since the end of the war.[24]

This particularly affected the country's confrontations with its geopolitical rivals Russia and China, but also its dealings with big companies like Amazon and Facebook, who saw Britain as just one of many middle-sized countries after Brexit. Instead of increasing its sovereignty, Britain lost international influence and found it increasingly difficult to assert its interests.

From an economic point of view, the gap between aspirations and reality was particularly big. Leave campaigners had promised that Britain would free itself from the supposedly weak, overregulated European national economies and strike 'huge new deals' and trade agreements with the growing markets of Asia. Five years later, the reality looked quite different. The only new trade deal struck since then was with Australia, which economists estimate will increase British economic output by 0.1 per cent at most. As Obama predicted, a similar deal with America was years away, while Britain's trade with its closest economic partners — the countries of the EU — fell off by more than 15 per cent. And what's more, rather than Britain freeing itself from European red tape, its exporters faced huge amounts of new paperwork after Brexit if they wanted to sell their products in the EU internal market.[25]

Although Britain has not yet implemented all the terms of its new trade agreement with the EU, Brexit already caused a drop in British economic performance of 1.6 per cent in 2021. According to a current estimate by the British government's own Office for Budget Responsibility, leaving the EU will result in a drop in the country's economic performance of around 4 per cent over the medium term. That's about twice as much as the projected losses caused by the COVID-19 pandemic, and is approximately equivalent to £80 billion (€90 billion) a year.[26] Across the whole population, assuming an average household size of 3.5 people, this is equivalent to around £4,200, which is almost exactly the amount predicted by Remain supporters during the referendum campaign, and many times more than the 'membership fee' that Britain supposedly 'saved'.

The absurdity of Brexit was most evident in the issue of immigration. As mentioned earlier, controlling the borders was one of the Leave campaign's central arguments. However, implementing that principle turned out to have several unforeseen consequences. The first was that more than 200,000 EU citizens left the country even before Britain's official exit. It quickly became apparent that most of those immigrants were not 'welfare migrants' as Leave supporters claimed; rather, they had filled jobs that were crucial for the running of society — in the retail, hospitality, and healthcare industries and, most vitally, in haulage.[27] When the country suddenly had no HGV drivers in autumn 2021, the economy ground to a halt and the government had to recruit thousands of East European drivers overnight to fill the gap.

Another consequence was that the remaining EU states now had far less interest in preventing asylum seekers from travelling on to Britain from their territories. The number of migrants crossing the English Channel from France to Britain in inflatable dinghies rose from just under 2,000 in 2019 to 8,000 in 2020, and almost 25,000 in 2021. This prompted Britain to accuse France of turning a blind eye to refugees crossing the Channel in this way. From the point of view of France, there was no longer any reason for refugees who clearly wanted to go to Britain to be held in France against their will, or to provide for them indefinitely. Instead of reaching an agreement among European partners, as was the case during previous waves of refugees, the immediate 'solution' to this was for Britain to pay the French state more than €60 million to beef up its coastguard.[28] Yet, even two years later, the migrant crossings have not stopped, and despite various efforts by British governments, no solution seems to be in sight.

The more Brexit was implemented in real terms, the more obvious it became that although Britain had been able to separate itself from the 'liberal project' of the European Union, it could not detach itself from the European continent, and that control and sovereignty could never be absolute in a complex world shaped by modern liberal ideas. Brexit had made Britain poorer rather than richer, and it had given the country less, rather than more control over its own fate. Instead of being a coherent alternative to the liberal vision of Europe, Brexit was nothing more than an attempt to reap the benefits of the European project without paying for them. The result was that none of the promises made by Leave supporters during the referendum campaign were kept. When asked in late 2022 what tangible advantages Brexit had brought the country so far, the former cabinet minister Edwina Currie answered, 'Two fingers to Brussels. It's fabulous.'[29]

CHAPTER 16
A Populist in the White House

AT THE SAME TIME THE BRITISH ELECTORATE WAS VOTING TO LEAVE the European Union, a similarly dramatic revolt was taking place on the other side of the Atlantic. The idea that Donald Trump — a real estate mogul, reality TV star, and 'thrice-married philanderer' with no experience in politics — would be elected president of the United States on his first attempt was, in the words of the American journalist Tim Alberta, 'pretty wild'.[1]

When Trump announced his candidacy in summer 2015, no one believed he was serious. Trump had no team, no election campaign, and hardly any supporters in the key primary states.[2] Most commentators were convinced that the whole thing was a publicity stunt to help sell his new book. When Trump was still ahead in the opinion polls six months later, it was believed that the Republican party would take him down at its nomination convention. And when he nonetheless won the party's presidential nomination, many people assumed his Democratic rival, Hillary

Clinton, would easily defeat him in the election. A few days before the vote in November 2016, most Republicans had virtually thrown in the towel, and Trump's staff had already started looking for new jobs.[3] No credible polls predicted a victory for Trump — not even those commissioned by the Republican Party. Shortly before the election, *The New York Times* put Clinton's chances of becoming the next American president at 91 per cent.[4]

For American political elites, Trump's victory was not just a surprise, but a major shock. More than 60 million Americans had voted for a candidate who portrayed himself as the radical antithesis of the entire political system. As it turned out, Trump was not only a skilful demagogue who used modern technology to stoke the fears of his mostly older white voters with divisive rhetoric, he also espoused political ideas that fundamentally challenged the modern liberal consensus on America's domestic, foreign, and social policies. Although Trump did not succeed in implementing much of his political programme, his presidency had devastating consequences. In his four years in office, American society became so polarised that its democratic institutions are still reeling today, and, in many respects, the country is so weakened that it is barely able to fulfil its role as a global leader.[5]

Back to the future

The Republicans' plans were actually quite different. Since George W. Bush's presidency if not before, the party elites were aware that white, ethnic 'Europeans' had been declining as a share of the population, while the share of Latinos and other non-European immigrant groups was increasing. Republican leaders understood that a party that failed to appeal to those 'new Americans' would find it increasingly difficult to win majorities. The turning point came in 2012, when Mitt Romney lost the election resoundingly to Obama. The party's so-called autopsy, a 100-page report commissioned by its then-chairman Reince Priebus, concluded that Romney's negative stance on immigration had cost him the election. The report's main recommendations were for the party to become champions of immigration reform, avoid divisive rhetoric, and project a more balanced, welcoming image to minorities.[6] By 2015, it had become a 'quasi-religious belief' among the party's establishment that its 'existing democratic base [of Republicans] could not stretch far enough', and that its next presidential candidate had to be someone who was seen as 'inclusive'.[7]

Trump was on the opposite journey. While he had been popular with Latino and African American audiences at the time of his television show, *The Apprentice*, which frequently featured minority contestants in positive, ambitious roles, this changed when he entered politics. The most dynamic political movement at the time was the Tea Party, whose populism and hostility towards the establishment fitted well with Trump's political views. Instead of projecting the idea of a multicultural America where people from different backgrounds had equal opportunities, from 2011 onwards, Trump articulated a negative, even pessimistic message, warning against diversity and equating demographic change with decline, which was aimed at people who had nothing to gain from the diverse, more multicultural America portrayed in shows like *The Apprentice*. In other words, his target audience was white Americans who felt threatened by the demographic change in their country. As the television journalist Hayes Brown explains, 'The core idea of the Tea Party was the same as Donald Trump's: a nostalgic appeal to old, white Americans. That was the meaning behind the slogan *Let's Make America Great Again!*'[8]

Migration became Trump's main issue. According to Sam Nunberg, a long-time Trump associate, Trump understood that his party's pivot towards the progressive had created a 'gap in the market': 'Every time Trump tweeted against amnesty [for illegal immigrants] in 2013, 2014, he would get hundreds and hundreds of retweets.'[9] No one would argue that Trump had developed a coherent world view by this time, but his statements on this issue, as well as his enthusiastic espousal of the 'birther' conspiracy claiming that Obama was not American-born, placed him clearly on the far-right fringe of the Republican Party. This gained him access to right-wing blogs, websites, and talk shows, where he quickly became a star.[10]

The people who got fired up by this message, and who believed that Trump would somehow 'bring back the jobs', or reverse the latest wave of immigration, or 'make America great again', were not radically different from Republican voters as a whole: in the end, 90 per cent of voters who defined themselves as Republican voted for Trump. As various studies have shown, they tended to be slightly older, more likely male, less educated, and based in rural areas and the so-called Rust Belt — the industrial areas of the Midwest and north-east that had particularly suffered from structural change. They were also more hostile towards 'political correctness' than Republicans in general, and were strongly opposed to what the political scientist Matt Grossmann described as 'group-based claims of structural disadvantage'; in other words, the idea that the country was inherently racist.[11]

Trump did not win the most votes in the election of November 2016. Contrary to what he has claimed, Trump's victory was neither 'decisive' nor 'crushing'. But his voters were more heavily located in battleground states and were — quite clearly — more likely to turn up at the polls than Clinton's supporters. With small majorities in several large (and previously Democratic) states such as Michigan, Wisconsin, and Pennsylvania, Trump gained more than enough votes in the electoral college to get elected. His campaign strategy had worked. Trump had become the voice of the 'whitelash', as the political analyst Van Jones called it, because he had found enough angry white men (and women) willing to support his revolt against the modern liberal version of America.

Rage machines

One important reason for Trump's success was the way he used the media to his advantage. Unlike his competitors in the Republican primary, Trump had been familiar to Americans for decades. His role in the TV show *The Apprentice* — as a businessman who fires one applicant after another — consolidated his image as a tough but successful entrepreneur. Although that image bore little relation to reality (dozens of Trump's companies had gone bankrupt),[12] many Americans saw him as the ideal political candidate. 'For a country sick of Washington gridlock and stasis,' says the historian Victor Davis Hansen, 'the idea of a firer-in-chief seemed intriguing.'[13]

Trump's colourful private life and his outspoken manner soon helped him become the darling of media channels such as Fox News and CNN, which often broadcast his entire campaign events — without breaks. While his competitors had to pay for their campaign ads, Trump received 5 billion dollars' worth of free airtime.[14]

Trump's social media presence was at least as important as his presence on other media, and his election victory — and his presidency — would have been hard to imagine without it. Trump's Twitter feed, as one *New York Times* commentator put it, 'flowed from the platform directly into the nation's psyche'.[15] During the election campaign, his follower base increased from 7 million to more than 30 million. Trump's statements sparked 'shitstorms' that went on for days and dominated the pages of supposedly serious media outlets such as *The New York Times* and *The Washington Post*. In many instances, the only way for his rivals to get media exposure was by responding to the latest thing Trump had tweeted.[16]

What made Trump such a successful 'influencer'? For Nick Pickles, a senior director at Twitter, it was the simple fact that he had a better understanding of how to use the platform than his rivals:

> Authenticity was crucial. When we explain to people how they should use Twitter, we always say, 'Be your authentic self.' That was definitely the case with Trump. It was as if you were talking to him in the same room. Secondly, speed. Because he wasn't surrounded by ten people checking his tweets, he could react to events immediately. Almost in real-time. And thirdly, interactivity. There were often instances when Trump responded to tweets from

normal users. That gave people the feeling that he took them seriously and wasn't part of some elite bubble.[17]

Nick Pickles fails to mention a fourth factor, of course: Trump was far more willing to break social taboos than any other politician — and no form of communication 'rewards' such behaviour in the way social media does. Many of Trump's tweets were demeaning or insulting, or attacked minorities, or contained false information.[18] All that was no problem for Trump. On the contrary, he realised that the only way he stood a chance of maintaining an advantage over his better organised, better funded rivals was by feeding his voters' rage — and he knew that there were no better media platforms for achieving that than Twitter and Facebook. According to the journalist Bob Woodward, Trump ordered printouts of his tweets every day to understand which ones had gained the most traction. And, says Woodward, 'the most effective tweets were often the most shocking'.[19]

Twenty years after it spread around the world, the internet had not lived up to the hope that it would be a universal instrument of democratisation and intercultural dialogue. More often, it served to deepen differences, contributed to the polarisation of societies, and helped cynical candidates like Trump whip up their voters. Rather than being a marketplace where reason would always prevail in confrontations between good and bad ideas — meaning the supposedly 'good' ideas would win out — social media became the arena for shouting matches from which the loudest and most extreme voices profited most. This was compounded by the fact that anti-Western powers made increasingly systematic use of the internet to weaken the West. According to an American investigation, for example, Russia waged a kind of 'information war' during the presidential election campaign, with thousands of fake accounts on Facebook, Twitter, Instagram, YouTube, and other platforms, which supported Trump and were designed to 'provoke [...] social discord'.[20]

There were many reasons why the internet became an instrument of negativity. Brian Fishman, a former Facebook executive, does not deny that the big tech companies bear responsibility for this — not least of all because of their use of algorithms that multiply controversial content. But the underlying problem, says Fishman, is the logic of the internet. 'If you give everyone a microphone, you hear everyone's voice. And the craziest ones are usually the loudest.'[21] This was advantageous for Trump, but for democratic discourse it was a disaster.

Populist nationalism

What was Trump's programme? The common view is that Trump was an intellectual blank slate, and so there is no point in searching for any kind of doctrine or conceptual framework in his politics. Even the journalist Joshua Green, who wrote one of the most important books on Trump's path to politics, concluded that Trump had no interest in political ideas:

> Trump doesn't believe in nationalism or any other political
> philosophy — he's fundamentally a creature of his own
> ego. Over the years, Trump repeated certain populist
> themes [...] These were expressions of an attitude — a

marketing campaign — rather than commitments to a set of policies.[22]

Green is probably right in that Trump is a narcissist, his views are not particularly subtle, and he says things because he thinks they will be popular. There is also no evidence that he reads very much or enjoys theoretical debate. At the same time, as Green admits, there is a certain consistency. For years — if not decades — Trump has repeatedly articulated the same or similar positions. These are neither complex nor intellectually challenging, but that does not make them any less 'genuine' or 'sincere'. Even if Trump may not be aware of their origin,[23] the resulting political framework is relatively coherent and has one thing in common: just like the ideas of Putin and Orbán, it represents a reactionary, albeit American-style, alternative to liberal modernity.

The overriding hallmark of Trump's world view is his populism, which in America is often compared to that during the presidency of Andrew Jackson (1767–1845). The historian Walter Russell Mead writes that Jackson articulated a kind of 'folk culture' that was first represented by Irish and Scottish immigrants. Mead says it was their view that, 'while problems are complicated, solutions are simple'; political ideas should be based on 'common sense'; and decisions are not to be made in the interest of large institutions, intellectuals, and (liberal) elites, but based on what is perceived to be the will of the people.[24] This was precisely the attitude that shaped Trump's presidency. Although, as the son of a successful real estate developer, and himself a billionaire and a TV star, he has been part of the elite all his life, Trump portrayed himself as an outsider and an advocate of the 'common man'. His entire rhetoric targeted the elites, established politicians, the liberal media, and minorities. And — just like Jackson — he was convinced that 'he alone' could 'fix the broken system'.[25]

Another influential force was 'paleoconservatism' — a political philosophy on the far-right fringe of the Republican Party that existed long before the Tea Party movement, but which for a long time had relatively little influence. As well as Jacksonian populism, the paleoconservatives represented an aggressive, but also isolationist, nationalism in foreign policy. Accordingly, paleoconservatives believed America should not be involved in foreign conflicts, but needed a strong military force to defend itself with overwhelming power against enemies when necessary. Paleoconservatives rejected international institutions, denied the validity of international law, and opposed free trade.[26] This corresponded to the positions already held by Trump many years before he entered politics. Back in the 1980s, he had complained that foreigners were 'taking advantage' of America; in the 1990s, he opposed the North American Free Trade Agreement; and in the 2000s, he was against the supposed 'forever wars' in Iraq and Afghanistan. Like the paleoconservatives, he wanted a militarily powerful America that dominated the world ('America First'), but which had as few obligations to that world as possible.[27]

The third source for Trump's programme was the European New Right, whose ideas Trump's chief strategist and campaign manager, Steve Bannon, had studied intensively. Bannon was a fan of European 'traditionalists' such as René Guénon and the Italian Julius Evola, who saw liberal modernism — and particularly such values as progress and equality — as the root of all evil. Bannon also admired their New Right heirs, such as the French intellectuals Alain de Benoist, Renaud Camus, and Guillaume Faye, who applied such ideas to the challenges faced by modern immigration societies.[28] In contrast to America's ethos of the 'melting pot' and a 'nation of immigrants', they argued that ethnic and religious diversity is not a strength, but a weakness, that it is the cause of conflicts, and that it leads to the demise of national identities. These were central ideas for Trump which defined his entire domestic, social, and immigration policies. According to Joshua Green, 'Anyone steeped in [these ideas] would recognise the terrifying spectre Trump conjured of marauding immigrants, Muslim terrorists, and the collapse of national sovereignty.'[29] Right at the start of his election campaign, Trump said Mexicans were 'rapists'; Muslims were 'terrorists';[30] and in the final year of his presidency he accused Chinese people of bringing the coronavirus to America.[31] In simple terms, harm came from abroad and the solution was not an open, diverse America, but one that sent illegal immigrants 'home', built a wall, and preserved its ethnic and religious composition.

In this respect, Trump's programme was made up of more or less the same ideas as those articulated by Orbán in Hungary and the AfD in Germany, which were used by right-wing populist politicians across the Western world to justify their opposition to liberal modernity. However, the difference was that Trump was not just some opposition politician or the head of government in a small European country. He was the leader of the West and president of the most powerful state in the world.

Radicalisation

And yet, for the most part, Trump failed to realise his anti-liberal vision. His administration did succeed in reducing the number of refugees taken in by America each year to the lowest level for decades, and in sabotaging international institutions, appointing ultraconservative judges to the Supreme Court, and undermining democratic processes wherever it could, but Trump's legislative successes were meagre and, with the exception of tax reforms that mainly benefitted corporations and high earners, he was unable to realise any of the projects he announced during his election campaign.

This was mainly due to the fact that Trump did not have a sufficiently large — or politically experienced — team to fill the numerous posts with which an American president puts his stamp on a new administration. Thus, he was forced to give many posts to veteran Republican politicians like the Defence Secretary James Mattis or the Director of National Intelligence Dan Coats, who were sceptical of Trump.[32] Another reason was that the division of powers was still functioning, and the judiciary watered down Trump's most radical ideas to such an extent that little remained of them in the end.[33] In short, American democracy turned out to be more robust than supposed, and even the most powerful man in the world — acting alone — could not turn the country into an authoritarian regime overnight.

That does not mean that Trump's presidency did not leave its mark. Trump destroyed trust in America and the (Western-dominated) international system.[34] Even more importantly, although his legislative successes were few, he succeeded in radicalising the American right. Rather than submitting to the leadership of his party as many had hoped he would, Trump forced the party establishment to adapt to him and his ideas — a process described by the journalist Tim Alberta as a 'hostile takeover'.[35] By the final period of his term in office, it had become impossible for Republican candidates to oppose Trump openly. His ideas about issues like migration, free trade, and military intervention had moved from the right-wing fringe into the mainstream. And he succeeded in tearing down the 'firewall' between Republicans and right-wing extremists. Rather than distancing himself from racists, conspiracy theorists, and right-wing militias, he signalled that they were accepted, or even welcomed, by the Republican Party. According to the American political scientist Stephen Tankel, Trump created the political 'conditions in which [right-wing] extremism thrives'.[36]

The consequence of this was not just a rise in right-wing extremist violence,[37] but also the storming of the Capitol on 6 January 2021, when more than a thousand Trump supporters invaded the seat of the US Congress to stop Trump's election defeat from being formalised. This was nothing less than an attempted insurrection, sanctioned by a sitting president, aimed at overthrowing the constitutional system. Trump had so successfully manipulated the discourse within the party that many Republicans saw nothing problematical in the attack. Surveys show that only just under 20 per cent of Republican voters believed it was a coup attempt, more than half expressed understanding for the actions of the demonstrators,[38] and more than 70 per cent still doubt to this day that Joe Biden was legitimately elected president.[39] Trump's influence and his refusal to accept electoral defeat resulted in around a third of Americans considering their current government to be illegitimate.

Added to this was the fact that Trump's presidency radicalised not only his supporters, but also many of his opponents. Although he was not responsible for introducing the issue of racial discrimination into the public discourse originally, and although the issue was not a purely American one, left-wing movements that were already seen as radical gained extra impetus due to Trump's presidency. The public debate on issues like race and identity grew more heated and the divide between the political camps grew deeper. Thus, Trump's presidency did not necessarily bring about a change in politics, but it did result in polarisation.[40] America was more politically divided than ever by the end of Trump's presidency, and there was virtually no issue on which Republicans and Democrats agreed.

Many of the fault lines in American society — between Black and white, rich and poor, left and right, liberal and conservative — existed long before Trump. But Trump was the first president in decades who tried to reinforce rather than overcome them. His 'business model' was not based on reconciliation but division, and, in the space of just a few years, he succeeded in splitting his country to such an extent that a large proportion of the population were no longer even willing to accept the results of a democratic election. In short, Trump had weakened his country and its institutions from the inside. That meant America was less prepared than it should have been for confronting global challenges, including growing geopolitical competition with China.

CHAPTER 17
China's Authoritarian Modernity

AT THE TURN OF THIS CENTURY, WESTERN POLITICAL ELITES FORESAW only two realistic scenarios for the future development of China. Both were based on Seymour Martin Lipset's modernisation theory (see chapter 1) and the idea that growth, prosperity, and integration into the worldwide economic system would lead to the establishment of a middle class and, with it, to liberalisation and democracy. The first scenario assumed the leadership of the Communist Party was aware of this dynamic and would attempt to increasingly integrate the demands of a richer and more self-confident population into its own processes and institutions. In the second scenario, the Party would resist change, provoking conflict with the people. While the first scenario would lead to a gradual process of liberalisation, the second would result in revolution. In both cases, increased economic openness would ultimately lead to democracy in China.[1] The only question was how long it would take and whether the communist leadership was smart enough to initiate the process itself. As Reinhard Bütikofer, who heads the European Parliament's China Relations Delegation, recalls: 'For a long time, very few people could imagine China developing the ambition not only to follow its own ideas about political order, but also to make them hegemonic. And even less that China would develop the power to enforce them globally.'[2]

As far as its economic development is concerned, China exceeded even the boldest of expectations. China's economy grew nine-fold in the 20 years after it joined the World Trade Organisation (WTO) in 2001. The country became the second biggest economy in the world in 2008, and some estimates see it overtaking America as the biggest economy by 2030.[3] 'Extreme poverty' (defined by the World Bank as living on less than $1.90 a day) has become virtually unknown in China since the turn of the millennium.[4] And, although income disparities have increased, the Chinese middle class grew from around 3 per cent of the population in the year 2000 to more than 50 per cent in 2020.[5] At no period in human history have the lives of so many people improved so much in so short a time as they did in those two decades in China.

However, although China left no stone unturned in terms of its economy, little political change took place. The hypothesis of modernisation theory that trade and economic interdependence will eventually lead to more political openness, proved to be wrong. The American journalist James Mann, one of the earliest critics of the West's policy towards China, sensed this as early as 2007:

> Trade is trade [...] It is not a magic political potion for
> democracy, nor has it brought an end to political repression

or to the Chinese Communist Party's monopoly on power, and there is not the slightest reason to think it will do so in the future.[6]

If anything, state repression increased as the economy opened up. While there were signs of liberalisation in the first few years,[7] China has become increasingly totalitarian, especially since Xi Jinping took power in 2012. This can be seen not only in the brutal suppression of minority groups like the Muslim Uyghurs, or the increasingly severe punishment of dissidents, but also, and primarily, in China's attempts to monitor its own population everywhere and at all times. Since Xi took office, the number of surveillance cameras in use in China has risen from 100 million to 600 million,[8] and by using an electronic social credit system, the government now controls all activities of its citizens in many cities. Experts no longer describe the system in China as an 'emerging democracy', but as an 'adaptive authoritarian regime', 'Market-Leninism' or even as a 'techno-dictatorship'.[9]

Economic success was coupled with an increased sense of China's ideological mission. In contrast to his predecessors, Xi is increasingly frequently speaking of China's own development and social model, which is in direct competition with Western liberal modernity. Not until the second half of the 2010s did Western political elites begin to realise that the West's support of China's rise had hindered the spread of democracy, rather than helping it as Fukuyama hoped.[10] They have also come to realise that China is not just going to integrate into the Western-created world order, as John Ikenberry had predicted (see chapter 3), but seeks to alter it to suit its own ideas. Yet, to this day, the West has developed no realistic strategy for dealing with China — one that reflects China's rise while limiting its influence as an authoritarian world power. Authoritarian modernity is still on the rise, therefore, not least of all due to China's global success.

The Chinese Dream

China's ambitions to become a world power and its political competition with the West were not, as is sometimes claimed, part of a long-planned strategy,[11] but came as a result of China's size and its huge economic growth. When Deng Xiaoping opened up China's economy in the late 1970s, no one, even in China itself, imagined how successful the policy would turn out to be. China was a bitterly poor country, and Deng wanted to use market-based economic tools to create prosperity and stabilise the communist system, which he believed in as strongly as his predecessor Mao Zedong. The West did not see this as a cause for concern. China was seen as being of secondary importance and, from an economic point of view, the opening of Chinese markets was more than welcome. The expectation was that China would become a 'moderately prosperous' country.[12]

Little initially changed in this respect until the turn of the millennium. While China's government was increasingly active in Asia, the Middle East, and Africa, the purpose of that activity was primarily economic, as China's needs for raw materials and energy had grown so great that it could no longer cover them with its own existing sources. However, this activity gradually developed into geopolitical rivalry. China was not only competing around the world with the West for raw materials, but it also offered an alternative to the 'universalist' approach in which Western funds and investments usually came with demands for transparency and respect for human rights. Unlike Western countries, China did not demand political reforms from its partners, had absolutely no interest in human rights, and did not even want to know whose pockets funds ended up in. In this way, the Chinese government rapidly developed good relations with authoritarian regimes such as Zimbabwe and Myanmar, which were under sanctions from the West due to their corrupt and oppressive policies.[13]

In the course of the 2010s, this rivalry mutated into open conflict. The turning point was the global financial crisis of 2008, which China saw as signalling the decline of America as a world power.[14] For the first time, Chinese government officials began to speak of their country as a 'leading global power' with a unique success story, great ambition, and its own 'development model'. From the middle of the decade onwards, they spoke increasingly of 'Chinese wisdom', a 'Chinese approach to problem solving', and even a 'Chinese dream' that the country wanted to share with others.[15]

At the centre of sharing that dream was economic modernisation — particularly in regions that had been neglected by the West, such as Africa. The aim was to create stability, albeit at the cost of political freedom. And the emphasis lay on non-interference and national sovereignty — not on universal rights. In other words, it was precisely the system that China had established successfully at home. As the China expert Raffaello Pantucci explains:

What they say is, 'Look how successful we are! Look at our model: developing infrastructure and opening up the markets in a controlled way, and it works. Everyone should emulate it.' And they say, 'We are prepared to help you. If you do as we do, you can become like us.' That's not exporting an ideology, at least not directly; it's far more subtle, like development aid together with a 'best practice' model.[16]

The best example of this was the so-called New Silk Road — a global development project initiated by Xi in 2013. The original intention was to create new trade routes in Central and South-East Asia. But so many countries wanted to be part of the project that it quickly expanded to encompass every continent.[17] The bigger the project grew, the more prominent its political motives became. Two years after it was first announced, the goal was no longer just to develop trade routes, but to completely realign the global economic system — with China at its centre. And rather than planning a purely physical infrastructure, with railways and ports, for example, the focus was increasingly placed on areas like digital networks, health, and even culture.[18] What started as an economic project had mutated into an all-encompassing political vision of the future, with which China pressed its claim to global leadership.

China also revealed its growing ambitions in other areas. It initiated a free trade agreement in Asia and established an investment bank to rival the Western-dominated World Bank. It built up its military capabilities, set up military bases, and its activities in the South China Sea became increasingly aggressive.[19] With its Shanghai

Organisation for Cooperation, the Chinese government promoted a diplomatic initiative that saw itself as an alternative to the West's G7 — uniting large, principally authoritarian states in an alliance, with China and Putin's Russia at the forefront.[20] 'The ideology has not changed over the years,' says the China expert Moritz Rudolf. 'What has changed is China's confidence and its opportunity to shape the world according to its views.'[21]

Dependency

Contrary to the expectations of Western political elites, China's success and its growing self-confidence created a situation in which the West had to open up to Chinese influence, and not the other way around.

This was particularly true of international companies, whose behaviour was increasingly oriented towards China's political agenda. From the start, the price of market access for Western companies was always an obligation to follow China's rules. This also applied to Western tech companies like Microsoft, Google, and Amazon, which portrayed themselves as champions of Western values at home in America, but were perfectly willing to allow their products to be censored on China's say-so.[22] Much of that censorship took place even before it was ordered by China. Facebook, for example, started developing extensive tools and algorithms in the mid-2010s to convince the Communist Party leadership that its platform was not ideologically dangerous.[23] Some Western companies even changed the products they made available *in the West* to comply with Chinese wishes.[24] Duncan Clark, an author and tech analyst who lives in China, says there is one simple reason for this obsequious behaviour: companies 'need to be part of this massive market somehow'.[25]

China increasingly began to make use of sanctions. The first time was in 2010 when China banned imports of salmon from Norway after the Norwegian Nobel Peace Prize committee gave the award to the Chinese dissident Liu Xiaobo. Similar actions followed in the subsequent years targeting Japan, the Philippines, Taiwan, Mongolia, South Korea, Canada, France, Australia, and others.[26] The latest example is Lithuania, which was hit with a comprehensive boycott by China in December 2021. A few months earlier, the Lithuanian government had announced the opening of an official Taiwanese representation office in its country. China, which considers Taiwan to be part of its territory, completely deleted Lithuania from its customs register, also affecting products that contain parts made in Lithuania, including cars and machinery, for example.[27] Instead of showing solidarity with the small country, many European governments remained tight-lipped or, as in the case of Germany, sent 'mixed signals'.[28] The German-Baltic Chamber of Commerce even threatened that German companies would halt production in Lithuania if the government didn't start to toe the Chinese government's line.[29]

China's growing influence is most clearly seen in the case of the conflict in the province of Xinjiang, which has seen repeated bouts of terrorism and separatist unrest since the 1990s. Following a period of renewed clashes in 2013 to 2016, the Chinese leadership decided to set up a huge penal and re-education system there. A de facto ban was placed on the Muslim Uyghurs practising their religion, and up to 1.5 million people were detained in internment camps.[30] However, there was little outcry from the international community. A letter in July 2019 from the UN's Human Rights Council criticising China's policy was signed by a mere 22 states, all of them from the West. A 'counter letter' defending the policy attracted more than 50 signatories, including many Muslim-majority countries that had benefited from Chinese investment, including Saudi Arabia, Egypt, Pakistan, Bahrain, the United Arab Emirates, and Qatar.[31] Even the Turkish president Recep Tayyip Erdoğan, who normally never misses an opportunity to denounce Islamophobia in the West, had words of praise for China's policy and stressed the country's right to non-interference.[32]

From the time of the euro crisis at the latest, the European Union was also not immune to Chinese influence. When several EU states had to submit to severe austerity measures, China spearheaded the group of countries offering aid. China bought up Portugal's national electricity grid and its biggest insurance company; it invested in Greece's telecommunications infrastructure and took over the country's biggest port.[33] China declared its own initiative to integrate 16 Central and Eastern European states into its New Silk Road project. Its most enthusiastic champion was Hungary's Viktor Orbán, who blocked an EU human rights resolution so as not to jeopardise the 'friendly relations with China'.[34]

Although not all China's efforts succeeded, and the European Union has so far refused to be split on major decisions, the intention is clear. As Janka Oertel of the European Council on Foreign Relations explains, 'Xi never made a secret of the fact that China intends to use its market power to make the world more dependent on it. And it is advantageous for China if Europe is split, as that prevents it from forming a united front with the USA.'[35]

Courses of action

Until the middle of the 2010s, China's growing political influence was of little concern to the vast majority of Western political elites. And even in the subsequent years, no convincing political vision emerged for how the West could continue to benefit from China's economic rise without also promoting the spread of its authoritarian technocratic social model. The most common comparison was with the Cold War, with China now in the Soviet Union's role.[36] But the differences were too great for any lesson to be learned for dealing with the current conflict. Unlike the Soviet Union, China was economically successful; it was integrated into the global market, and many Western countries' economies were now dependent on China — albeit to varying degrees. Also, Xi and his party were in a far more secure position than the Soviet leadership had been. The combination of economic success, nationalist indoctrination, and technological control had enabled them to create a system that made widespread rebellion either very unlikely or downright impossible. By the start of the 2020s, the chances of democratic 'regime change' were therefore almost zero.[37] Even the policy of 'containment' had become difficult to implement due to the many economic ties to China.

The first possible course of action was therefore to carry on with 'business as usual'. Companies and industry associations that had profited from the opening of Chinese markets advocated for the continuation of the industrial policy that focused principally on closer economic integration. They called for more trade and investment rather than less[38] — often with the justification that there might be political change in China sometime in the future.[39] Even if that were not to happen, the economic benefits of such relations were considered far more important than any political concerns. Europe must not allow itself to be dragged into 'a new Cold War with Beijing', warned the former German Chancellor Gerhard Schröder. 'China is simply too important to us for that.'[40]

However, in reality, China had long-since distanced itself from the 'business model' that was so profitable for Western companies. From the middle of the 2010s onward, the Chinese government pursued a strategy of making its economy less dependent on trade with the West, and producing more key technologies at home.[41] This involved the strategic expansion of its own capabilities, massive investment in research and development, and the targeted acquisition of foreign companies,[42] but also a systematic programme of industrial espionage and the widespread use of state-controlled hacker attacks.[43] This shows that the idea that the 'division of labour' between China and the West could simply continue unchanged was an illusion. China had long ago ceased to see itself as nothing but a sales market and the cut-price 'workshop of the world', as it had during the 1990s and early 2000s. Now it was doing everything it could to compete with the West — in all areas. Even with a willingness to ignore China's political ambitions, a purely economic-based 'business as usual' was no longer an option.

The opposite course of action was called 'decoupling'. That

meant the West extricating itself from dependent relationships or, where necessary, cutting ties with China — the opposite of stronger integration and more interdependence. Almost all the proponents of this option stress that they do not want a complete shutdown of trade relations with China, but at most a 'partial disengagement' or a 'reorientation' in strategic areas like the flow of finances, supply chains, national security, research, and telecommunications.[44] Even the American think tank the National Bureau of Asian Research, which had become a gathering place for China hawks, shied away from concepts like a 'new Cold War' or isolating China completely, speaking only of increased competition, diversification, and a 'tougher policy'.[45]

In practice, however, even partial, selective disengagement turned out to be difficult. In many areas, economic integration was already so advanced that it could no longer be reversed. The supply chains for almost all technological products in particular involved China in some way.[46] This was compounded by the fact that China was pursuing its own decoupling policy and the areas in which the West wanted to reduce economic interdependence tended to be those where China wanted cooperation to continue, and vice versa. What would remain, then, after both sides had decoupled according to their own ideas and interests?

Another key factor was that the West needed cooperation to continue in many policy areas, such as fighting climate change (see chapter 18) and global pandemics, and so could not afford to risk losing China's cooperation due to open hostility or an overly tough stance. In short, slogans like 'decoupling' and 'reducing dependency' may have sounded good, but as actual policies they presented so many difficulties and hindrances that it remained unclear what they meant in practice.

A united front?

By around the end of the 2010s, a large proportion of the Western political elites had finally ceased thinking of China just as a competitor or partner, and now saw it principally as a 'systemic rival'.[47] In 2015, when Biden was vice president, America's national security strategy still stated, 'The United States welcomes the rise of a stable, peaceful and prosperous China.'[48] Six years later, the same document described China as the greatest threat to 'the stability and openness of the international system'.[49] America's position had done a complete about-turn in the space of a few years. The primary goal had changed from cooperation to containment as part of a global coalition. However, attempts to forge that coalition exposed many of the West's weaknesses and disadvantages compared to authoritarian China.

One of the most important attempts at formulating a 'common agenda' was undertaken in 2021 by the Munich Security Conference, working together with the think tanks, The Aspen Institute and the Mercator Institute for China Studies. Under the leadership of Wolfgang Ischinger and Joseph Nye, the three organisations brought together twenty prominent experts from both sides of the Atlantic to identify problem areas and come up with concrete proposals for action. They gave their 60-page report the title *Mind the Gap: Priorities for Transatlantic China Policy*. In it, they identified seven areas that urgently required a common approach by the West. This resulted in almost 30 priorities, identified by the authors as possible 'quick wins'.[50]

At first glance, the report read like a kind of instruction manual for competing with China. A closer look revealed that many of the goals would be neither quick nor easy to achieve. There were serious disputes, sometimes going back years, in areas such as tariffs, technical standards, and the digital market, *within* the West. Other issues, such as who should fill international posts, required a degree of coordination that would have been unusual even during the Cold War era. And challenges like building transnational infrastructures and joint resistance to economic sanctions required the creation of completely new mechanisms and institutions. The problem was that the West — unlike China — was not a single, hierarchical state pursuing a clear policy line in all areas. Instead, it was made up of dozens of large, medium-sized, and small states that all had their own interests, with varying degrees of harmony in their relations, and that even competed with each other in some areas. Before it could devote itself to the issue of China, the West had to expend large amounts of energy on tackling its own problems.

This was further complicated by the fact that the West's dependency on China was primarily the result of trade and investment by private companies. For decades, industrialised nations like Germany had treated their policy towards China as a kind of national industrial policy and so, for many years, the pace and direction of engagement with China had been dictated by companies with investments there, most importantly in the automotive and machinery sectors. Jan Weidenfeld of the Mercator Institute explains: 'Not all of Germany's industry is dependent on

China, but the dependency of individual, very weighty companies is huge. And in the past, those companies have had special access to policymakers.'[51] So it was not enough for national governments to just agree amongst themselves. They also had to convince industry associations and companies to act against their own instincts and 'sacrifice short-term gains for long-term economic security and less dependency on China'.[52] China did not have this problem as the Communist Party still controlled the national economy and even seemingly private companies had no choice in practice but to follow the rules set by the party leadership.[53]

A third disadvantage for the West was the narrow timeframe of its planning. While the party leadership in China had been thinking in terms of decades since at least Xi's assumption of power and had oriented all its long-term planning towards the year 2049 — the centenary of Mao's revolution — any commitments from Western governments were valid for a few years at best, before a new government with different priorities and political ideas came to power. In the case of Donald Trump, who had sparked conflicts with several European states, this was an advantage from the European point of view. But even in 2023, the possibility that he, or a candidate with a similar orientation, could be back in the White House within just a few years already hung like the sword of Damocles over all negotiations with America.[54]

The prospects for a 'united front' — or even for 'quick wins' — were thus very dim. The party leadership in China had succeeded where the Soviet Union never did: it managed to develop an authoritarian social model that was economically successful, produced growth and innovation, and helped the country to shape the world order according to its own ideas. Western political elites reacted to this too late, and their response so far has been self-contradictory and timid. The West still lacks a vision for a world order that takes into account China's rise and its increasing importance within the international system, without promoting its authoritarian tendencies, never mind its territorial ambitions, most immediately in the case of Taiwan. If the proponents of modernisation theory don't turn out to be correct after all, and China doesn't collapse under the strain of internal tensions, it could be authoritarian — rather than the liberal — modernity that dominates the battle between different political systems in the 21st century.

CHAPTER 18
Climate Emergency

UNLIKE THE COMPETITION BETWEEN GREAT POLITICAL POWERS, which has played out in the same — or a similar — way for centuries, anthropogenic climate change is a novel existential threat that affects not just the West, but the entire world. As the political economist Maja Göpel shows, the intellectual roots of the environmental crisis are to be found in the West and in the ideas of the Enlightenment. In the course of the seventeenth century, scientists and philosophers such as Galileo Galilei, René Descartes, and Isaac Newton created a new worldview, centred on man — or more accurately, on the individual. Their central message was that since humans have the capacity to reason, they can take their destiny into their own hands. God's will or fate were no longer absolute. This gave birth to the concepts of human rights, democracy, and the other achievements of liberal modernity. But it also engendered capitalism and the idea that humans should tame nature and subdue it. Göpel argues that this created a utilitarian world, in which economic growth is synonymous with progress and nature can be exploited for as long as humans profit from it.[1]

The resulting prosperity was based on the exploitation of natural resources and the use of fossil fuels such as coal, gas, and oil. By the late 1970s at the latest, it was clear that this economic model was not sustainable as it consumed more resources than it gave back to nature and thus jeopardised the existence of future generations. Practically all climate scientists agreed that the carbon dioxide released by burning fossil fuels was the main cause of the global warming that had been measurable since the first half of the twentieth century and which dramatically picked up pace in the second half of the century.[2]

That realisation did little to change things, however. Since the Club of Rome, an organisation of leading politicians and academics, published its ground-breaking report *The Limits to Growth* in 1972,[3] the world's population has grown from 4 billion to almost 8 billion. The West has continued its economic activity unchanged, while both China and India — the two most populous nations in the world — have adopted a similarly 'dirty' economic model to the West's. Rather than falling, human-generated carbon emissions have more than doubled in the last 50 years.[4]

The Intergovernmental Panel on Climate Change (IPCC), a United Nations body that reviews the academic literature on climate change and uses it to make projections, found in its fifth report in 2014 that the previous 40 years had been the hottest period since the early Middle Ages and predicted that the Earth would heat up by up to 4.8 degrees centigrade compared to pre-industrial levels by the year 2100 — if the global community does not radically and immediately cut carbon emissions. The report warns that even a smaller increase than that, of two to three degrees, could have catastrophic consequences, many of which have already begun to be seen, such as the melting of the polar icecaps, leading to rising sea levels, and an increase in the frequency of extreme weather events like heatwaves, droughts, storms, and floods. The consequences of that, says the report, would be famine, water shortages, desertification, the spread of infectious disease, migration, and violent conflict.[5] Human life would become far more difficult in many countries, while in others, it could become impossible.

As climate change progresses, the West is destroying not just itself, but the entire planet. And although the majority of Western political elites have now realised this, the logic of their own economic and political model makes it impossible for them to take effective action to stop it. It is probably already too late to achieve the climate goals it has set itself, and all realistic future scenarios include the threat of massive ecological, social, and political consequences. Even liberal modernity's supposed ability to correct itself will not be of help, since many of the effects of climate change are irreversible.

Contradictions

It is no coincidence that the West has such difficulty reacting to climate change with adequate measures. The economic and political model that developed as a consequence of liberal modernity fundamentally and severely contradicts the necessities that arise from the climate emergency.

The first contradiction lies in the economic system, even the most socially and ecologically aware version of which is based on constant growth, consumption, and the exploitation of natural resources. Despite recycling and environmental taxes and levies, Western countries consume twice to three times as much of the environment as their size and population would entitle them to.[6] In 2022, Germany already reached 'overshoot day' on 3 May, the date when a population's demand for ecological resources and services exceeds what the Earth can regenerate in that year — so, every day of prosperity in Germany after that date comes at a cost to future generations.[7] It is patently clear that the economic system that created such great prosperity in the West cannot easily be reconciled with ideas like sustainability and climate neutrality. Thus, any measures that would reverse climate change or slow it down to such an extent that it no longer poses an existential threat would necessitate abandoning the logic of constant growth and consumption.

The second problem is the cyclical democratic system. It has always been relatively easy for Western politicians to enter into wide-ranging commitments because they know it will be their successors and not themselves who will have to honour them. For example, in the summer of 2019, in the final weeks before she resigned, the British Prime Minister Theresa May passed legislation obliging the country to become climate neutral by the year 2050. She was applauded for that by environmental groups, but critics pointed out that no realistic plan for achieving that goal existed.[8] This is not just the case in Britain. Enthusiasm for climate protection has always declined rapidly when concrete measures that cost money and additionally burden citizens or businesses were suggested. This is presumably because, natural disasters notwithstanding, there were always more immediate problems whose negative effects were more tangible. While climate change was associated with terrible consequences, they would not occur during the current legislative period but in the far future, and that has made it difficult for democratic politicians to persuade their voters to accept the necessity of financial sacrifices or immediate action.

This is further complicated by the fact that climate change is a global threat. While Western states were still responsible for more than half of the carbon emissions in 1990, that share fell to less than a third in the following decade. This trend will continue because although the West's emissions have been declining slightly for 20 years, those produced by China, India, and other Asian states continue to rise.[9] That means that, even if the West were to adopt dramatic measures to reduce its own levels of consumption, that would not necessarily bring about a reduction in global carbon emissions. China and India (with a total combined population of 2.8 billion) have made it clear that they will need at least ten (for China) to 20 (for India) years to make up their 'development deficit' compared to the West. Although the West created the problem of anthropogenic climate change, it is not (any longer) in a position to solve it alone.

Strategies

Climate change has been a topic on the international agenda since 1992, when more than 150 states met in Rio de Janeiro for the first global climate conference. Further conferences followed — in Kyoto in 1997 and Copenhagen in 2009 — but the real breakthrough did not come until the conference in Paris in 2015, when virtually every country in the world committed to limiting global warming to a maximum of two, or ideally 1.5, degrees centigrade compared to preindustrial levels by the end of the century. It was an ambitious goal, as IPCC calculations showed that global warming had already reached 1.1 degrees by that time, meaning that the increase in carbon emissions would have to be cut drastically and immediately.[10] Spurred on by the Swedish climate activist Greta Thunberg and the Fridays for Future movement she initiated, reaching the Paris climate goals became a political priority in the following years. However, although almost everyone believed in the need for drastic action, all of the strategies discussed so far have been insufficient or unfeasible.

The most radical proposals come from the so-called degrowth movement. One of its champions is the anthropologist Jason Hickel, who argues in his book *Less Is More: how degrowth will save the world* that economic growth can never be completely 'decoupled' from the exploitation of natural resources, and the only solution is therefore to limit growth to such an extent that it no longer causes damage to the environment.[11] Hickel says developing countries should be allowed to grow to a certain point, while industrialised nations must reduce the size of their economies gradually year by year. Hickel claims that this would not only solve the problem of climate change, but also redress the prosperity imbalance between North and South. 'We live on an abundant planet and we can all flourish on it together, but to do so we have to share it more fairly,' is Hickel's message.[12]

The problem is that Hickel and his fellow campaigners have no real idea of how to realise their vision. Although those who criticise growth constantly claim that consumption doesn't bring happiness to people and that Western standards of living could be maintained even if economic performance is drastically reduced, it is obvious that there is no support in Western societies for a systematic dismantling of prosperity. Any practical implementation would therefore have to take the form of a kind of 'eco-dictatorship', in which many people were forced to radically change their way of life.[13] Even in countries like China, which Hickel would allow to grow a certain amount, limiting economic output would be met with resistance — not least of all because the legitimacy of the government there is dependent on a promise of prosperity. In other words, large parts of the world are already too inextricably caught in the modern liberal 'growth trap' to accept the systemic change demanded by Hickel.

There is another school of thought that says growth should be accelerated rather than stopped. In techno-optimistic America especially, it is often said that the problem of climate change can only be reined in using innovation, and that no system is better suited to developing the necessary technology than capitalism. The growth critic Maja Göpel describes this approach sarcastically as 'carrying on as before, but on steroids'.[14] And indeed, with the aid of billions in venture capital investment and state incentives, a booming branch of industry has rapidly developed to search for technological solutions to climate change. Many concentrate on renewable energy, batteries, and electric vehicles. Others study the possibility of sequestering or recycling carbon. The most adventuresome are attempts to change the climate directly by means of so-called geoengineering, including gigantic mirrors to reflect the sun's rays back into the atmosphere, or artificial clouds to prevent the melting of the polar icecaps.[15]

There have been many breakthroughs in the development of renewable energies and electric vehicles in recent years in particular. The price of solar panels has fallen dramatically and vehicle batteries have become ever-more efficient.[16] More than 20 per cent of the European Union's energy needs were already covered by renewable sources in 2020, and almost 10 per cent of newly registered vehicles were electric.[17] But there has been little progress in other areas, and despite all the successes, the expansion of renewable energy use has been far too slow to completely transform within one generation an energy system, 80 per cent of which still relies on fossil fuels. Even the most optimistic estimates predict that fossil fuels will still account for 60 to 70 per cent of global energy consumption by the year 2040. And because the number of people in Asia who consume energy and want to drive cars is constantly increasing, it is probable that carbon emissions and the number of cars with internal combustion engines will also continue to increase.[18] In other words, although it is moving quickly, technological development is still progressing too slowly to keep up with global economic growth and the rising demand for energy.

A third approach, which is especially popular among Western governments, is based on hybrid strategies, which combine state interventions, such as tougher environmental legislation, setting (usually relatively moderate) prices for carbon emissions, or investments in green technologies, with market-based instruments, such as carbon emissions trading or novel financial tools and lending mechanisms.[19] International climate diplomacy takes on a central role in this context, which means persuading as many states as possible to commit to more real action on climate change. A good example of this was the Glasgow climate conference in November 2021, which produced a range of new agreements on, among other things, phasing out coal, ending deforestation, achieving climate neutrality by 2050, and a 45-per-cent reduction in global emissions by 2030.[20]

It is anyone's guess whether such commitments will ever be honoured — not least of all because they include no sanctions for states that fail to meet their targets. According to an independent study by the Climate Analytics think tank, none of the major states that took part in the Glasgow conference have yet presented a realistic plan for achieving climate neutrality by 2050; the reduction goals for 2030 will be missed by a wide margin at present rates of progress; the performance of several Western countries, such as Australia, is explicitly rated as 'poor'; and there is no sign of a phasing out of coal.[21] Countries like China, India, Indonesia, and Vietnam are bringing dozens of new coal-fired power stations online, and in places where such facilities are being decommissioned, the replacement source is usually not renewable energy, but gas, which is also a fossil fuel.[22] In America, which has re-entered the Paris Climate Agreement since Donald Trump's election defeat, even President Joe Biden's ambitious Infrastructure Investment and Jobs Act of November 2021 will only have a small impact on emissions.[23] As the American president's special envoy for the climate, John Kerry, admits, the two dozen countries responsible for a large share of global emissions are simply carrying on with 'business as usual'.[24]

Scenario 1: Climate conflicts

Regardless of whether the Paris climate goals are met or not, anthropogenic climate change will have severe economic and political consequences in the coming decades. These are seldom discussed, and Western governments are totally unprepared to face them.

The most likely scenario is that the goal of limiting global warming to a maximum of 1.5 or two degrees will be missed — although it is not yet clear by how much. The immediate consequences will be a continued sharp rise in sea levels and a further increase in the frequency of extreme weather events. This development is already under way and has been documented for many years. According to the World Meteorological Organisation and other governmental agencies, sea levels have already risen by an average of 23 centimetres since 1880 — nine centimetres of that increase have taken place since the middle of the 1990s. Heatwaves, storms, and floods have not only become more frequent, but they have also increased in intensity and duration.[25]

Almost all experts agree that this will lead to more wars. As early as 2005, think tanks began to treat climate change as a security issue and started warning that the impact of environmental factors would become increasingly significant in causing conflicts. They pointed out that states in Africa and Asia would be particularly vulnerable to this as they were already seen as fragile due to poverty, internal tensions, and weak governments.[26] Both the UN and the European Union conceive of climate change as a 'threat multiplier', making wars more likely or more severe, even if it was usually not the only — or most direct — cause of the respective conflict. The conflict in the Sudanese region of Darfur, which began in the early years of this century with disputes over water and grazing rights, claimed 300,000 lives, and forced an estimated 3 million people from their homes, was described by Ban Ki-moon, the UN secretary-general at the time, as 'the first modern climate war'.[27]

Even soldiers have now started to become interested in climate change. The best-known example is the former commander of the Dutch Armed Forces, Tom Middendorp, who witnessed the consequences of climate change during his overseas missions:

> We felt the effects of the climate every day in Afghanistan. The heat was so intense in summer that we had to use our heavier helicopters because the lighter ones didn't work. We were dealing with villages where the root of the conflict was water distribution […] It was similar in Somalia, where we were fighting piracy. The pirates were actually farmers or fishermen who were no longer able to earn a living because the warming of the waters had driven the fish away. When you're desperate because you can no longer feed your family, it's only a very short step into organised crime or extremism.[28]

When Middendorp first spoke publicly in 2016 about the consequences of climate change for security policy, many of his military colleagues were surprised:

> Climate change was seen as a 'left-wing' issue and the security policy community wanted to have nothing to do

with it [...] But that is a mistake. Climate change is not *only* a security problem, but it has serious implications for security.[29]

The climate emergency can have a polarising effect and lead to conflict even in Western societies. An entire generation of young activists sees anthropogenic global warming as an existential threat that older generations did not take seriously enough and which now threatens the survival of the entire planet. Alongside Fridays For Future, more radical organisations like Extinction Rebellion and Just Stop Oil have emerged recently, which have much in common with degrowth campaigners and whose members demand an immediate policy change from Western governments. Members of Extinction Rebellion have staged spectacular protests in many places, often involving illegal actions, to raise public awareness of their cause. Although the group espouses the principle of non-violent protest, there have been repeated statements that cast doubt on that. For example, one of the group's founders told journalists 'I am willing to be arrested. I am willing to be jailed. And [...] I am willing to die for this movement.'[30] Andreas Malm, a Swedish professor of human ecology and one of the movement's pioneers, published a book that he titled *How to Blow Up a Pipeline*.[31]

Scenario 2: Energy revolution(s)

Even the more positive scenario — i.e., if it was somehow possible to meet the Paris climate goals — includes the threat of great upheavals.[32] The International Energy Agency predicts that demand for the raw materials needed to manufacture batteries will rise steeply over the next two decades — by 2,500 per cent in the case of cobalt and nickel, and by as much as 4,300 per cent for lithium.[33] This offers countries that have such resources the opportunity to become very rich very quickly. However, as has often been the case in the Middle East, having rich deposits of raw materials can be a 'curse', leading to conflict and promoting autocratic and corrupt regimes.[34] In addition, the West has already fallen behind China in the competition for these resources,[35] potentially enabling China to use access to certain raw materials for political leverage.[36]

The effect such a global energy revolution would have on fossil-fuel-producing countries is still a matter of debate. Even if there were a radical switch to renewable energy, it can still be assumed that demand for oil and gas would remain relatively stable for at least a decade or two due to the continued rise in energy consumption in Asia. It is also likely that relatively expensive producer countries like America and Canada would be more heavily affected by a reduction than Russia or Saudi Arabia, for example.[37] But a shift away from fossil fuels would also eventually impact those economies, and countries whose prosperity is based almost exclusively on oil and gas would suddenly be faced with an existential problem. It is no coincidence that efforts to slow down or stop measures to protect the climate in recent years have often come from Russia and Saudi Arabia.[38]

The political complexity of phasing out fossil fuels for energy production can be seen not least of all in the West. When, in the early 2010s, Obama pushed for an end to the use of coal, it was like a declaration of war on the traditional coal states like West Virginia, where many mines were closing, and once-thriving cities were now becoming deserted. Many of the former coal communities saw Donald Trump as their saviour because he opposed climate protection measures and promised a return to fossil fuels.[39] A similar scenario is currently playing out in the East German region of Lusatia, where the number of people employed in coal mining is now one tenth of that before German Reunification. That has led to an exodus of people from the region. Germany has pledged to become coal-free by 2038, which the new government was planning to bring forward to 2030, and that has not only raised questions about the economic future of that region, but also led to political disaffection. The German sociologist Klaus Dörre explains, 'We were the heroes of the nation during communist times. Now we are seen as the fools or the villains of the nation and have even been accused of being Nazis, murderers, and polluters. That hurts.'[40]

However, the most realistic — and most dangerous — scenario is neither the first nor the second of those described above, but a combination of both: the introduction of half-hearted and long-overdue measures to counter climate change, leading to social, economic, and political upheavals without actually reducing the rise in sea levels or the frequency of extreme weather events to a manageable level. In a certain sense, liberal modernity would then have defeated itself: strong enough to subdue nature, but ultimately too weak to deal with the consequences of doing so.

Towards a More Sustainable Modernity

NO SOONER HAD THE WAR IN UKRAINE BEGUN THAN FRANCIS FUKUYAMA came out with another self-confident assessment. Because the Russian advance was progressing less quickly than expected, he promptly declared the invasion, and with it Vladimir Putin's entire presidency, to be a failure. According to Fukuyama, Putin's appeal lay in his strength, and as soon as he could no longer demonstrate that, his entire project would be in question. Not only would Putin fall, Fukuyama believed, but he would also take down with him the entire network of right-wing populists who had chosen him as their figurehead. Putin's attack had achieved the precise opposite of what he had intended: after years of division, the West was now united, and even traditionally cautious Germany had finally brought itself to resist the aggressor. Tragic though it was, the conflict would eventually result in a 'rebirth of liberalism'.[1]

What should we make of that prognosis? Just as he had after the end of the Cold War ('The End of History?') and the Arab

Spring ('Is China Next?'), Fukuyama had reduced a highly complex conflict to a clash between liberal modernity and its enemies, while ignoring all the other driving forces — such as nationalism, religion, ethnic identity, and the pursuit of power and material advantage.[2] His resulting predictions were always optimistic, but also almost always wrong. Eastern Europe did become democratic, but most of the Soviet Union's successor states, including Russia, reverted to autocratic rule after one or two free elections. The attempt to bring democracy to the Middle East by means of force was a total failure. And, rather than engendering more democracy, the Arab Spring led to a revival of dictators and jihadists. Despite trade and dialogue, China failed to become freer and more democratic, instead further cementing its authoritarian model of rulership. In the West itself, there was an erosion of democratic values and a rise of reactionary, anti-liberal forces that not infrequently — and not coincidentally — sympathised with Putin's Russia. In 2021, the democracy index published by the British journal *The Economist* was at its lowest level in fifteen years: only 6.4 per cent of the world's population were considered to be living in full democracies, while more than half — 54.3 per cent — were in countries classified as 'authoritarian' or 'hybrid' regimes.[3]

This shows that, irrespective of the outcome of the war in Ukraine, there is no reason to dream of an imminent 'rebirth of liberal democracy'. Indeed, particular caution should be exercised here. As this book has shown, the naïve and often completely unrealistic ideas of Western political elites have played a considerable part over the past three decades in the gradual demise of the quasi-hegemonic position taken by the West after the end of the Cold War and the continuous rise in anti-liberal forces — both within and outside of the West. The conclusion must be that carrying on with 'business as usual' under these conditions would be dangerous, not to say fatal. If the West wants to preserve itself and the achievements it has made, then it urgently needs to reinvent itself.

The new world (dis)order

From the present perspective, it is almost impossible to understand the level of optimism among Western elites a generation ago when it came to the future of their political and social model. Barely anyone was able to imagine that a system that resolutely espoused freedom and human self-realisation could ever come under existential pressure. Hadn't the West just defeated the Soviet Union — the most powerful, dangerous, and ideologically determined opponent of all times? Compared to that all other threats were trivial, and there was no cause for serious concern over the supremacy of the West. As late as 1997, the current US president, Joe Biden, mocked the idea that Russia could turn away from the West and towards an autocratic China, replying with words to the effect of 'Yeah, good luck with that!' to the Russian journalist who asked the question.[4]

The terrorist attacks of 11 September 2001 were a wake-up call, but rather than scrutinising its own ideologically based assumptions, the West sought to promote their spread with even more zeal. America's reaction was the War on Terror, which not only failed to solve the problem, but also dragged the West into a 20-year conflict in the Middle East and challenged the credibility of the Western ideas of democracy and liberty around the world. This was accompanied by a process of internal erosion that — starting with the global financial crisis — exposed the fragility of the Western economic and financial model and deepened political rifts within Western societies. Fukuyama sees these as excesses that have nothing to do with the good liberalism he has in mind.[5] In reality, however, those developments were a direct consequence of the West's exaggerated belief in the superiority of its own system, which Fukuyama himself had fuelled with his theory of 'the end of history'.

The crisis of liberal modernity was already obvious by the year 2010, but the West's reaction was not to do anything decisive to address it, but rather to enter into a long phase of self-doubt and uncertainty in which America in particular no longer seemed to have a clear idea of what the supremacy of the West meant, or of how it should exercise its leadership role. This was most apparent during the popular uprisings of the Arab Spring. The West did welcome the desire of Arab populations for modernisation, and it did encourage the people to strive for freedom, but its support was so inconsistent and timid that it made the ensuing conflicts worse rather than better, and strengthened the hand of those who oppose liberal modernity. This benefitted not only the Islamic State, but also Vladimir Putin, who began to challenge the West wherever he could and in ever-more brazen ways. And in the West itself, a process of erosion began. This was particularly pronounced in Europe, where monetary union and Schengen, the two most ambitious unification projects, almost failed, leaving the modern liberal idea of Europe severely damaged.

By the middle of the 2010s, the backlash was in full swing. Threats to liberal democracy had emerged from three directions. The first was external. Although Russia continued to be a geopolitical troublemaker, the most serious strategic competition came from China. It was the world's most populous country and its fastest-growing economy, with an authoritarian political system that ruthlessly enforced domestic stability, and a development model that could compete with the West in many parts of the world without seeking direct conflict. While it was culturally more distant than Russia, China's 'authoritarian modernity' has become the West's main rival — especially on the two most dynamic and economically fastest growing continents, Africa and Asia, and even within parts of the West, such as in Australia and New Zealand.

The second threat, the internal one, consisted of the ever-deepening division and polarisation of Western societies. Many countries experienced the rise of highly vocal minorities who were unsettled by the political and social changes occurring around them and who actively opposed the liberal social model. Britain's exit from the EU and Donald Trump's election victory proved that such minorities can turn into voting majorities, with the consequence that all assumptions about what constitutes a liberal democracy were suddenly called into question. This was compounded by an activist left, which carried its demands for equality to extremes, further fuelling the growing radicalisation on the right of the political spectrum with its own kind of radicalism. Even the liberal *New York Times* noted that the political left and the political right were trapped in a 'destructive spiral' which threatened to destroy public debate.[6] It was primarily in this respect that Russia became a threat, since Putin not only embodied the same anti-liberal, ultranationalist ideas as Trump, Orbán, and the right-wing populist parties, he also actively promoted the spread of those ideas.

The third threat transcended both internal and international political issues. The origins of anthropogenic climate change lie in the Western model of economics and growth, but it now threatens the entire planet. Although that was already clear by the 1980s, it was not until a generation later that the consequences became so tangible that the need for immediate action became undeniable. However, the states of the West were not able to reduce their dependency on fossil fuels quickly enough, and the newly industrialised nations in Asia did not want to try. Now, notwithstanding an unexpected technological breakthrough, there is little hope of the Paris climate targets being met, and all societies therefore face dramatic social, economic, and political upheavals. More so even than the internal or external threats, this jeopardises not just the supremacy of the West, but its very existence.

A more sustainable modernity

The West is in crisis, but what is the solution? As established at the start of this book, there are currently three schools of thought on this: the anti-imperialists, who want to 'abolish' the West; the liberals, who believe in liberal modernity's self-healing powers; and the (neo-)realists, who advocate for a more interests-driven kind of politics. None of those solutions are convincing. The vision of the anti-imperialists disregards the West's achievements, the liberals pretend everything is fine, and the (neo-)realists want to force the West to abandon the values that define it.

This book argues for a new approach. Instead of carrying on as before, the West must begin to learn in a much more purposeful way from its mistakes, and instead of abandoning its values, it must reinterpret them. This would result in a type of modernity that retains its liberal and pluralist values but acts in a humbler, more honest and inclusive way when applying them. It would be the opposite of a self-destructive modernity; it would be a more sustainable modern age.

The most important value in this regard is honesty. After decades of failed attempts to export democracy, Western elites need to accept that not all societies think the same way or want to emulate the West. Although liberal ideas have universal appeal, they are filtered through different historical, cultural, and political experiences. What's more, religion, nationalism, or ethnic identity shape the political preferences — and actions — of many people at least as much as the desire for a liberal system of government. The West's difficulty in understanding these supposedly deep-rooted forces has made it easy for its opponents to mobilise them.

Furthermore, Western elites should realise that they are generally not perceived to be as selfless as they see themselves. In the Middle East and Africa in particular, Western interventions have often been the trigger for chaos and even oppression, rather than a force for good. The lesson to be learned from this is not that promoting Western values is always wrong, or that the West is a profoundly immoral project, but that its actions and the ideological assumptions it is based on should be questioned more often — and more intensely. In simple terms, it means placing yourself in others' shoes.[7]

Closely related to this is the need for more humility. As has been shown, liberal democracies tend to consider themselves the centre of the universe, but 'perpetual peace' is not achieved simply because Western societies say so; and economic globalisation does not automatically lead to global dependency on the West, but can indeed have the opposite effect. The most unrealistic expectation is that Western ideas — and the system of rules shaped by the West — will simply prevail, even as the proportion of the world's population and of global economic activity represented by the West continues to shrink.

A humbler West would ask itself in each instance whether its goals can be achieved with the available means. Doing so might have led to a much earlier realisation that the goal of a secure, stable and — more or less — democratic Afghanistan was illusory; or that the West's half-hearted engagement in Syria only served to make the war worse. A humbler, more pragmatic West would have understood that a turbo-capitalist 'shock therapy' was not going to promote the emergence of democracy in Russia; or that overly hasty attempts at integration would not create a 'European consciousness'.

Finally, a sustainable modernity would also be more inclusive. Western political elites are often so convinced of the blessings brought by modern liberal ideas that they forget that political change usually generates both winners *and* losers. This was apparent in the intervention in Iraq, which turned once-privileged Sunni Muslims into an embittered minority overnight. It was also manifested in the regions of Western Europe and North America that were left behind by economic change and international free trade, where once-proud workers were suddenly robbed of a future and put the blame on minorities and liberal elites. An inclusive modernity would take seriously the needs of those whose economic, political, and psychological loss could form the basis for the next backlash to follow the Brexit vote and the election of Donald Trump in 2016. This will be particularly important if the entire global economy is to be rebuilt according to ecological principles — a massive undertaking that will produce both winners and losers on every continent.

No doubt, a humbler, more honest, and inclusive approach would make liberal modernity more sustainable. Its ultimate intent and purpose should never be forgotten, however: the promotion of human rights, freedom, and prosperity — the achievements of which have allowed the West to become the most successful political, economic, and social system in human history. A more sustainable modernity should avoid making lazy compromises with its enemies — irrespective of whether they are religiously motivated, reactionary, or authoritarian. Those who reject, oppose, or propagate an alternative to a pluralistic model of society can never be permanent partners. However, those who move towards pluralism, who open up their own societies and are willing to tolerate other political and social ideas should be welcomed by the West with open arms. Not least because that would make identifying common interests and forging robust alliances much easier, especially in relation to common global challenges such as climate change and the fight against pandemics.

There is no doubt that the West has gambled away a lot of its capital since the end of the Cold War. However, its ideas are still the right ones, and they can continue to be the most attractive ideology in the world in the twenty-first century — as long as the West represents them in a consistent, credible, and sustainable way.

Notes

Introduction

1   See Volker Steenblock, *Geschichte der Philosophie*, Stuttgart 2019, pp. 168–222; Franz J. Bauer, *Das ‹lange› 19. Jahrhundert*, Reclam, Stuttgart 2010, pp. 33–50.

2   Niall Ferguson, *Civilization: the West and the rest*, Penguin Books, London 2011, p. 1 ff.

3   See Jamal A. Nassar, *Globalization and Terrorism: the migration of dreams and nightmares*, Rowman & Littlefield, Lanham, Maryland 2009.

4   See Zygmunt Bauman, *Liquid Modernity*, Polity Press, Cambridge 2000; idem., *Modernity and Ambivalence*, Polity Press, Cambridge 1993.

5   René Guénon, *The Crisis of the Modern World*, Sophia Perennis, Hillsdale, NY 2001.

6   See Daniel Deudney and G. John Ikenberry, 'The Logic of the West', *World Policy Journal* 10 (4) (1993), pp. 17–25; Gunther Hellmann and Benjamin Hellborth (Eds.), *Uses of 'the West': security and the politics of order*, Cambridge University Press, Cambridge 2017; William H. McNeill, 'What we mean by the West', *Orbis*, Autumn 1997, pp. 513–524.

7   See e.g. Noam Chomsky, *Who Rules the World?* Hamish Hamilton, London 2016; Michael Lüders, *Blowback: how the West f*cked up the Middle East (and Why it was a Bad Idea)*, Old Street Publishing, London 2017.

8   See Ferguson, *Civilization*; Heinrich August Winkler *Geschichte des Westens. Die Zeit der Gegenwart*, C.H. Beck, Munich 2016.

9   Winkler, *Geschichte des Westens*, p. 610.
10 See Carlo Masala, *Weltunordnung. Die globalen Krisen und das Versagen des Westens*, C.H. Beck, Munich 2018; John Mearsheimer, *The Tragedy of Great Power Politics*, Norton & Company, New York 2014.
11 Masala, op. cit. p. 154.
12 Interviewees were given the chance to speak either on- or off-the-record. All interviews were conducted in accordance with King's College London War Studies Group Research Ethics guidance.
13 These are the three most populous Western European states. However, this selection primarily reflects the language abilities of the author.

1. The New World Order

1   'September 11, 1990: Address Before a Joint Session of Congress', *UVA Miller Center*; https://millercenter.org/the-presidency/presidential-speeches/september-11-1990-address-joint-session-congress.
2   Don Oberdorfer, 'Bush's Talk of a "New World Order". Foreign Policy Tool or Mere Slogan?' *Washington Post*, 26 May 1991, https://www.washingtonpost.com/archive/politics/1991/05/26/bushs-talk-of-a-new-world-order-foreign-policy-tool-or-mere-slogan/7d6dd1a2-7ad2-4b90-a206-f6fcd75a6e26/.
3   George Bush and Brent Scowcroft, *A World Transformed*, Vintage Books, New York, 1998.
4   Quoted from Oberdorfer, 'Bush's Talk'.
5   Cf. Alasdair Spark, 'Conjuring order: the new world order and conspiracy theories of globalization', *The Sociological Review* 48 (2) (2000), p. 48 ff.
6   Interview with Klaus Naumann, May 2021.
7   Francis Fukuyama, 'The End of History?', *The National Interest*, Summer 1989, pp. 3–18.
8   Ibid. p. 18.
9   James Atlas, 'What Is Fukuyama Saying? And to Whom Is He Saying It?', *New York Times*, 22 October 1989.
10 Henry R. Nau, 'Why "The Rise and Fall of the Great Powers" Was Wrong', *Review of International Studies* 27 (4) (2001), p. 590.
11 Cf. Jeane J. Kirkpatrick, 'A Normal Country in a Normal Time', *The National Interest*, Autumn 1991.
12 See Kenneth Waltz, 'The Emerging Structure of International Politics', *International Security* 18 (2) (1993), pp. 44–79.
13 Joseph S. Nye, 'What New World Order?', *Foreign Affairs*, Spring 1992, pp. 83–96.
14 See Charles Krauthammer, 'The Unipolar Moment', *Foreign Affairs*, Winter 1990, pp. 23–33.
15 William Kristol and Robert Kagan, 'Toward a Neo-Reaganite Foreign Policy', *Foreign Affairs*, Summer 1996, pp. 18–32.

16   Martin Seymour Lipset, 'Some Social Requisites of Democracy:
      Economic Development and Political Legitimacy', *American Political
      Science Review* 53 (1) (1959), pp. 69–105.

17   See Ronald Inglehart and Christian Welzel, 'How Development Leads
      to Democracy. What We Know about Modernization', *Foreign Affairs*,
      Spring 2009, pp. 33–48.

18   See Samuel P. Huntington, *Political Order in Changing Societies*, Yale
      University Press, New Haven 1968.

19   Friedman borrowed the expression 'creative destruction' from the
      Austrian economist Joseph Schumpeter. See Thomas L. Friedman,
      The Lexus and the Olive Tree, Harper Collins, New York 2000, p. 11 ff.

20   Ibid. p. 69 ff.

21   Ibid. pp. 105, 169–193.

22   Quoted in Paul E. Peterson, 'Is America Still the Hope of the Earth?',
      in Thomas W. Gilligan (Ed.), *American Exceptionalism in a New Era*,
      Hoover Institution Press, Stanford, 2017, p. 10.

23   'A National Security Strategy of Engagement and Enlargement', The
      White House, July 1994, p. 3.

24   Madeleine Albright, *Madam Secretary: a memoir*, Harper Perennial,
      New York 2003, p. 641.

25   Interview with Ted Piccone, February 2021.

26   Ibid.

27   Quoted in Albright, *Madam Secretary*, p. 449.

28   Quoted in ibid. pp. 449 ff.

29   Interview with Hansjörg Geiger, February 2021.

30   Interview with Wolfgang Ischinger, February 2021.

31   Poland, the Czech Republic, Slovakia, Hungary, Slovenia, Lithuania,
      Latvia and Estonia became members of the EU in 2004. Romania and
      Bulgaria joined in 2007.

32   Quoted in *Erklärung der Bundesregierung – Aktuelle Fragen der
      Europapolitik* [Federal Government Statement — Current Issues in
      European Policy], German Federal Government, 11 December 1995.

33   See Michael Dauderstädt, 'EU-Osterweiterung. Wirkungen,
      Erwartungen und Interessen in den Beitrittsländern' ['EU Enlargement
      to the East. Impacts, Expectations, and Interests in the Accession
      States'], *Integration* 21 (3) (1998), pp. 149–167.

34   Carmen González Enriquez, 'EU enlargement as seen from Eastern
      Europe. Expectations, experiences, disappointments, and Euro-
      enthusiasm', *Real Instituto Elcano, Working Paper* 15 – 2002,
      December 2002

35   Interview with Bernd Mützelburg, February 2021.

36   Enriquez, op. cit.

37   Interview with Bernd Mützelburg, February 2021.

2. Perpetual Peace

1   See Colin McInnes, 'Labour's Strategic Defence Review', *International Affairs* 74 (4) (1998), pp. 823–845.

2   Theo Farrell, *Unwinnable: Britain's war in Afghanistan, 2001–2014*, Bodley Head, London 2017, p. 120.

3   See 'Strategic Defence Review', Ministry of Defence, July1998, chapter 2; https://web.archive.org/web/20060201093228/http://www.mod.uk/issues/sdr/wp_contents.htm.

4   Jack S. Levy, 'Domestic Politics and War', *The Journal of Interdisciplinary History* 18 (4) (1988), p. 662.

5   Immanuel Kant, *Perpetual Peace: a philosophical sketch*, The Gutenberg Project, p. 134, https://www.gutenberg.org/files/50922/50922-h/50922-h.htm.

6   Montesquieu, quoted in Friedman, *The Lexus*, p. 249.

7   See Dean V. Babst, 'Elective Governments. A Force for Peace', *The Wisconsin Sociologist* 3 (9) (1964), p. 1–14.

8   At least a hundred articles on this topic were published in academic journals between 1987 and 1997. See William Thompson and Richard Tucker, 'A Tale of Two Democratic Peace Critiques', *Journal of Conflict Resolution* 19 (3) (1997), p. 51.

9   Zeev Maoz and Bruce Russett, 'Normative and Structural Causes of Democratic Peace, 1946–86', *American Political Science Review* 92 (1) (1998), p. 625.

10 Michael W. Doyle, 'Kant, Liberal Legacies, and Foreign Affairs, Part 1', *Philosophy and Public Affairs* 12 (3) (1983), pp. 205–235.

11 Christopher Layne, 'Kant or Cant. The Myth of the Democratic Peace', *International Security* 19 (2) (1994), pp. 5–49.

12 Edward Mansfield and Jack Snyder, 'Democratization and War', *Foreign Affairs*, Summer 1995, p. 80.

13 John M. Owen, 'How Liberalism Produces Democratic Peace', *International Security* 19 (2) (1994), pp. 87–125.

14 Friedman, *The Lexus*, chapter 12.

15 'Address before a Joint Session of the Congress on the State of the Union', The White House, 25 January 1994.

16 Samuel P. Huntington, *The Clash of Civilizations and the Remaking of World Order*, Simon & Schuster, New York 1996, p. 59.

17 Samuel P. Huntington, 'A Clash of Civilizations?', *Foreign Affairs*, Summer 1993.

18 See 'Noam Chomsky on the Clash of Civilizations', YouTube, 2 March 2007; https://www.youtube.com/watch?v=qT64TNho59I.

19 Joschka Fischer, *Die Rückkehr der Geschichte. Die Welt nach dem 11. September und die Erneuerung des Westens*, Kiepenheuer & Witsch, Cologne 2005, p. 20.

20 Robert Kaplan, 'The Coming Anarchy', *The Atlantic*, February 1994.

21 Interview with Robert Kaplan, February 2021.

22 See Gareth Evans, 'The Evolution of the Responsibility to Protect. From Concept and Principle to Actionable Norm', in Rameh Thakur and William Maley (Eds.), *Theorising the Responsibility to Protect*, Cambridge University Press, Cambridge 2015, pp. 16–37.

23 Farrell, *Unwinnable*, p. 118.

24 See Jürgen Habermas, *The Divided West*, Polity Press, Cambridge 2004, p. 170–76.

25 Quoted in Bruce Hoffman, 'Rethinking Terrorism and Counterterrorism Since 9/11', *Studies in Conflict and Terrorism* 25 (5) (2002), p. 310 ff.

26 Bill Clinton, *My Life*, Hutchinson, London 2004, p. 593.

27 Albright, *Madam Secretary*, p. 152.

28 Lawrence Freedman, 'Force and the international community. Tony Blair's Chicago speech and the criteria for intervention', *International Relations* 31 (2) (2017), pp. 107–124.

29 Interview with Lawrence Freedman, February 2021.

30 Habermas, *The Divided West*, p. 33.

31 Fukuyama, 'The End', p. 18; Friedman, *The Lexus*, chapters 15 and 16.

32 Benjamin Barber, *Jihad vs. McWorld*, Ballantine Books, New York, p. 157.

33 Interview with Boris Ruge, February 2021.

34 Interview with James Gow, March 2021.

35 Albright, *Madam Secretary*, p. 414; cf. Clinton, *My Life*, p. 509.

36 Albright, *Madam Secretary*, p. 404

37 Hobart Rowen, 'Making the 'Peace Dividend' a Reality', *Washington Post*, 3 October 1991.

38 The defence budgets of Italy and Greece, for example, remained more or less constant. See Todd Sandler and Justin George, 'Military Expenditure Trends for 1960–2014 and What They Reveal', *Global Policy* 7 (2) (2016), pp. 174–184.

39 Interview with Hansjörg Geiger, February 2021.

40 Kristol, 'Toward a Neo-Reaganite Foreign Policy', p. 24.

3. Who's Afraid of Russia and China?

1 Quoted in Strobe Talbott, *The Russia Hand: a memoir of presidential diplomacy*, Random House, New York 2002, p. 7 ff.

2 Condoleezza Rice, 'Promoting the National Interest', *Foreign Affairs*, January 2000.

3 Quoted in 'Conversations with History. Yegor Gaidar', University of California Television, 1996; https://www.youtube.com/watch?v=fa_Yf52GCYk.

4 Andrei Shleifer and Daniel Treisman, *Without a Map: political tactics and economic reform in Russia*, MIT Press, Cambridge 2000, p. vii.

5 David Lipton and Jeffrey D. Sachs, 'Prospects for Russia's Economic Reform', Brookings Institution, 1992, p. 213.

6   Ibid. pp. 266–280.

7   Paul Klebnikov, *Godfather of the Kremlin: the decline of Russia in the age of gangster capitalism*, Harcourt, Orlando 2000, p. 80.

8   Celestine Bohlen, 'Yeltsin Outlines Sale of Industry', *New York Times*, 20 August 1992.

9   Interview with Mark Galeotti, March 2021.

10   Gazprom, for example, was auctioned off for a mere 250 million dollars, although the gas deposits it owned were estimated to be worth between 300 and 700 billion dollars. See Klebnikov, *Godfather of the Kremlin*, p. 135.

11   One of the most infamous was Boris Berezovski, who was even made a national security advisor. See Klebnikov, *Godfather of the Kremlin*, pp. 257–264.

12   Ibid. pp. 103–109.

13   Michael Mandelbaum, *The Dawn of Peace in Europe: a twentieth century fund*, New York 1996, p. 143.

14   Klebnikov, *Godfather of the Kremlin*, pp. 106 ff.

15   Interview with Michael Hurley, February 2021.

16   Federico Varese, *The Russian Mafia: private protection in a new market economy*, Oxford University Press, Oxford 2001, p. 56.

17   Interview with John Scarlett, February 2021.

18   Interview with Mark Galeotti, February 2021.

19   See Strobe Talbott, *The Russia Hand: a memoir of presidential diplomacy*, Random House, New York 2002.

20   Clinton, *My Life*, p. 571.

21   Ibid. p. 502.

22   Interview with Moritz Rudolf, February 2021.

23   Quoted in James Baker, *The Politics of Diplomacy: revolution, war and peace, 1989–1992*, G.P. Putnam's Sons, New York 1995, p. 591.

24   See G. John Ikenberry, 'Why Export Democracy?', *The Wilson Quarterly*, Spring 1999.

25   G. John Ikenberry, 'New Grand Strategy Uses Lofty and Material Desires', *Los Angeles Times*, 12 July 1998.

26   Friedman, *The Lexus*, pp. 184–189.

27   Interview with Jeffrey Bader, March 2021.

28   The 'Asian Tigers' were much smaller than China and all were American allies. The US government had significant influence over them. See James Mann, *The China Fantasy*, Penguin, London 2007, pp. 12 ff.

29   Quoted in 'Remarks at the Yale University Commencement Ceremony', *Public Papers of the Presidents of the United States*. George H.W. Bush, 27 May 1991.

30   Quoted in 'President Clinton's Remarks on the Passage of the China Trade Bill', Associated Press, 25 May 2000.

31   Rice, 'Promoting the National Interest', p. 55.

32   Interview with Nigel Inkster, February 2021.
33   Friedman, *The Lexus*, pp. 184–189, 260.
34   See Gordon G. Chang, 'The Coming Collapse of China', *New York Times*, 9 September 2001. Cf. Gordon C. Chang, *The Coming Collapse of China*, Random House, New York 2001.
35   Quoted in 'Clinton's Words on China. Trade Is the Smart Thing', *New York Times*, 9 March 2000. See also 'Remarks by the President in Address on China and the National Interest', The White House, 24 October 1997.
36   See Evgeny Morozov, *The Net Delusion: how not to liberate the world*, Allen Lane, London 2011, pp. 13, 25.
37   See Jonathan Zittrain and Benjamin Edelman, 'Internet Filtering in China', Harvard Law School, Research Paper No. 62, March/April 2003; Elizabeth C. Economy, *The Third Revolution: Xi Jinping and the new Chinese State*, Oxford University Press, Oxford 2018, pp. 60–65.
38   See James Fallows, *Looking at the Sun: the rise of the new East Asian economic and political system*, Pantheon Books, New York 1994, pp. 405 ff.
39   Interview with Kerry Brown, February 2021.
40   Ibid.
41   Interview with Jeffrey Bader, March 2021.
42   Ibid.
43   Interview with Moritz Rudolf, February 2021.

4. Techno-Optimism

1   Robert Anderson et al., *Universal Access to Email: feasibility and societal implications*, The RAND Corporation, Santa Monica, 1995, p. iii.
2   John Gray, *Al Qaeda and What It Means to Be Modern*, Faber and Faber, London 2003, p. 27.
3   Benjamin R. Barber, 'Three Scenarios for the Future of Technology and Strong Democracy', *Political Science Quarterly*, 113 (4) (1998), pp. 573–589.
4   Gray, *Al Qaeda*, p. 42.
5   Cory Doctorow, 'Techno-Optimism', *Locus Mag*, 2 May 2011; https://locusmag.com/2011/05/cory-doctorow-techno-optimism/.
6   See Howard P. Segal, *Technological Utopianism in American Culture*, Syracuse University Press, Syracuse 2005, p. 173.
7   Ibid.
8   See Howard Rheingold, *The Virtual Community: homesteading on the electronic frontier*, MIT Press, New York 1993, chapter 3.
9   See Dale Carrico, 'Technoprogressivism beyond Technophilia and Technophobia', *Amor Mundi*, 30 June 2005; https://amormundi.blogspot.com/2005/06/technoprogressivism-beyond.html.
10   See Paulina Borsook, 'Cyber Selfish', *Prospect Magazine*, November 1996.

11 See Larissa MacFarquhar, 'The Gilder Effect', *The New Yorker*, May 2000.

12 Richard Barbrook, 'The Californian Ideology', *Science as Culture*, January 1996.

13 Quoted in John Schwartz, 'Court Upholds Free Speech on Internet, Blocks Decency Laws', *Washington Post*, 13 June 1996.

14 Jerry Berman and Daniel J. Weitzner, 'Technology and Democracy', *Social Research* 64 (3) (1997), pp. 1313–1319. See also Ralf Lindner, 'Wie verändert das Internet die Demokratie?', *Gesellschaft, Wirtschaft, Politik* 4 (2012), pp. 517–525.

15 Rheingold, *The Virtual Community*, p. 14.

16 Ibid. p. 26.

17 Quoted in Anderson, *Universal Access*, p. 131. The findings of a larger-scale study carried out in 1997 were the same: 'Far from creating a nation of strangers, the internet is creating a nation richer in friendships and social relationships.' See James Katz and Philip Asden, 'A Nation of Strangers?', *Communications of the ACM*, December 1997.

18 Barber, 'Three Scenarios', pp. 582–584.

19 Jeffrey M. Ayres, 'From the Streets to the Internet. The Cyber-Diffusion of Contention', *The Annals of the American Academy of Political Science*, November 1999, pp. 132–143.

20 See Matthew Eagleton-Pierce, 'The Internet and Seattle WTO Protests', *Peace Review* 13 (3) (2001), pp. 331–337.

21 John Arquilla and David Ronfeldt, *The Emergence of Noopolitik: toward an American information strategy*, The RAND Corporation, Santa Monica, 1999.

22 Joseph S. Nye, *Soft Power. The Means to Success in World Politics*, PublicAffairs, New York 2004, p. 91.

23 Ibid. pp. 92 ff.

24 Lawrence K. Grossman, *The Electronic Republic: reshaping American democracy for the information age*, Penguin Books, New York 1996, p. 3.

25 Richard Wiggins, 'Al Gore and the Creation of the Internet', *First Monday* 5 (10) (2000); https://firstmonday.org/ojs/index.php/fm/article/download/799/708/.

26 Robert Kahn and Vinton Cerf, 'Al Gore and the Internet', *The Register*, 2 October 2000; https://www.theregister.com/2000/10/02/net_builders_kahn_cerf_recognise/.

27 'Inauguration of the First World Telecommunication Development Conference. Remarks prepared for delivery by Mr. Al Gore, US Vice President', *International Telecommunication Union*, 21 March 1994.

28 See 'Leader's Speech, Brighton 1995', *British Political Speeches*; http://www.britishpoliticalspeech.org/speech-archive.htm?speech=201.

29 Quoted in 'Tony Blair's Full Speech', *The Guardian*, 7 March 2000.

30 Plenarprotokoll des Deutschen Bundestages [Official Record of

Plenary Proceedings of the German Bundestag] 13/170, 28 April 1997.

31   Plenarprotokoll des Deutschen Bundestages [Official Record of Plenary Proceedings of the German Bundestag] 13/95, 14 March 1996.

32   Abel Reiberg, *Netzpolitik. Genese eines Politikfelds*, Nomos Verlag, Baden-Baden, 2018, p. 105

5. The New Terrorism

1   Friedman, *The Lexus*, p. 402.

2   Jytte Klausen, *Western Jihadism: a thirty-year history*, Oxford University Press, Oxford 2021, pp. 74–104.

3   Ibid.

4   Of course, the same accusations have also been made against America and Western states.

5   Claire Sterling, *The Terror Network: the secret war of international terrorism*, Holt, Rinehart and Winston, New York 1981.

6   Interview with Mark Stout, March 2021.

7   Once again, the terrorists encountered technical problems, and the attack killed 'only' thirteen people.

8   See Walter Laqueur, *The New Terrorism: fanaticism and the arms of mass destruction*, Oxford University Press, Oxford 1999.

9   See Brian Michael Jenkins, 'The New Age of Terrorism', in David G. Kamien (Ed.), *The McGraw-Hill Homeland Security Handbook*, McGraw-Hill, Boston 2006, p. 118.

10   See Peter R. Neumann, *Old and New Terrorism*, Polity Press, Cambridge 2008.

11   Cf. Walter Laqueur, *No End to War: terrorism in the twenty-first century*, Continuum, London 2004, p. 9.

12   Fukuyama, 'The End', p. 18.

13   See John Arquilla, David Ronfeldt and Michele Zanini (Eds.), *Countering the New Terrorism*, RAND Corporation, Santa Monica, 1999; Peter L. Bergen, *Holy War Inc.: inside the secret world of Osama bin Laden*, Simon & Schuster, London 2001; Simon Reeve, *The New Jackals: Ramzi Yousef, Osama bin Laden and the future of terrorism*, Northeastern University Press, Boston 1999.

14   Kepel, *Jihad: the trail of political Islam*. The Belknap Press, Cambridge, Mass. 2002; Olivier Roy, *The Failure of Political Islam*, Harvard University Press, Cambridge, Mass. 1996.

15   Interview with Guido Steinberg, April 2021.

16   See Charles Krauthammer, 'The Unipolar Moment', *Foreign Affairs*, Winter 1990; Charles Krauthammer, 'The Unipolar Moment Revisited', *The National Interest*, Winter 2002.

17   Stephen M. Walt, 'Building Up New Bogeymen', *Foreign Policy*, Spring 1997, pp. 176–189.

18   Patrick E. Tyler, 'Pentagon Imagines New Enemies to Fight in Post-

Cold War Era', *New York Times*, 17 February 1992.

19   Thomas Barfield, *Afghanistan: a cultural and political history*, Princeton University Press, Princeton 2010, p. ix.

20   See 'Conversations with History. Michael Scheuer', *University of California Television*, 2008; https://www.youtube.com/watch?v=gxdb5nnRMrU.

21   Farrell, *Unwinnable*, pp. 31 ff.

22   Interview with Michael Hurley, February 2021.

23   Interview with David Omand, February 2021.

24   Interview with Gerhard Conrad, February 2021.

25   Ibid.

26   Ibid.

27   Interview with Ali Soufan, February 2021.

28   Clinton, *My Life*, p. 925.

29   Daniel P. Bolger, *Why We Lost: a general's inside account of the Iraq and Afghanistan wars*, Houghton Mifflin Harcourt, New York 2014, p. 23.

30   Interview with Ali Soufan, February 2021.

31   *U. S. Foreign Policy Agenda* 6 (1) (2001), pp. 5–18.

32   Richard A. Clarke, *Against All Enemies: inside America's war on terror*, Free Press, London 2004, p. 226.

33   Larry C. Johnson, 'The Declining Terrorist Threat', *New York Times*, 10 July 2001.

6. Wake-Up Call 9/11

1   Paul Auster, 'Random Notes – September 11, 2001, 4 PM', *Die Zeit*, September 13, 2001. See Paul Auster, *Collected Prose*, Picador/Henry Holt, New York 2003, pp. 505–506.

2   Terrorists crashed another hijacked plane into the US Pentagon building at almost the same time. A fourth plane, which the terrorists probably planned to fly into the Capitol or the White House, crashed in a field in Pennsylvania after the hijackers were overcome by passengers. A total of almost three thousand people were killed in the coordinated attacks.

3   Bernard Lewis, 'The Revolt of Islam', *The New Yorker*, 19 November 2001.

4   The USA was maintaining no-fly zones over Iraq at the time, which were mandated by the UN Security Council. The US and Britain carried out air strikes in late 1998 to force Iraq to comply with the sanctions imposed on it.

5   Susan Sontag, in 'Tuesday, and After', *The New Yorker*, 24 September 2001.

6   Ralph Giordano, 'Wie gut, dass es Amerika gibt!', in *Dienstag, 11. September 2001*, p. 144.

7   Michael Ehrke, '11. September 2001. Anschläge auf welche Zivilisation?', *Internationale Politik und Gesellschaft*, January 2002, pp.

16 ff.

8   Jean-Marie Colombani, 'Nous sommes tous Américains', *Le Monde*, 13
        September 2001.

9   'Full Text of President Bush's Address to a Joint Session of Congress
        and the Nation', The White House, 20 September 2001.

10   Charles Krauthammer, 'The Real New World Order', *The Weekly
        Standard*, 12 November 2001.

11   Quoted in Farrell, *Unwinnable*, p. 47.

12   According to Raymond Kelly; see Michael Chandler and Rohan
        Gunaratna, *Countering Terrorism: can we meet the threat of global
        violence?*, Reaktion Books, London 2008.

13   Rohan Gunaratna, *Inside al-Qaeda: global network of terror*, Hurst,
        London 2002, p. 172].

14   Harvey Kushner, *Holy War on the Home Front: the secret Islamic terror
        network in the United States*, Sentinel, New York 2004.

15   Paul L. Williams, *Al Qaeda: brotherhood of terror*, Alpha, Boston 2002,
        p. 172.

16   Paul L. Williams, *Dunces of Doomsday: 10 blunders that gave rise to
        radical Islam, terrorist regimes, and an American Hiroshima*, Nashville,
        Washington, D.C. 2008, chapter 6.

17   Interview with Jonathan Evans, April 2021.

18   Interview with Michael Hurley, April 2021.

19   Interview with David Frum, April 2021.

20   Interview with Peter Bergen, May 2021.

21   See 'Wolfowitz Interview with *Vanity Fair*'s Tannenhaus', US
        Department of Defense, 30 May 2003.

22   Quoted in Ivo Daalder and James Lindsay, *America Unbound: the Bush
        revolution in foreign policy*, Wiley, Hoboken, NJ 2003, p. 82.

23   Quoted in Steve Coll, *Directorate S: the C. I. A. and America's secret
        wars in Afghanistan and Pakistan, 2001–2016*, Penguin, New York
        2018, p. 175.

24   In this context, 'the Middle East' refers to the twenty-two states
        defined by the United Nations as the 'Arab Region'.

25   Gary Schmitt, 'A Case of Continuity', *National Interest*, Autumn 2002.

26   The reports can be found on the Arab Human Development Report
        website: https://arab-hdr.org/.

27   'Arab Human Development Report 2002. Creating Opportunities
        for Future Generations', United Nations Development Programme,
        August 2002; https://arab-hdr.org/report/opportunities-2002/.

28   Michael Mandelbaum, 'The Inadequacy of American Power', *Foreign
        Affairs*, September 2002.

29   Robert I. Rotberg, 'Failed States in a World of Terror', *Foreign Affairs*,
        July 2002.

30   Fouad Ajami, 'Iraq and the Arabs' Future', *Foreign Affairs*, January
        2003. The liberal professor Charles Kupchan had a similar view; see

Charles A. Kupchan, 'Misreading September 11th', *The National Interest*, Autumn 2002.

31   Michael Scott Doran, 'Somebody Else's Civil War', *Foreign Affairs*, January 2002.
32   Fischer, *Die Rückkehr der Geschichte*, p. 20.
33   Ibid. p. 227.
34   Ibid.
35   Ibid. p. 209.
36   Ibid. p. 20.
37   Ibid. p. 224
38   Quoted in 'Defense Policy', *National Interest*, November 2001.
39   Quoted in 'Full Text. Bush's Speech', *The Guardian*, 18 March 2003.

7. The Good War

1   Farrell, *Unwinnable*, p. 48.
2   Coll, *Directorate S*, p. 134.
3   Bush, quoted in Daalder & Lindsay, *America Unbound*, pp. 103 ff.
4   Ibid. p. 103.
5   Josef Joffe, 'Of Hubs, Spokes and Public Goods', *The National Interest*, Autumn 2002.
6   Interview with Michael Hurley, April 2021.
7   Farrell, *Unwinnable*, p. 104; see also Coll, *Directorate S*, p. 127.
8   Bolger, *Why We Lost*, p. 94.
9   Ibid. p. 95.
10   Dov S. Zakheim, *A Vulcan's Tale: how the Bush administration mismanaged the reconstruction of Afghanistan*, Brookings Institution Press, Washington D.C. 2011, pp. 168–170.
11   Quoted in 'Full text of Tony Blair's speech to parliament', *The Guardian*, 4 October 2001.
12   Quoted in 'Full transcript of Tony Blair's statement', *The Guardian*, 11 September 2001.
13   Interview with Christoph Heusgen, April 2021.
14   Interview with Ulrich Schneckener, April 2021.
15   This was questionable because, as lawmakers from the Left Party pointed out, this 'separation' was based on nothing but a promise from the British Prime Minister, Tony Blair, and was not regulated by any international treaties. If it came to a conflict, the Americans would have the final word. See Minutes of Plenary Proceedings of the German Bundestag (Plenarprotokoll des Deutschen Bundestages) 14/210, 22 December 2001.
16   Foreign Minister Fischer, quoted in ibid.
17   Ibid.
18   Interview with Theo Farrell, April 2021.
19   Minutes of Plenary Proceedings of the German Bundestag, op cit.
20   Minutes of Plenary Proceedings of the German Bundestag

(Plenarprotokoll des Deutschen Bundestages) 14/210, 22 December 2001.

21   Fischer, Die Rückkehr der Geschichte, p. 211.
22   Reid later claimed that these (often-cited) words have been misremembered, and that he was actually saying that the conflict might continue. Quoted in Julian Borger, 'Why we went into Helmand', *The Guardian*, 23 April 2012.
23   Ben Anderson, *No Worse Enemy: the inside story of the chaotic struggle for Afghanistan*, Oneworld Publications, Oxford 2011, p. xvii. 24 Interview with Theo Farrell, April 2021.
25   Thomas Barfield, *Afghanistan. A Cultural and Political History*, Princeton University Press 2010, p. 316.
26   Ibid.; Hassan Abbas, *The Taliban Revival. Violence and Extremism on the Pakistan-Afghanistan Frontier*, Yale University Press, New Haven 2014, pp. 92 ff.
27   Interview with August Hanning, April 2021.
28   See Seth Johnston, 'NATO's Lessons from Afghanistan', *Parameters*, Autumn 2019; https://www.belfercenter.org/publication/natos-lessons-afghanistan.
29   Seth G. Jones, *In the Graveyard of Empires: America's war in Afghanistan*, W.W. Norton & Company, New York 2009, p. 165; Farrell, *Unwinnable*, p. 165.
30   Interview with Bernd Mützelburg, April 2021.
31   Interview with Stefan Kornelius, April 2021.
32   Interview with Bernd Mützelburg, April 2021.
33   Interview with Tim Wilsey, April 2021.
34   Jason Burke, *The 9/11 Wars*, London 2012, pp. 81–84.
35   Quoted in Chris Johnson and Jolyon Leslie, *Afghanistan: the mirage of peace*, Zed Books, London 2004, p. 26.
36   Ibid. p. 31.
37   Barfield, *Afghanistan*, p. 317.
38   Johnson & Leslie, *Afghanistan*, p. 33.
39   Hassan, *The Taliban Revival*, p. 91.
40   Rory Stewart, 'Are we failing in Afghanistan?', *Prospect Magazine*, 20 January 2008.
41   Interview with Hannah Neumann, April 2021.

8. Regime Change

1   Cf. Habermas, *The Divided West*, chapter 2.
2   See The Iraq Inquiry, The Chilcot Report. Executive Summary, Kingston upon Thames 2016.
3   See Bob Woodward, *Bush at War*, Simon & Schuster, New York 2002; Daalder/Lindsay, *America Unbound*, p. 143.
4   James Mann, *Rise of the Vulcans: the history of Bush's war cabinet*, Viking Penguin, New York 2004, p. 238.

5   Interview with David Frum, April 2021.

6   Thomas E. Ricks, *Fiasco: the American military adventure in Iraq*, Penguin, New York 2006, p. 31.

7   As the head of the German Federal Intelligence Service (BND) at the time, August Hanning, explains: 'It was about chemical weapons that had suddenly gone missing after the First Gulf War (1991). No one really knew whether they were still being stored somewhere or had been destroyed.' Interview with August Hanning, April 2021.

8   Ricks, *Fiasco*, p. 49.

9   Kenneth M. Pollack, *The Threatening Storm: the case for invading Iraq*, Random House, New York 2002, p. 158.

10   Lawrence F. Kaplan and William Kristol, *The War over Iraq: Saddam's tyranny and America's mission*, Encounter Books, San Francisco 2003, chapters 1–3.

11   'Wolfowitz Interview with *Vanity Fair*'s Tannenhaus', US Department of Defense, 30 May 2003.

12   Ajami, 'Iraq and the Arabs' Future', p. 2.

13   'Wolfowitz Interview'.

14   Ken Adelman, 'Cakewalk in Iraq', *Washington Post*, 13 February 2002.

15   Ricks, *Fiasco*, p. 71 ff.

16   Interview with Michael Doran, April 2021.

17   Ricks, Fiasco, p. 109; Iraq Inquiry, The Chilcot Report, p. 120.

18   Interview with Emma Sky, April 2021.

19   Quoted in Bing West, *The Strongest Tribe: war, politics, and the endgame in Iraq*, Random House, New York 2009, p. 24.

20   Ricks, *Fiasco*, p. 160. See Ali A. Allawi, *The Occupation of Iraq: winning the war, losing the peace*, Yale University Press, New Haven 2008, p. 148.

21   Ricks, *Fiasco*, p. 162.

22   Allawi, *The Occupation*, p. 158.

23   Interview with Emma Sky, April 2021.

24   James A. Baker and Lee H. Hamilton, *The Iraq Study Group Report*, Vintage Books, New York 2006, p. 35.

25   'Iraq. The Human Cost', Massachusetts Institute of Technology; http://web.mit.edu/humancostiraq/. See Philip Bump, '15 years after the Iraq war began, the death toll is still murky', *Washington Post*, 20 March 2018.

26   Besides Iraq, these included Syria, Libya, Lebanon, Iran, Sudan and Yemen. See Perle, quoted in 'Defense Policy', *National Interest*.

27   Peter R. Neumann, 'Suspects into Collaborators', *London Review of Books*, 3 April 2014.

28   Interview with Michael Doran, April 2021.

29   Peter R. Neumann, *Radicalized: new jihadists and the threat to the West*, I.B. Tauris, London 2016, pp. 58–60.

30   Interview with Jonathan Evans, April 2021.

31   Quoted in Richard Norton-Taylor, 'Former MI5 chief delivers damning verdict on Iraq invasion', *The Guardian*, 20 July 2020.

32   Interview with Guido Steinberg, April 2021.

33   'Annual Arab Public Opinion Survey 2010', University of Maryland with Zogby International, 5 August 2010; https://www.brookings.edu/wp-content/uploads/2016/06/0805_arabic_opinion_poll_telhami.pdf.

34   Amaney Ahmad Jama and Mark Tessler, 'Attitudes in the Arab World', *Journal of Democracy* 19 (1) (2008), pp. 97–110.

35   Joseph Stiglitz, *The Three Trillion Dollar War: the true cost of the Iraq conflict*, W.W. Norton and Company, New York 2008.

36   See Joschka Fischer, 'The Middle East's Lost Decade', *Project Syndicate*, 18 March 2013.

9. Market Excesses

1   'Real GDP Forecast', Organisation for Economic Cooperation and Development (OECD); https://data.oecd.org/gdp/real-gdp-forecast.htm; Martin Wolf, *The Shifts and the Shock:. what we've learned – and have still to learn – from the financial crisis*, Penguin Books, London 2014, p. 90.

2   See Dani Rodrik, 'Goodbye Washington Consensus, Hello Washington Confusion? A Review of the World Bank's Economic Growth in the 1990s. Learning from a Decade of Reform', *Journal of Economic Literature* 44 (2006), pp. 973–987.

3   Quoted in Wolf, *The Shifts and the Shocks*, p. 138.

4   Alan S. Blinder, *After the Music Stopped: the financial crisis and response, and the work ahead*, Penguin Books, New York 2008, p. 57.

5   'China GDP Growth Rate, 1961–2021, Macrotrends; https://www.macrotrends.net/countries/CHN/china/gdp-growth-rate. 'China Exports, 1960–2021'; Macrotrends; https://www.macrotrends.net/countries/CHN/china/exports. 'Ratio of residents living below the poverty line in China from 2000 to 2020', Statista; https://www.statista.com/statistics/1086836/chinapoverty-ratio/.

6   Thomas L. Friedman, *The World Is Flat: the globalized world in the twenty-first century*, Allen Lane, London 2005, p. 150.

7   Martin Wolf, *Why Globalization Works*, Yale University Press, New Haven 2005, p. 120.

8   Robert E. Lucas, 'Macroeconomic Priorities', *The American Economic Review*, March 2003.

9   Quoted in Stephen King, 'No more boom and bust' – an epitaph for Chancellor Brown', *The Independent*, 11 December 2006.

10   'How China's Entry Led to Lower Prices in the U.S.', National Bureau of Economic Research Digest, 8 August 2017; https://www.nber.org/digest/aug17/how-chinas-wto-entry-led-lower-prices-us.

11   See Susan Houseman, 'Understanding the Decline in Manufacturing Employment', W. E. Upjohn Institute for Employment Research,

January/June 2018; https://www.upjohn.org/research-highlights/
understanding-decline-manufacturing-employment. The introduction
of new technologies was, however, not the sole reason for this
development, which was exacerbated by radical labour market reforms,
cuts to the welfare state and the absurd returns on investments in the
financial markets. See Michael Aklin, Andreas Kern and Mario Negre,
'Does Central Bank Independence Increase Inequality?', *World Bank
Policy Research Working Paper* 9522, January 2021.

12   See Juliana Horowitz et al., 'Trends in Income and wealth inequality',
      Pew Research Center, 9 January 2020.
13   See OECD.stat, https://stats.oecd.org/Index.
      aspx?DataSetCode=IDD#.
14   Thomas Piketty, *Capital in the Twenty-First Century*, Harvard
      University Press, Cambridge, MA2014, p. 263
15   See Christoph Lakner and Branko Milanović, 'Global Income
      Distribution. From the Fall of the Berlin Wall to the Great Recession',
      World Bank Policy Research Working Paper 6719, December 2013.
16   See 'Der letzte Macho', *Stuttgarter Nachrichten*, 5 April 2019.
17   Quoted in Oliver Moody, 'Britons take a generous view of filthy rich',
      The Times, 11 February 2019.
18   Friedman, *The World*, pp. 265–268.
19   Wolf, *Why Globalization Works*, pp. 170 f.
20   See Raghuram G. Rajan, *Fault Lines: how hidden fractures still threaten
      the world economy*, Princeton University Press, Princeton 2011.
21   Blinder, *After the Music Stopped*, pp. 3–27.
22   Quoted in Chip Berlet, 'Reframing Populist Resentments in the Tea
      Party Movement', in Lawrence Rosenthal and Christine Trost (Eds.),
      Steep: the precipitous rise of the Tea Party, University of California
      Press, Berkeley 2012, p. 59.
23   Blinder, *After the Music Stopped*, p. 68.
24   Ibid., pp. 3–27.
25   Ibid., p. 6.
26   Wolf, *The Shifts*, p. 125.
27   Quoted in ibid., p. 21.
28   Christopher Sebastian Parker, 'The Radical Right in the United States
      of America', in Jens Rydgren (Ed.), *The Oxford Handbook of the
      Radical Right*, Oxford University Press, Oxford 2018, p. 636.
29   See David Kirby and Emily Ekins, 'Libertarian Roots of the Tea Party',
      Policy Analysis, 6 August 2012.
30   Parker, 'The Radical Right', p. 637.
31   See Michael Cox and Martin Durham, 'The politics of anger. The
      extreme right in the United States', in Paul Hainsworth (Ed.), The
      Politics of the Extreme Right. From the Margins to the Mainstream,
      Bloomsbury Academic, London 2000, pp. 287–311.
32   Richard Hofstadter, 'The Paranoid Style in American Politics', Harper's

Magazine, November 1964. See Seymour Martin Lipset and Earl
Raab, The Politics of Unreason. Right-Wing Extremism in America,
1790–1970, Harper & Row, New York 1970, pp. 13–17.

33   Christine Trost and Lawrence Rosenthal, 'The Rise of the Tea Party',
in Rosenthal, Steep, p. 9.

34   See Peter R. Neumann, Bluster. Donald Trump's War on Terror,
Oxford University Press New York 2020, p. 143.

35   Quoted in Charles Postel, 'The Tea Party in Historical Perspective. A
Conservative Response to a Crisis of Political Economy', in Rosenthal,
Steep, p. 42.

36   Ronald P. Formisano, The Tea Party, The Johns Hopkins University
Press, Baltimore 2012, p. 114.

37   Lisa Disch, 'The Tea Party. A "White Citizenship" Movement?', in
Rosenthal, Steep, p. 143.

38   Formisano, The Tea Party, p. 106 f.

10. Arab Spring?

1   In Western countries, that figure stood at less than 10 per cent. James
L. Gelvin, The Arab Uprisings: what everyone needs to know, Oxford
University Press, Oxford 2015, pp. 21 ff.

2   Christopher Phillips, The Battle for Syria: international rivalry in the
Middle East, Yale University Press, New Haven 2016, p. 46.

3   Gelvin, The Arab Uprisings, p. 50.

4   See Juan Cole, The New Arabs: how the millennial generation is
changing the Middle East, Simon & Schuster, New York 2014, chapter
1.

5   Marc Lynch, The Arab Uprising: the unfinished revolutions of the new
Middle East, PublicAffairs Books, New York 2012, p. 3.

6   See Introduction.

7   'Egypt's Moment', New York Times, 11 February 2011.

8   See Philip N. Howard and Muzammil Hussain, Democracy's Fourth
Wave?: digital media and the Arab Spring, Oxford University Press,
Oxford 2013.

9   Tariq Ali, quoted in Srećko Horvat, Nach dem Ende der Geschichte.
Vom Arabischen Frühling zur Occupy-Bewegung, LAIKA Verlag,
Hamburg 2013, p. 43.

10   See 'From Prague Spring to Arab Spring. Global and Comparative
Perspectives on Protest and Revolution, 1968–2012', Stanford
University Center on Democracy, Development, and the Rule of Law
Conference, 2 March 2012; https://cddrl.fsi.stanford.edu/events/
from_prague_spring_to_arab_spring__global_and_comparative_
perspectives_on_protest_and_revolution_19682012_3_2_2012.

11   See Annette Jünemann, 'Vor dem Scherbenhaufen einer verfehlten
Regionalpolitik. Europa und der Arabische Frühling', in Thorsten
Gerald Schneiders (Ed.), Der Arabische Frühling. Hintergründe und

Analysen, Springer Fachmedien, Wiesbaden 2013, p. 95.

12   Interview with Daniel Gerlach, November 2021.

13   Interview with Bernard Rougier, November 2021.

14   See Barack Obama, *A Promised Land*, Penguin, New York and London 2020, p. 643; Ben Rhodes, *The World As It Is: inside the Obama White House*, Bodley Head, London 2018, p. 142; Fouad Ajami, 'How the Arabs Turned Shame Into Liberty', *New York Times*, 26 February 2011; Ceyda Nurtsch, 'The West is Terrified of Arab Democracies. Interview with Noam Chomsky', Qantara, 17 June 2011; https://en.qantara.de/content/interview-with-noam-chomsky-the-west-is-terrified-of-arab-democracies.

15   Francis Fukuyama, 'Is China Next?', *Wall Street Journal*, 12 March 2011.

16   Emmanuel Todd, *Frei! Der arabische Frühling und was er für uns bedeutet*, Piper, Munich 2011, blurb.

17   See Cole, *The New Arabs: how the millennial generation is changing the Middle East*, Simon & Schuster, New York 2014; 'Wael Ghonim and Egypt's New Age Revolution', *CBS News*, 16 February 2011; https://www.cbsnews.com/news/wael-ghonim-and-egypts-new-age-revolution/.

18   Quoted in Mark Landler, 'Obama Seeks Reset in the Arab World', *New York Times*, 11 May 2011. See also Obama, *A Promised Land*, p. 643.

19   Lynch, *The Arab Uprising*, p. 16.

20   Jean-Pierre Filiu, *The Arab Revolution: ten lessons from the democratic uprising*, Oxford University Press, Oxford 2011, pp. 25, 73.

21   Interview with John Sawers, November 2021.

22   Filiu, *The Arab Revolution*, p. 113.

23   Fawaz A. Gerges, 'How the Arab Spring Beat al-Qaeda', *Daily Beast*, 13 July 2012.

24   Quoted in Shiraz Maher and Peter R. Neumann, *Al-Qaeda at the Crossroads: how the terror group is responding to the loss of its leaders and the Arab Spring*, ICSR, London 2012, p. 14; https://icsr.info/wp-content/uploads/2012/10/ICSR_Maher-Neumann-Paper_For-online-use-only.pdf

25   See Bruce Hoffman, 'The Arab Spring and Its Influence on al-Qaida', *CTC Sentinel*, May 2012; https://www.ctc.usma.edu/the-arab-spring-andits-influence-on-al-qaida/; Aron Zelin, *Your Sons Are at Your Service: Tunisia's missionaries of jihad*, Columbia University Press, New York 2020.

26   Jünemann, 'Vor dem Scherbenhaufen', pp. 95–114.

27   'Remarks by the President at Cairo University', The White House, 4 June 2009.

28   Obama names the reasons for this as not only the wars in Afghanistan and Iraq, but also the consequences of the financial crisis and the Fukushima nuclear accident. See Obama, *A Promised Land*, p. 655.

29   Quoted in Lara Marlowe, 'Obama turns focus to nation-building at

home', *Irish Times*, 24 June 2011.

30   Michael Lüders, *Wer den Wind sät. Was westliche Politik im Orient anrichtet*, C.H. Beck, Munich 2020, p. 176.

31   Interview with Hussein Ibish, October 2021.

32   See David Rothkopf, 'Obama's 'Don't Do Stupid Shit' Foreign Policy', *Foreign Policy*, 4 June 2014.

33   'Remarks by the President on the Middle East and North Africa', The White House, 19 May 2011. See also Lynch, *The Arab Uprising*, p. 193 ff.

34   Interview with Emile Hokayem, November 2021.

35   Volker Perthes, 'Politische Perspektiven der arabischen Revolutionen', in Schneiders (ed.), *Der Arabische Frühling*, p. 82.

36   Interview with Daniel Gerlach, November 2021.

37   Morozov, *The Net Delusion*, pp. xiii, 233.

38   Ibid., p. xii.

39   Interview with Gerhard Schindler, November 2021.

40   See Jytte Klausen, *Western Jihadism: a thirty year history*, Oxford University Press, Oxford 2021, chapter 11.

41   See Charlie Winter, *The Virtual 'Caliphate': understanding Islamic State's propaganda strategy*, Quilliam, London 2015, pp. 28–32.

42   Jon Greenberg, 'Does the Islamic State Post 90,000 Messages a Day?', Politifact, 19 February 2015. See also J.M. Berger and Jonathon Morgan, The ISIS Twitter Census. Defining and Describing the Population of ISIS Supporters on Twitter, The Brookings Institution, Washington D.C. 2015.

43   Morozov, *The Net Delusion*, pp. 10–25.

11. France's Adventure

1   See Alison Pargeter, *Libya. The Rise and Fall of Qaddafi*, Yale University Press, New Haven 2012.

2   Ibid., chapters 3 and 6.

3   Ibid., chapter 5.

4   Quoted in 'Libya's Gaddafi: "I will cleanse Libya house by house".', *Sky News*, 23 February 2011; https://www.youtube.com/watch?v=9WQ1gm30RxM.

5   Quoted in 'Gaddafi's son: "There will be rivers of blood in Libya"', *Channel 4 News*, 21 February 2011; https://www.youtube.com/watch?v=Z9SJc1PcOfE.

6   See Alex Crawford, *Colonel Gaddafi's Hat. A Tyrant Falls and a Nation Rises*, HarperCollins, London 2012.

7   It was later revealed that Alliot-Marie had business interests connected to the Tunisian government, and that she had taken several flights in a private jet belonging to a close friend of Ben Ali. See 'Michèle Alliot-Marie critiquée pour ses relations amicales avec un proche de Ben Ali', *France 24*, 2 February 2011.

8   Quoted in 'La voix de la France a disparu dans le monde', *Le Monde*, 22 February 2011.

9   See Samantha Power, *The Education of an Idealist*, William Collins, London 2019, chapter 17.

10   Interview with Mark Hecker, November 2021.

11   Interview with Bernard Rougier, November 2021.

12   Quoted in Natalie Nougayrède, 'La guerre de Nicolas Sarkozy', *Le Monde*, 23 August 2011.

13   Quoted in ibid.

14   Interview with Bernard Rougier, November 2021.

15   Renaud Girard, 'La campagne libyenne de Bernard-Henri Lévy', *Le Figaro*, 18 March 2011; Steven Erlanger, 'By His Own Reckoning, One Man Made Libya a French Cause', *New York Times*, 1 April 2011.

16   Bernard-Henri Lévy, 'Pourquoi la guerre de Libye est le contraire de la guerre d'Irak', *La Règle du Jeu*, 7 August 2011. Cf. Nougayrède, 'La guerre de Nicolas Sarkozy'.

17   Quoted in 'Bernard-Henri Lévy raconte son conflit libyen', *Le Monde*, 7 November 2011.

18   Quoted in Jason W. Davidson, 'France, Britain, and the Intervention in Libya. An Integrated Analysis', *Cambridge Review of International Affairs* 26 (2) (2013), p. 324.

19   See Samantha Power, *A Problem from Hell. America and the Age of Genocide*, Harper Perennial, London 2010.

20   Quoted in Rhodes, *The World*, p. 113.

21   See Obama, *A Promised Land*, p. 667.

22   Frederic Wehrey, 'NATO's Intervention', in Cole, *The Libyan Revolution*, p. 116.

23   'Obama: We should not be afraid to act', *CBS News*, 29 March 2011.

24   Quoted in Wehrey, 'NATO's Intervention', p. 111.

25   Ibid., p. 116.

26   Ibid., p. 116 f.

27   Barack Obama, David Cameron and Nicolas Sarkozy, 'Libya's Pathway to Peace', *New York Times*, 14 April 2011.

28   Interview with John Sawers, November 2021.

29   Interview with Bernard Rougier, November 2021.

30   'Libya: Examination of intervention and collapse, and the UK's future policy options. Third Report of Session 2016–17', *House of Commons, HC 119*, September 2016, pp. 18–23.

31   Interview with Bernard Rougier, November 2021.

32   Ibid.

33   'Libya: Examination of', *House of Commons*, pp. 25 ff.

34   Interview with John Sawers, November 2021.

35   Quoted in 'Libya: Examination of', *House of Commons*, p. 26.

36   See Jean-Baptiste Jeangène Vilmer, 'Ten Myths about the 2011 Intervention in Libya', *The Washington Quarterly*, Summer 2016, pp.

32 f.

37 Over five years, Britain provided a fraction of the money it spent on the intervention for state-building. See 'Libya: Examination of', *House of Commons*, p. 27.

38 Interview with Emile Hokayem, November 2021.

39 Olivier Schmitt, 'A war worth fighting? The Libyan intervention in retrospect', *International Politics Review* 3 (1) (2015), p. 9.

40 Quoted in Jeffrey Goldberg, 'The Obama Doctrine', *The Atlantic*, April 2016.

41 Interview with Florence Gaub, November 2021.

42 'Sarkozy: Discours à Benghazi avec Cameron', *Public Sénat*, 15 September 2011; https://www.youtube.com/watch?v=0bhtPbkbKCA.

43 Interview with Daniel Gerlach, November 2021.

44 Interview with Gerhard Schindler, November 2021.

45 'Country Reports: Middle East and North Africa Overview', *U. S. Department of State, Country Reports on Terrorism*, 2013

46 Frederic Wehrey, *The Burning Shores. Inside the Battle for the New Libya*, Farrar, Straus and Giroux, New York 2018, p. 86.

47 Ibid., pp. 147 f.

48 Nicolas Marsh, 'Brothers Came Back with Weapons. The Effects of Arms Proliferation from Libya', *Prism* 6 (4) (2017), pp. 79 f.

49 Simon McMahon and Nando Sigona, 'Boat Migration across the Central Mediterranean. Drivers, Experiences, and Responses', *MEDMIG Research Brief*, September 2016; Patrick Kingsley, *The New Odyssey. The story of the twenty-first-century refugee crisis*, Liveright Publishing Corporation, New York 2017.

50 See Mary Fitzgerald, 'Finding Their Place. Libya's Islamists During and After the Revolution', in Cole, *The Libyan Revolution*, pp. 177–204.

51 At this time, the Libyan coastal city of Sirte was 'the group's main urban base outside Syria and Iraq'. Interview with US security officials, November 2021.

52 See Inga Trauthig, 'Assessing the Islamic State in Libya', *Europol*, April 2019; https://www.europol.europa.eu/sites/default/files/documents/inga_trauthig_islamic_state_libya.pdf.

53 Interview with Gilles de Kerchove, December 2021.

12. The Syrian Disaster

1 Economic growth in Syria stood at between 4 and 6 per cent in the first decade of this century – more than before, but still far from enough to create sufficient jobs for the growing population. See John McHugo, *Syria. A Recent History*, Saqi Books, London 2014, p. 216.

2 Quoted in 'Interview with Syrian President Bashir al-Assad', *Wall Street Journal*, 31 January 2011.

3 Phillips, *The Battle*, pp. 56 f.

4   McHugo, *Syria*, p. 228.
5   See 'Syria war: UN calculates new death toll', *BBC News*, 24
     September 2021; 'Over 600,000 people killed in Syria since beginning
     of the "Syrian Revolution"', *SOHR*, 1 June 2021.
6   Stefan Luft, *Die Flüchtlingskrise. Ursachen, Konflikte, Folgen*, C.H.
     Beck, Munich 2016, p. 27.
7   Sharmila Devadas, Ibrahim Elbadawi and Norman Loayza,
     'Growth after War in Syria', *World Bank Policy Research Working
     Paper*, August 2019; https://documents1.worldbank.org/curated/
     en/424551565105634645/pdf/Growth-after-War-in-Syria.pdf.
8   Michael Lüders, *Die den Sturm ernten. Wie der Westen Syrien ins
     Chaos stürzte*, C.H. Beck, Munich 2019, p. 11.
9   Ibid.
10   Ibid. p. 167.
11   See Jane Mayer, 'Outsourcing Torture', *The New Yorker*, 6 February
     2005.
12   See McHugo, *Syria*, p. 214; Phillips, *The Battle*, p. 49.
13   Phillips, *The Battle*, p. 65.
14   Hokayem, *Syria's Uprising*, p. 154.
15   Phillips, *The Battle*, p. 67.
16   'Syria's Ramadan Massacre', *Washington Post*, 1 August 2011.
17   See Scott Wilson, 'How the US Message on Assad Shifted',
     Washington Post, 18 August 2011.
18   Interview with Haid Haid, November 2021.
19   Phillips, *The Battle*, p. 82.
20   Interview with Hussein Ibish, October 2021.
21   Interview with Gerhard Schindler, November 2021.
22   Phillips, *The Battle*, p. 74.
23   Ibid., p. 67.
24   Ibid., p. 77.
25   Quoted in Rhodes, *The World*, pp. 198–200.
26   Samer Abboud, *Syria*, Polity Press, Cambridge, 2018, pp. 185–187.
27   Phillips, *The Battle*, p. 76.
28   Interview with Bernard Rougier, November 2021.
29   Ibid., pp. 186, 204.
30   Ibid., pp. 168, 177.
31   Interview with Emile Hokayem, November 2021.
32   Interview with John Sawers, November 2021.
33   See 'Syria Countrywide Conflict Report #1', *Carter Center*, August 2013.
34   Abboud, *Syria*, pp. 102 f.
35   Ibid., pp. 106 f.
36   Interview with Haid Haid, November 2021.
37   Ibid.
38   Interview with John Sawers, November 2021.
39   Quoted in Phillips, *The Battle*, p. 125.

40   Rhodes, *The World*, p. 197.
41   See Phillips, *The Battle*, p. 141; McHugo, *Syria*, p. 252; Nikolaos van
      Dam, *Destroying a Nation. The Civil War in Syria*, I.B. Tauris, London
      2017, p. 71; Robert F. Worth, *A Rage for Order. The Middle East in
      Turmoil, from Tahrir Square to ISIS*, Pan Macmillan, London 2017,
      chapter 3.
42   Peter R. Neumann, *Radicalized: New Jihadists and the Threat to the
      West*, I.B. Tauris, London 2016, pp. 65–84.
43   See Joana Cook and Gina Vale, *From Daesh to Diaspora. Tracing the
      Women and Minors of the Islamic State*, ICSR, London 2018, p. 4.
44   See Lorenzo Vidino, Francesco Marone and Eva Entenmann, *Fear Thy
      Neighbor. Radicalization and Jihadist Attacks in the West*, ISPI, Milan
      2017.
45   See Peter R. Neumann, *Bluster. Donald Trump's War on Terror*, Oxford
      University Press, Oxford and New York 2020, chapter 6.
46   Angela Stent, *Putin's World. Russia against the West and with the Rest*,
      Grand Central Publishing, New York 2020, p. 349. See also Hokayem,
      Syria's Uprising, p. 172.
47   Interview with Hussein Ibish, October 2021.
48   See Abboud, *Syria*, p. 198.
49   Interview with John Sawers, November 2021.

13. German-Russian Illusions

1   Interview with Mark Galeotti, March 2021.
2   Quoted in 'Wortprotokoll der Rede Wladimir Putins im Deutschen
      Bundestag am 25. 09. 2001', Deutscher Bundestag, 25 September
      2001; https://www.bundestag.de/parlament/geschichte/gastredner/
      putin/putin_wort-244966.
3   Interview with Wolfgang Ischinger, February 2021.
4   Quoted in 'Putin's famous Munich speech 2007', YouTube; https://
      www.youtube.com/watch?v=hQ58Yv6kP44.
5   Interview with Wolfgang Ischinger, February 2021.
6   See Fyodor Lukyanov, 'Putin Has Stumbled in Ukraine', *Russia in
      Global Affairs*, 11 August 2014; Aschot L. Manutscharjan, 'Russlands
      Weg in die 'postwestliche Welt', *Aus Politik und Zeitgeschichte* 67 (21)
      (2017), p. 14; Kathryn Stoner and Michael McFaul, 'Who Lost Russia
      (This Time)? Vladimir Putin', *The Washington Quarterly*, Summer
      2015, p. 178.
7   Jonathan Tepperman, 'War of the Worlds. Michael McFaul on Russia
      and Ukraine', *The Octavian Report*, 24 February 2022.
8   John J. Mearsheimer, 'Why the Ukraine Crisis Is the West's Fault',
      Foreign Affairs, September 2014.
9   Quoted in Charlie Rose, 'All Eyes on Putin', *CBS News*, 27 September
      2015; 'Interview with Oliver Stone', *President of Russia*, 19 July 2019.
10   Interview with Wolfgang Ischinger, February 2021.

11   See Gavin Hall, 'Ukraine: the history behind Russia's claim that Nato promised not to expand to the East', *The Conversation*, 14 February 2022.

12   Interview with Klaus Naumann, May 2021.

13   Andreas Umland, 'Die deutsche Russlandpolitik im Lichte des Ukraine-Konflikts. Schein und Sein des interdependenztheoretischen Ansatzes zur Friedenssicherung in Europa', *Forum für osteuropäische Ideen und Zeitgeschichte* 24 (2) (2020), pp. 94 f.

14   Stoner, 'Who Lost Russia', p. 176.

15   Ibid., p. 173.

16   See Marlene Laruelle, 'Alexander Dugin and Eurasianism', in Mark Sedgwick (Ed.), *Key Thinkers of the Radical Right*, Oxford University Press, Oxford 2019, pp. 155–169.

17   Stoner, 'Who Lost Russia', p. 181.

18   Andreas Heinemann-Grüder, 'Wandel statt Anbiederung. Deutsche Russlandpolitik auf dem Prüfstand', *Osteuropa* 63 (7) (2013), p. 187.

19   Stoner, 'Who Lost Russia', pp. 182 f.

20   See Heinrich August Winkler, *Geschichte des Westens. Vom Kalten Krieg zum Mauerfall*, C.H. Beck, Munich 2019, Part 3.

21   Egon Bahr, 'Verantwortungspartnerschaft mit Moskau und Washington - Rede anlässlich der Verleihung des Dr.-Friedrich-Joseph-Haass-Preises 2015', in Adelheid Bahr (Ed.), *Warum wir Frieden und Freundschaft mit Russland brauchen*, Westend, Frankfurt 2018, p. 13.

22   See Thorsten Benner, 'Olaf Scholz is Coming to America on a Salvage Mission', *Foreign Policy*, 4 February 2022; https://foreignpolicy.com/2022/02/04/olaf-scholz-germany-united-states-ukraine-credibility/.

23   Although they are usually attributed collectively to Russia, almost half of the Soviets who died were from Ukraine, Belarus and the Baltic states.

24   Matthias Platzeck, 'Zurück zu politischer Vernunft. Deutschland muss endlich Initiative für ein sicheres Europa ergreifen', in Bahr (Ed.), *Warum wir Frieden*, Westend, Frankfurt 2018, p. 134.

25   Ibid., p. 136.

26   Peter Gauweiler, 'Ein anderer Umgang mit Russland ist nötig', in ibid., p. 98.

27   Sigmar Gabriel, 'Wandel durch Annäherung. Zur Aktualität der Rede Egon Bahrs vor 55 Jahren in Tutzing', in ibid., p. 95.

28   See Matthias Dembinski and Hans-Joachim Spanger, 'Plural Peace. Principles of a New Russia Policy', Peace Research Institute Frankfurt (PRIF), 2017.

29   Quoted in 'Kretschmer wirbt für Ende der Russland-Sanktionen', *Tagesspiegel*, 7 June 2019.

30   Ibid.

31   See Hans Adomeit, 'Bilanz der deutschen Russlandpolitik seit 1990',

Sirius 4 (3) (2020), p. 286.

32   See for example Frank-Walter Steinmeier, quoted in 'Interview mit
      der Tageszeitung Rheinische Post', Der Bundespräsident, 6 February
      2021; https://www.bundespraesident.de/SharedDocs/Reden/DE/Frank-
      Walter-Steinmeier/Interviews/2021/210206-Interview-Rheinische-
      Post.html.

33   Umland, 'Die deutsche Russlandpolitik', p. 96.

34   Quoted by Angelika Hellemann in 'Steinmeier gibt zum ersten Mal
      Fehler zu', BILD, 4 April 2022.

35   Umland, 'Die deutsche Russlandpolitik', p. 104.

36   See Jeffrey Mankoff, 'Russia's Latest Land Grab. How Putin Won
      Crimea and Lost Ukraine', *Foreign Affairs*, May 2014.

37   See 'Hunting the Hunters. How We Identified Navalny's FSB
      Stalkers', Bellingcat, 14 December 2020; https://www.bellingcat.com/
      resources/2020/12/14/navalny-fsb-methodology/.

38   See Michael Schwirtz, 'Top Secret Russian Unit Seeks to Destabilize
      Europe, Security Officials Say', *New York Times*, 8 October 2019.

39   See Andrew S. Bowen, 'Coercive Diplomacy and the Donbas.
      Explaining Russian Strategy in Eastern Ukraine', *The Journal of
      Strategic Studies* 42 (3) (2019), pp. 312–343.

40   Sune Engel Rasmussen, 'Russia accused of supplying Taliban as power
      shifts create strange bedfellows', *The Guardian*, 22 October 2017.

41   Quoted in 'Address by President of the Russian Federation', *President
      of Russia*, 18 March 2014.

42   Interview with Gerhard Schindler, November 2021.

43   See Lars Haferkamp, 'Darum sind Putin und die AfD Verbündete',
      Vorwärts, 28 April 2016; Holger Roonemaa, Martin Lane and Michael
      Weiss, 'Exclusive: Russia Backs Europe's Far Right', *Newlines
      Magazine*, 24 March 2022.

44   "'I am the anti-Merkel": Marine Le Pen on Brexit, EU, Putin, and Nato
      – BBC Newsnight', YouTube, 29 March 2017; https://www.youtube.
      com/watch?v=SeEHQhARESU.

14 Europe Under Pressure

1   Fukuyama, 'The End of History?', p. 5.

2   Ibid., p. 18.

3   Robert Kagan, *Of Paradise and Power. America and Europe in the New
      World Order*, Alfred A. Knopf, New York 2003.

4   See Mark Franklin, Michael Marsh and Lauren McLaren, 'Uncorking
      the Bottle. Popular Opposition to European Unification in the Wake of
      Maastricht', *Journal of Common Market Studies* 32 (1994), pp. 455–
      473.

5   Interview with Nathalie Tocci, December 2021.

6   The first stage, in 1999, was the fixing of exchange rates, and the
      second stage, in 2002, was the abolition of national currencies and the

introduction of euro notes and coins.

7 Interview with Charles Grant, November 2021.

8 Joseph Huber, *Der Euro. Grundlagen, Krise, Aussichten*, Springer Gabler, Wiesbaden 2018, pp. 1 f.

9 Quoted in Helmut Kohl and Kai-Alexander Schlevogt, 'Supranational Visionary and Builder of Euroland', *The Academy of Management Executive* 16 (1) (2002), p. 11.

10 Interview with Ruprecht Polenz, November 2021.

11 When Greece joined in 2001, budgetary and economic data were accepted which had very clearly been embellished. See 'Griechenland räumt Betrug bei Euro-Beitritt ein', *Der Tagesspiegel*, 16 November 2004.

12 Interview with Charles Grant, November 2021.

13 Quoted in Antje Wiener, Antje A. Börzel and Thomas Risse, *European Integration Theory*, Oxford University Press, Oxford 2019, p. 121.

14 Ibid.

15 See Huber, *Der Euro*, p. 9.

16 See Olli Rehn, *Walking the Highwire. Rebalancing the European Economy in Crisis*, Springer International Publishing, Wiesbaden 2020, chapter 4.

17 Ibid., chapter 6. See also Huber, *Der Euro*, pp. 17–27.

18 'Escaping the Stagnation Trap. Policy Options for the Euro Area and Japan', *OECD*, January 2015; https://www.oecd.org/eu/escaping-the-stagnation-trap-policy-options-for-the-euro-area-and-japan.pdf.

19 Eurobarometer, see Rosa Balfour and Lorenzo Robustelli, 'Why did Italy Fall Out of Love with Europe?', *Istituto Affari Internazionali*, July 2019; https://www.iai.it/en/pubblicazioni/why-did-italy-fall-out-love-europe.

20 Ibid.

21 See Michaeli Pantelouris, 'Schulden und Schuld – die Euro-Krise aus der Perspektive der Medien', *Bundeszentrale für Politische Bildung*, 3 February 2014; https://www.bpb.de/geschichte/zeitgeschichte/griechenland/178337/euro-krise-aus-der-perspektive-der-medien.

22 Ulrike Guerot and Victoria Kupsch, 'Deutschland kann auf sich allein gestellt sein', in Henning Meyer and Andrew Watt (Eds.), *Die 10 Mythen der Eurokrise*, Macroeconomic Policy Institute, Düsseldorf 2014, pp. 134 f.

23 See Hugo Brady, 'Openness versus helplessness. Europe's 2015–2017 border crisis', *Group d'Etudes Géopolitiques*, June 2021; https://geopolitique.eu/en/2021/06/28/openness-versus-helplessness-europes-2015-2017-border-crisis/.

24 Quoted in 'Es war mit das wichtigste Werk meines Lebens', *Neue Westfälische Zeitung*, 14 June 2010.

25 Interview with Charles Grant, November 2021.

26 Luft, *Die Flüchtlingskrise*, pp. 47–64.

27   Robin Alexander, *Die Getriebenen. Merkel und die Flüchtlingspolitik: Report aus dem Inneren der Macht*, Siedler Verlag, München 2017, p. 90.

28   Interview with Ruprecht Polenz, November 2021.

29   Luft, *Die Flüchtlingskrise*, p. 27.

30   See Gerald Knaus, *Welche Grenzen brauchen wir?*, Piper, München 2020, p. 287.

31   Brady, 'Openness versus helplessness'.

32   Alexander, *Die Getriebenen*, p. 7.

33   Interview with Gerald Knaus, November 2021.

34   Interview with Gerhard Schindler, November 2021.

35   In 2014, for example, 70 and 80 per cent of the populations the Czech Republic and Hungary respectively said they were opposed to any kind of immigration. See Harold D. Clarke, Matthew Goodman and Paul Whiteley, *Brexit. Why Britain Voted to Leave the European Union*, Cambridge University Press, Cambridge 2017, pp. 224 f. See also Luft, *Die Flüchtlingkrise*, p. 82.

36   Alexander, *Die Getriebenen*, chapter 6.

37   Interview with Herbert Reul, November 2021.

38   Interview with Gerald Knaus, November 2021.

39   'Viktor Orbán's speech at the 14th Kötcse civil picnic', 5 September 2015; http://2010-2015.miniszterelnok.hu/in_english_article/viktor_orban_s_speech_at_the_14th_kotcse_civil_picnic.

40   Ibid.

41   As late as 2014, Sweden was considered the 'most foreigner-friendly' country in Europe. See Clarke, *Brexit*, p. 224.

15. The Brexit Revolt

1   Quoted in Tim Shipman, *All Out War. The Full Story of Brexit*, HarperCollins, London 2017, p. 432.

2   Quoted in Elisabeth Perlman, 'Brexit: Boris Johnson Admits Defeat on the Tube', *Newsweek*, 23 June 2016.

3   Interview with Nathalie Tocci, December 2021.

4   Clarke, *Brexit*, p. 19.

5   Ibid., p. 3.

6   See Rachel Ellehuus, 'Did Russia Influence Brexit?', Center for Strategic and International Studies, 21 July 2020; https://www.csis.org/blogs/brexitbits-bobs-and-blogs/did-russia-influence-brexit.

7   Interview with David Goodhart, December 2021.

8   See Clarke, *Brexit*, p. 155.

9   Roger Eatwell and Matthew Goodwin, *National Populism. The Revolt against Liberal Democracy*, Pelican Books, London 2018.

10   See Sarah Poppleton et al., 'Social and Public Service Impacts of International Migration at the Local Level', *Home Office Research Report* 72, July 2013.

11   Interview with Mark Leonard, December 2021.

12   Ibid.

13   Shipman, *All-Out War*, p. 299–301.

14   Ibid.

15   Shipman, *All-Out War*, p. 583.

16   Quoted in ibid., p. 250.

17   See Shipman, *All-Out War*, p. 303–306.

18   Quoted in ibid., p. 374.

19   The expressions 'hard Brexit' and 'soft Brexit' changed their meanings over time, but in general referred to more limited or less limited access to the EU's internal market respectively. See Chris Grey, *Brexit Unfolded. How no one got what they wanted*, Biteback Publishing, London 2021, p. 9.

20   Interview with David Miliband, January 2022.

21   Grey, *Brexit Unfolded*, p. 15.

22   Timothy Oliver, 'British people now define themselves as 'Leavers' or 'Remainers', *The Conversation*, 31 January 2020.

23   See David M. Andrews (Ed.), *The Atlantic Alliance under Stress. US-Europe Relations after Iraq*, Cambridge University Press, Cambridge 2005.

24   Interview with David Miliband, January 2021.

25   Joe Mayes, 'Just a Year of Brexit Has Trumped UK's Economy and Businesses', *Bloomberg*, 22 December 2021. See also John Springford, 'The Cost of Brexit: October 2021', *Centre for European Reform*, 13 December 2021; https://www.cer.eu/insights/cost-brexit-october-2021.

26   Robert Shrimsley, 'Boris Johnson Cannot Escape the Costs of Brexit', *Financial Times*, 3 November 2021. See also Anand Menon, 'The Never-Ending Brexit. The True and Mounting Costs of Leaving the EU', *Foreign Affairs*, 30 December 2021; https://www.foreignaffairs.com/articles/united-kingdom/2021-12-30/never-ending-brexit.

27   Mayes, 'Just a Year'.

28   See 'UK to pay French border police €62.7 million in migrant clampdown', *France 24*, 21 July 2021; https://www.france24.com/en/europe/20210721-uk-to-pay-french-border-police-%E2%82%AC62-7-million-in-migrant-clampdown.

29   Quoted in '"Two fingers to Brussels" is "tangible" Brexit benefit, Edwina Currie declares', *LBC*, 3 January 2022.

16. A Populist in the White House

1   Tim Alberta, *American Carnage: on the frontlines of the Republican civil war*, HarperCollins, New York 2019, p. 1.

2   See Michael Kranish and Marc Fisher, *Trump Revealed: the definitive biography of the 45th president*, Simone & Schuster, London and New York 2016, p. 316.

3   See Michael Wolff, 'Donald Trump Didn't Want to Be President', *The

Intelligencer, 5 January 2018; https://nymag.com/intelligencer/
2018/01/michael-wolff-fire-and-fury-book-donald-trump.html.

4   'Hillary Clinton has a 91% chance to win', *New York Times*, 18
     October 2016; https://www.nytimes.com/newsgraphics/2016/10/18/
     presidentialforecast-updates/newsletter.html.

5   This chapter contains passages from my book *Bluster: Donald Trump's
     war on terror*, Oxford University Press, Oxford and New York 2019, in
     particular chapters 1 and 2.

6   See Jennifer Rubin, 'GOP autopsy report goes bold', *Washington Post*,
     18 March 2013.

7   Salena Zito and Brad Todd, *The Great Revolt: inside the populist
     coalition reshaping American politics*, Crown Publishing Group, New
     York 2018, p. 16 f.

8   Interview with Hayes Brown, January 2022.

9   Quoted in Joshua Green, *Devil's Bargain: Steve Bannon, Donald
     Trump, and the nationalist uprising*, Penguin, London 2017, p. 106.

10   See Ed Pilkington, 'How the Drudge Report Ushered in the Age of
     Trump', *The Guardian*, 24 January 2018.

11   Matt Grossmann, 'Racial Attitudes and Political Correctness in the
     2016 Presidential Election', Niksanen Center, 10 May 2018.

12   'Trump's Ailing Empire', *Bloomberg*, https://www.bloomberg.com/
     graphics/2021-donald-trump-net-worth-business/.

13   Victor Davis Hanson, *The Case for Trump*, Basic Books, New York
     2019, pp. 108 f.

14   See Emily Stewart, 'Donald Trump Rode $5 Billion in Free Media to
     the White House', *The Street*, 20 November 2016.

15   Sarah Lyall, 'A Hundred Days without Trump on Twitter', *New York
     Times*, 17 April 2021.

16   Neumann, *Bluster*, p. 30.

17   Interview with Nick Pickles, January 2022.

18   See Kevin Quealy, 'The Complete List of Trump's Twitter Insults
     (2015–2021)', *New York Times*, 19 January 2021; https://www.nytimes.
     com/interactive/2021/01/19/upshot/trump-complete-insult-list.html.

19   Bob Woodward, *Fear: Trump in the White House*, Simon & Schuster,
     New York and London 2019, p. 207.

20   See 'Report on the Investigation into Russian Interference in the 2016
     Election' (Muller Report), U.S. Department of Justice, March 2019;
     https://www.justice.gov/archives/sco/file/1373816/download.

21   Interview with Brian Fishman, January 2022.

22   Green, *Devil's Bargain*, p. 241.

23   For more on the specifically American tradition of those ideas, see
     Edward Ashbee, *The Trump Revolt*, Manchester University Press,
     Manchester 2017, chapter 3.

24   Walter Russell Mead, 'The Jacksonian Tradition and American Foreign
     Policy', *The National Interest* 58 (3) (1999), pp. 5–29.

25 Shortly after taking office, Trump placed a bust of Jackson in the Oval Office. See Susan B. Glasser, 'The Man Who Put Andrew Jackson in Trump's Oval Office', *Politico*, 22 January 2018; Yoni Appelbaum, 'I Alone Can Fix It', *The Atlantic*, 22 July 2016.

26 See Seth Bartee, 'Paul Gottfried and Paleoconservatism', in Mark Sedgwick, *Key Thinkers of the Radical Right*, Oxford University Press, Oxford 2019, pp. 102–120; Edward Ashbee, 'Patrick J. Buchanan and the Death of the West', in ibid., pp. 121–136.

27 Neumann, *Bluster*, pp. 17–19.

28 Green, *Devil's Bargain*, pp. 220–223. See Jean-Yves Camus, 'Alain de Benoist and the New Right', in Sedgwick, *Key Thinkers*, pp. 73–90; Renaud Camus, *You Will Not Replace Us*, Chez l'auteur, Plieux 2018; Guillaume Faye, *Why We Fight: manifesto of the European resistance*, Arktos Media, London 2011.

29 Green, *Devil's Bargain*, p. 223.

30 See Neumann, *Bluster*, pp. 36–39.

31 See Mishal Reja, 'Trump's Chinese Virus helped lead to rise in racist anti-Asian Twitter content', *ABC News*, 18 March 2021; https://abcnews.go.com/Health/trumps-chinese-virus-tweet-helped-lead-rise-racist/story?id=76530148.

32 Neumann, *Bluster*, pp. 48–55.

33 An example of this was the so-called Muslim ban; see ibid., chapter 4.

34 See David Frum, *Trumpocracy: the corruption of the American Republic*, Harper, New York 2018, chapter 8.

35 Alberta, American Carnage, p. ix.

36 Stephen Tankel, 'Riding the Tiger. How Trump Enables Right-Wing Extremism', *War on the Rocks*, 5 November 2018.

37 Neumann, *Bluster*, pp. 148–150.

38 See William Saletan, 'Republicans Still Sympathize with the Insurrection', *Slate*, 15 April 2021.

39 See Max Greenwood, 'Nearly three quarters of GOP voters doubt legitimacy of Biden's win: poll', *The Hill*, 30 December 2021.

40 Interview with Zack Beauchamp, January 2022.

17. China's Authoritarian Modernity

1 James Mann, *The China Fantasy: why capitalism will not bring democracy to China*, Penguin Books, London 2007, chapter 1.

2 Interview with Reinhard Bütikofer, February 2022.

3 'Chosun Ilbo – China's Economy Could Overtake U.S. Economy by 2030', Center for Economics and Business Research, 5 January 2022.

4 See Jack Goodman, 'Has China Lifted 100 million People Out of Poverty?', *BBC News*, 28 February 2021; https://www.bbc.com/news/56213271.

5 'How Well-Off Is China's Middle-Class', China Power Project, CSIS, 30 September 2021; https://chinapower.csis.org/china-middle-class/.

6   Mann, *The China Fantasy*, p. 110.

7   See Elizabeth Economy, *The Third Revolution: Xi Jinping and the new Chinese state*, Oxford University Press, Oxford 2018, p. 71.

8   Stefan Aust and Adrian Geiges, *Xi Jinping: the most powerful man in the world*, Polity Press, Cambridge 2022, p. 103.

9   'Adaptive authoritarian regime': Andrew J. Nathan, 'China at the Tipping Point? Foreseeing the Unforeseeable', *Journal of Democracy* 24 (1) (2013), pp. 20–25. 'Market-Leninism': Nicolas Kristof, quoted in Jeffrey N. Wasserstrom, *China in the 21st Century*, Oxford University Press, Oxford 2013, p. 109. 'Techno-dictatorship': Victor Shih, 'China's Techno-Dictatorship', *The Wire China*, 1 November 2020; https://www.thewirechina.com/2020/11/01/chinastechno-dictatorship/.

10   Fukuyama, 'Is China Next?'.

11   See Rush Doshi, *The Long Game: China's grand strategy to dislodge American power*, Oxford University Press, Oxford 2021; Robert Blackwell and Ashley Tellis, 'Revising U.S. Grand Strategy toward China', Council on Foreign Relations, April 2015.

12   See Wasserstrom, *China in the 21st Century*, p. 140.

13   Mann, *The China Fantasy*, p. 25.

14   Economy, *The Third Revolution*, p. 188.

15   Ibid., pp. 10–12, 17 f.

16   Interview with Raffaello Pantucci, February 2022.

17   Economy, *The Third Revolution*, pp. 190–193; Jacob J. Law and Gary Roughead, 'China's Belt and Road. Implications for the United States', Independent Task Force Report No. 79, Council on Foreign Relations, 2021.

18   Interview with Moritz Rudolf, February 2021.

19   Economy, *The Third Revolution*, pp. 199–205, 213.

20   Ibid., p. 213.

21   Interview with Moritz Rudolf, February 2022.

22   See Jeremy Fuster, 'Amazon Shuts Down Reviews of Xi Jinping's Book', *The Wrap*, 20 December 2021.

23   Mike Isaac, 'Facebook Said to Create Censorship Tool to Get Back into China', *New York Times*, 22 November 2016.

24   See 'U.S. Airlines Are Editing Their Websites to Remove Taiwan's Name', *Bloomberg*, 25 July 2018; Erich Schwartzel, 'How China's Growing Clout Led Hollywood to Look for a New Villain', *Wall Street Journal*, 5 February 2022.

25   Quoted in Hannah Beech, 'A Brief History of Facebook's Courtship in China', *Time*, 21 March 2016.

26   See Gary Clyde Hufbauer and Euijin Jung, 'China plays the sanctions game, anticipating a bad US habit', *China Economic Watch*, 14 December 2020; Bonnie S. Glaser, 'Time for Pushback against China's Economic Coercion', CSIS Global Forecast, 13 January 2021.

27   Eva Lamby-Schmitt, 'Litauen bringt die EU ins China-Dilemma',

Tagesschau, 22 January 2022.

28	Interview with Janka Oertel, February 2022.

29	'Deutsche Unternehmen üben in China-Streit Druck auf Litauen aus', *Handelsblatt*, 21 January 2022.

30	Stephanie Nebehay, '1.5 million Muslims could be detained in China's Xinjiang: academic', Reuters, 13 March 2019.

31	Qatar later withdrew its signature. See Roie Yellinek and Elizabeth Chen, 'The "22 vs. 50" Diplomatic Split between China and the West over Xinjiang and Human Rights', Jamestown Foundation China Brief, 31 December 2019; https://jamestown.org/program/the-22-vs-50-diplomatic-split-between-the-west-and-china-over-xinjiang-and-human-rights/

32	See ibid.

33	See 'Portugal: A China-friendly EU nation driven by need', *Deutsche Welle*, 12 March 2019; Elena Varvitsioti, 'Piraeus port deal intensifies Greece's unease over China links', *Financial Times*, 19 October 2021.

34	Quoted in Hans von der Burchard and Jacopo Barigazzi, 'Germany slams Hungary for blocking EU criticism of China on Hong Kong', *Politico*, 10 May 2021.

35	Interview with Janka Oertel, February 2022.

36	See David E. Sanger, 'Washington Hears Echoes of the 50's and Worries: Is this a Cold War with China?', *New York Times*, 17 October 2021.

37	Interview with Jan Weidenfeld, February 2022.

38	See Li Fusheng, 'VW CEO calls for more cooperation with China', *China Daily*, 21 December 2021.

39	Interview with Jan Weidenfeld, February 2022.

40	Gerhard Schröder, 'Wer das glaubt, hat China nicht verstanden', T-Online, 3 February 2022; https://www.t-online.de/nachrichten/deutschland/id_91579212/china-und-olympia-gerhard-schroeder-warnt-vor-neuemkalten-krieg.html.

41	J. Stewart Black and Allen J. Morrison, 'The Strategic Challenges of Decoupling', *Harvard Business Review*, May 2021.

42	See Max J. Zenglein and Anna Holzmann, 'Evolving Made in China 2025: China's industrial policy in the quest for global tech leadership', MERICS Papers on China, July 2019.

43	Interview with Sandro Gaycken, February 2022.

44	See 'Decoupling. Severed Ties and Patchwork of Globalisation', European Union Chamber of Commerce in China, January 2021; Interview with Thorsten Benner, February 2022.

45	See Charles W. Boustany and Aron L. Friedberg, 'Partial Disengagement. A New U.S. Strategy for Economic Competition with China', NBR Special Report #82, November 2019.

46	Interview with Raffaello Pantucci, February 2022.

47	See Heiko Maas, quoted in 'China is a partner, competitor and rival', German Federal Foreign Office, 12 July 2020; https://www.auswaertiges-amt.de/en/newsroom/news/maas-rnd/2367552.

48　Quoted in Daniel Yergin, *The New Map: energy, climate, and the clash of nations*, Penguin Books, London 2022, p. 445.

49　Quoted in ibid., p. 446.

50　'Mind the Gap. Priorities for Transatlantic China Policy', MSC, Aspen and MERICS, July 2021.

51　Interview with Jan Weidenfeld, February 2022.

52　'Mind the Gap', MSC, p. 26.

53　See Economy, *The Third Revolution*, p. 211 f.; Aust & Geiges, Xi Jinping, p. 135.

54　Interview with Jan Weidenfeld, February 2022.

18. Climate Emergency

1　Maja Göpel, *Unsere Welt neu denken. Eine Einladung*, Berlin 2021, p. 39.

2　See Jeffrey Mazo, *Climate Conflict. How global warming threatens security and what to do about it*, Taylor & Francis, Abingdon 2010, p. 19.

3　Donella Meadows, Dennis Meadows, Jørgen Randers and William Behrens, *The Limits to Growth*, Universe Books, Los Angeles 1972.

4　'Global Carbon Atlas 2021', *Global Carbon Project*; http://www.globalcarbonatlas.org/en/content/welcome-carbon-atlas.

5　Tony Juniper, *The Science of Our Changing Planet. From Global Warming to Sustainable Development*, Penguin Random House, London 2021, pp. 122 f.

6　Ibid., pp. 198 f.

7　Göpel, *Unsere Welt*, p. 28.

8　See Peter Walker, Rowena Mason and Damian Carrington, 'Theresa May commits to net zero UK carbon emissions by 2050', *The Guardian*, 11 June 2019.

9　'Global Carbon Atlas', *Global Carbon Project*.

10　'AR5 Synthesis Report. Global Climate Change 2014', *Intergovernmental Panel on Climate Change*; https://www.ipcc.ch/report/ar5/syr/.

11　Jason Hickel, *Less is More: How Degrowth Will Save the World*, Penguin Books, London 2020.

12　Quoted in Kelsey Piper, 'Can We Save the Planet by Shrinking the Economy?', *Vox*, 3 August 2021.

13　Ibid.

14　Göpel, *Unsere Welt*, p. 49.

15　Yergin, *The New Map*, pp. 403–405.

16　Ibid., p. 398.

17　'New registrations of electric vehicles in Europe', *European Environment Agency*, 18 November 2021; https://www.eea.europa.

eu/ims/new-registrations-of-electric-vehicles; 'Renewable Energy 2020', *Eurostat*, 18 January 2022; https://ec.europa.eu/eurostat/statistics-explained/index.php?title=File:Renewable_energy_2020_infographic_18 – 01 – 2022.jpg.

18   Yergin, *The New Map*, p. 412.

19   Germany's foreign minister, Annalena Baerbock, spoke of a 'toolbox' in this context. See 'Good COPS. Aligning International Climate Diplomacy', *Munich Security Conference*, 19 February 2022, https://securityconference.org/en/msc-2022/.

20   The point of reference for this reduction is the year 2010. See 'Cop 26 Outcomes', *UN Climate Change Conference UK 2021*; https://ukcop26.org/the-conference/cop26-outcomes/.

21   'Warming Projections Global Update', *Climate Action Tracker*, November 2021; https://climateanalytics.org/what-we-do/climate-action-tracker/cat-updates/. See also 'Australia', *Climate Action Tracker*, 2 August 2022; https://climateactiontracker.org/countries/australia/.

22   Yergin, *The New Map*, p. 436.

23   See 'Preliminary Report: The Climate Impact of Congressional Infrastructure and Budget Bills', *REPEAT Project,* October 2021; https://repeatproject.org/docs/REPEAT_Preliminary_Report_102021.pdf.

24   Quoted in ibid.

25   See 'Weather-related disasters increase over past 50 years, but cause fewer deaths', *World Meteorological Organisation*, 31 August 2021; https://public.wmo.int/en/media/press-release/weather-related-disasters-increase-over-past-50-years-causing-more-damage-fewer; 'Climate Change Indicators. Weather and Climate', *Environmental Protection Agency*; https://www.epa.gov/climate-indicators/weather-climate; Christina Nunez, 'Sea Level Rise, explained', *National Geographic*, 15 February 2022; https://www.nationalgeographic.com/environment/article/sea-level-rise-1.

26   Mazo, *Climate Conflict*, p. 32.

27   Ibid., p. 35.

28   Interview with Tom Middendorp, February 2022.

29   Ibid.

30   Quoted in Tim Wilson and Richard Walton, 'Extinction Rebellion. A review of ideology and tactics', *Policy Exchange*, 2019; https://policyexchange.org.uk/wp-content/uploads/2019/07/Extremism-Rebellion.pdf.

31   Andreas Malm, *How to Blow Up a Pipeline: Learning to Fight in a World on Fire*, Verso, London 2021.

32   Jason Bordoff and Meghan O'Sullivan, 'Green Upheaval', *Foreign Affairs*, January 2022.

33   Quoted in Yergin, *The New Map*, p. 344.

34   See Jeffrey Sachs and Andrew Warner, 'Natural Resource Abundance and Economic Growth', *NBER Working Paper Series*, No. 5398, December 1995; Thomas Havranek, Roman Horvath and Ayaz Zeynalov, 'Natural resources and economic growth. A meta-analysis', *IOS Working Papers*, No. 350, October 2015.

35   Yergin, *The New Map*, pp. 340–344.

36   Bordoff, *Green Upheaval*.

37   Ibid.

38   See Ellen Knickmeyer and Helena Alves, 'Saudi Arabia denies playing climate saboteur at Glasgow', *Associated Press*, 11 November 2021; Dmitri Trening, 'After COP26. Russia's Path to the Global Green Future', *Carnegie Moscow Centre*, 16 November 2021; https://carnegiemoscow.org/commentary/85789.

39   Alec MacGillis, 'Brown Out', *The New Yorker*, 7 February 2022.

40   Quoted in ibid.

A Turning Point? What Comes Next.

1   Francis Fukuyama, 'Preparing for Defeat', *American Purpose*, 10 March 2022; https://www.americanpurpose.com/articles/preparing-for-defeat/; Francis Fukuyama, 'Putin's War on the Liberal Order', *Financial Times*, 3 March 2022.

2   For other interpretations of the Ukraine conflict see Elliott Abrams, 'The New Cold War', *National Review*, 4 March 2022; Steven Erlanger, 'Putin's War on Ukraine is about Ethnicity and Empire', *New York Times*, 16 March 2022; Ivan Krastev, 'We Are All Living in Putin's World Now', New York Times, 27 February 2022; William S. Smith, 'Ukraine and the Clash of Civilizations', *The National Interest*, 12 May 2020.

3   'Democracy Index 2021: less than half the world lives in a democracy', The Economist Intelligence Unit, 10 February 2022; https://www.eiu.com/n/democracy-index-2021-less-than-half-the-world-lives-in-a-democracy/.

4   Quoted in 'When Russians told Biden', *Insider Paper*; https://twitter.com/TheInsiderPaper/status/1501028978785763329.

5   Fukuyama, 'Putin's War'.

6   'America Has a Free Speech Problem', *New York Times*, 18 March 2022.

7   In academic debate, this is known as reflexivity. See Inanna Hamati-Ataya, 'Reflectivity, Reflexivity, Reflexivism. IR's 'Reflexive Turn' – and beyond', *European Journal of International Relations* 19 (4) (2012), pp. 669–694.

Index